THE SIGNIFICANCE OF HUMANS IN THE UNIVERSE

THE PURPOSE AND MEANING OF LIFE

LUKE VANDENBERGHE

ISBN 978-1-953223-85-2 (paperback)
ISBN 978-1-953223-84-5 (digital)

Rushmore Press LLC
1 800 460 9188
www.rushmorepress.com

Printed in the United States of America

CONTENTS

PREFACE

This book is a history about the religious, philosophical, and scientific thought since the first civilisation. It is a non-fiction essay for the lay reader and forms a sequel to my previous book, *God, Fact or Fiction*, in which I concluded that God does not exist. After all, the supernatural does not exist, God is an entity of the supernatural, and so God does not exist either.

The book is a research study to unravel the significance of human in the universe and determine whether there is any purpose or meaning to life.

The historicity of the facts often demands a verbatim copying of the sources. Unavoidably, I bear the stain of being a plagiarist. The compilation allowed me to form a canvas on which I pinned my own thoughts. I am a well-read man, having a library of more than three thousand books collected during seventy years, however the information and knowledge contained in my books do not match the information available on the Internet, particular in Wikipedia, of which I have made great use. The research demanded an extensive investigation of all possible religious and philosophical texts on the matter. With the help of scientific data, it may be stated that all religions are nonsense and that philosophy is senselessness. Consequently, the theme of the book can only be approached in a scientific way in order to provide a satisfactory answer.

I confront the reader with the reality and terse questions that demonstrate that human evolution is still in its early stage, that humans' knowledge is still limited, and that humans are still susceptible to placebos. Modesty is so highly recommended.

Religions provide arguments which are based on the existence of a transcendent and immanent deity. In the philosophy through the ages, viewpoints differ according to whether the author is a theist or an atheist.

Through the ages, thinkers have been the victims of the time of their existence, a limited knowledge, and a limited cultural environment. They have always suffered from a lack of scientific and technological knowledge in such a way that their philosophy, regardless of their intelligence, often led to great falsehoods and misunderstandings.

Civilisations have existed since more than ten thousand years ago, but it is only in the twentieth century that we can speak of ground-breaking work in the sciences and that technology that has made it possible to unravel the secrets of the universe. Quality of life has greatly improved by the advances of science and technology. Unfortunately, there are too few people in the world who benefit from this progress and therefore stagnate further in difficult living conditions.

Famous religious thinkers like Augustine and Thomas Aquinas can still be appreciated today but can hardly be taken credibly. Believers will not like to hear it, but founders of religions must be regarded as naïve or false prophets who believe their own dreams or are even regarded as charlatans. The most recent religions, like those of the Mormons or of Scientology, are even founded by imposters.

Life is the most important thing on earth. Up till now, life has not been detected elsewhere in the universe, but there is no reason at all to presume there are no life forms on other planets in the universe.

As rational beings, we have a deep need to know why we are here, being thrown into the world without consent. The enigma of the universe and its nature bothers us. In the past, religions answered these questions but now have been proven to be utter nonsense.

In my new book, I try to deal with all aspects of life, and from there I approach the purpose and meaning of life. Purpose and meaning are closely related but are still different. My research starts with the origin of life on earth around 3.7 billion years ago and then goes to the evolution of life and humans. The life stance to some extent determines the meaning of life but is not the actual understanding. It's quite possible that my approach is not satisfactory, but it will at least contribute to an objective discussion. The universal and rational human deserve a discussion outside of a religious context and averse of the supernatural.

My atheistic belief brings me, as in my last book, once more in conflict with the Church and all religions. To make it clear, no deity has intervened in the creation of heaven and earth; the scientific proof of the origin of the universe and of the earth is motivated extensively.

The first line of John Keats's famous poem "Endymion" reads, "A thing of beauty is a joy forever." He refers to the beauty of women but forgets that this beauty is short-lived because all things in the universe are temporal, even if they seem timeless.

Language is a means of communicating. Neat language is simply more accurate and more pleasant. My training as a fiscal jurist has not given me the gift of a novelist.

In the last 150 years, the sciences including biology, medical sciences, chemistry, and physics had an unprecedented bloom, making technology. As a consequence, the quality of life greatly improved. However, the material progress does not mean that the people are nowadays happier than before. In addition, one should note that in many regions of the world where the people are not able to profit from scientific and technical progress, the quality of life remains unchanged.

Since the nineteenth century, all branches of physics are handled mathematically, and from 1900 the structure of classical physics—with a description of the matter on a macroscopic scale and at relatively low speeds—was largely completed. Since then, however, the theories of modern physics, and particular the special theory of relativity, quantum theory, and string theory, have thoroughly changed our overall understanding of the universe, even to the extent to make God redundant.

The urge to improve his destiny is necessary to rise humans up from mediocrity. Political systems, which rightly aim to remedy humans out of poverty and spread prosperity, sin quite often to limit the freedom of people by taking measures which indirectly counteract initiatives, causing mediocrity and inhibiting evolution. Evolution requires freedom of action to beget inspiration. Freedom is the highest good of man, but it's not absolute in the sense that it may impair the equality of people.

If we are honest with ourselves, then we must admit that we are rather hypocrites. The truth is usually difficult to digest, and therefore we camouflage it in such a way that its meaning is lost.

Religion shuns the truth like the plague because it is the breakdown of her thought process, destroying the fairy tale. The same applies to the theistic philosophy. Only compliance with the scientific discipline admits the truth, though this is not always possible.

Humans are in the current stage of evolution as weak creatures that are only too happy to swallow placebos.

I challenge the reader by pointing out aberrations in the memorabilia. I outline the thinking of the prominent former and current thinkers about the purpose and meaning of life, and I examine whether these can apply in the face of the present scientific knowledge. Religions go constantly against the grain and use utter nonsense to prove their stances.

I confront the reader with questions about the lack of purpose and meaning of life and the seemingly absurdity of life in face of the scientific logic of the universe.

CHAPTER 1

Death of Goldilocks

In astrobiology, the Goldilocks zone refers to the habitable zone around a star. The Goldilocks principle defined that a planet must be neither too far away from nor too close to a star and galactic centre. Either extreme would result in a planet incapable of supporting life.

The sun[82] is the star at the centre of the solar system and is by far the most important source of energy for life on Earth. Its diameter is 109 times that of Earth, and its mass is about 330,000 times that of Earth, accounting for about 99.86 per cent of the total mass of the solar system. About three-quarters of the sun's mass consists of hydrogen; the rest is mostly helium, with much smaller quantities of heavier elements such as oxygen, carbon, neon, and iron.

The sun is a G-type star or a yellow dwarf. It formed approximately 4.6 billion years ago from the gravitational collapse of matter within a region of a large molecular cloud consisting mostly of hydrogen and helium. The sun may have been triggered by shockwaves from one or more nearby supernovae. The sun is roughly middle-aged and has not changed dramatically for over four billion years; it will remain fairly stable for at least another five billion years. However, after hydrogen fusion in its core has stopped, the sun will undergo severe changes and become a red giant. It is calculated that the sun will become sufficiently large to engulf the current orbits of Mercury, Venus, and possibly Earth.

The sun does not have enough mass to explode as a supernova. Instead, it will become a red giant. The luminosity of the sun will have nearly doubled, and Earth will be hotter than Venus is today. Once the core hydrogen is exhausted in 5.4 billion years, the sun will expand into a subgiant phase and slowly double in size over about half a billion years. It will then expand more rapidly over another half a billion years until it is over two hundred times larger than it is today and a couple thousand times more luminous. This then starts the red-giant-branch phase, whereby the sun will spend around a billion years and lose around one-third of its mass.

After the red-giant branch, the sun has approximately 120 million years of active life left, but much happens. First, the core, full of degenerate helium, ignites violently in the helium flash. It is estimated that 6 per cent of the core, itself 40 per cent of the sun's mass, will be converted into carbon within a matter of minutes through the triple-alpha process (Ostlie, D.A. & Carroll, B.W., *An Introduction to Modern Stellar Astrophysics*, Addison Wesley, San Francisco, 2007).The sun then shrinks to around ten times its current size and fifty times the luminosity, with a temperature a little lower than today. It will then have reached the red clump or horizontal branch, but a star of the sun's mass does not evolve bluewards along the horizontal branch. Instead, it becomes moderately larger and more luminous over about 100 million years as it continues to burn helium in the core.

When the helium is exhausted, the sun will repeat the expansion it followed when the hydrogen in the core was exhausted, except this time it all happens faster, and the sun becomes larger and more luminous. This is the asymptotic-giant-branch phase; the sun is alternately burning hydrogen in a shell or helium in a deeper shell. After about 20 million years on the early asymptotic giant branch, the sun becomes increasingly unstable with rapid mass loss and thermal pulses that increase the size and luminosity for a few hundred years every 100,000 years or so. The thermal pulses become larger each time, with the later pulses pushing the luminosity to as much as 5,000 times the current level and the radius of over one astronomical unit.

According to a 2008 model[82], Earth's orbit is shrinking due to tidal forces (and, eventually, drag from the lower chromosphere), so that it is engulfed by the sun near the end of the asymptotic-giant-branch phase. Models vary depending on the rate and timing of mass loss. Models that have a higher mass loss on the red-giant branch produce smaller, less luminous stars at the tip of the asymptotic giant branch, perhaps only 2,000 times the luminosity and less than two hundred times the radius. For the sun, four thermal pulses are predicted before it completely loses its outer envelope and starts to make a planetary nebula. By the end of that phase—lasting approximately 500,000 years—the sun will only have about half of its current mass.

The post-asymptotic-giant-branch evolution is even faster. The luminosity stays approximately constant as the temperature increases, with the ejected half of the sun's mass becoming ionised into a planetary nebula as the exposed core reaches 30,000 kelvins. The final naked core temperature will be over 100,000 kelvins, after which the remnant will cool towards a white dwarf that contains an estimated 54.05 per cent of the sun's present-day mass. The planetary nebula will disperse in about 10,000 years, but the white dwarf will survive for trillions of years before fading to black dwarf.[82]

Long before the sun becomes a red giant, Goldilocks—the Earth—will have become a cinder not sustaining any life form. What happened to humankind? Did humans perish like all life forms on Earth, or did they evolve from Homo *sapiens* to Homo *superior* and dominate the universe? Who knows? Five billion years—nearly an eternity—is a very long way to go!

The evolution of primitive man to the current Homo *sapiens* took a few million years, which is a trifle in perspective with the universe's billions of years.

CHAPTER 2

Nature

Nature, in the broadest sense, is the natural, physical, or material world or synonym of universe.[129]

Nature includes not only the living nature (biosphere, fauna, and flora) but also the non-living nature that is purely material (the terrestrial stratosphere, atmosphere, and lithosphere).

The size of the universe is unknown as it is constantly expanding, so the universe may be infinite, though infinity seems to conflict with mathematics.

Matter and energy are subject to certain physical laws, which means that physics is the most fundamental science; it dominates all knowledge. The universe totally consisting of matter and energy is likewise subject to natural laws.

On a small scale, physics governs the quantum mechanics, whereas physics on a large scale is dominated by gravity, which is determined by the general theory of relativity of Albert Einstein.[1] The matter with mass—which is equivalent to energy ($M = E/C^2$) — consists of atoms that undergo chemical compounds.

Nature is synonym of universe. Life and man are parts of nature. Is there a purpose and a meaning attached to nature? The answer is definitely negative. Nature consists of the universe, life and man which all came spontaneously into being and therefore can have no purpose or meaning. The fate of man, as part of nature, is inseparable from the fate of the universe that has neither purpose nor meaning.

A stone on Earth is lifeless but a part of nature. This may be very materialistic but remains the naked truth that must be accepted even if it has little tenor for man.

CHAPTER 3

Origin of the universe

The universe is the description of all matter and energy within the whole space-time continuum in which we exist. The universe is all time and space and its contents.[130]

In 1908, Hermann Minkowski, one of the math professors of the young Einstein, introduced a geometric interpretation of special relativity that fused time and the three spatial dimensions of space into a single, four-dimensional continuum now known as Minkowski space-time. A key feature of this interpretation is the definition of a space-time interval that combines distance and time. Although measurements of distance and time between events differ for measurements made in different reference frames, the space-time interval is independent of the inertial frame of reference in which they are recorded.

Minkowski's geometric interpretation of relativity was to prove vital to Einstein's development of his 1915 general theory of relativity, wherein he showed that space-time becomes curved in the presence of mass or energy. Before Einstein's work on relativistic physics, time and space were viewed as independent dimensions.

The initial singularity, a small change which causes a large effect, was the gravitational singularity of infinite density thought to have contained all of the mass and space-time of the universe before quantum fluctuations caused it to expand in the Big Bang and subsequent inflation, creating the present-day universe.

In mathematics, a singularity is a point at which a given mathematical object is not defined or erratic (infinite or not differentiable). An essential singularity is a singularity near which a function exhibits extreme behaviour.

It is impossible to see the singularity or the actual Big Bang itself because time and space did not exist inside the singularity. Therefore, there would be no way to transmit any radiation from before the Big Bang to the present day. However, evidence for the existence of an initial singularity, and the Big Bang theory itself, comes in the form of the cosmic microwave background and the continued expansion of the universe. In 2011, the astrophysicist and Nobel Prize laureate Brian Schmidt proved the acceleration of the universe's expansion.

Generally, it is assumed that the universe was created according to the Big Bang theory of the Belgian priest Georges Lemaître, a theory even the Vatican does not dispute. (In 1951, Pope Pius XII declared that the Big Bang was in line with the Catholic concept of creation.) However, the Catholic Church couples the Big Bang with an intervention of God, which Lemaître did not approve because he considered that science and religion were two different things. The Big Bang theory is the prevailing cosmological model of the universe from the earliest known periods through its subsequent large-scale evolution. The model accounts for the fact that the universe expanded from a very high-density and high-temperature state and offers a comprehensive explanation for a broad range of phenomena, including the abundance of light elements, the cosmic microwave background, the large-scale structure, and the findings (Hubble's laws) by the astronomer Edwin Hubble. If the known laws of physics are extrapolated beyond where they are valid, there is a singularity. Modern measurements place this moment at approximately 13.8 billion years ago. After the initial expansion, the universe cooled sufficiently to allow the formation of subatomic particles and later simple atoms. Giant clouds of these primordial elements later coalesced through gravity to form stars and galaxies.[83]

The general theory of relativity of Albert Einstein and Lemaître's Big Bang theory assume that the whole universe has emerged from an exceedingly small point, or particle, which must have been enormously dense and hot. Something must have been the object of the Big Bang, matter or energy (E=MC2). Space and time were created in the Big Bang, and these were imbued with a fixed amount of energy and matter. As space expands, the density of that matter and energy decreased.

The question of where the universe came from remains unanswered. Two theories exist as to exactly what happened 13,8 billion years ago when the universe, which is now unaccountably huge, emerged from something so unimaginably small – according to the new research one hundred billionth the size of a proton. First there is the theory of cosmic inflation-a period before the Big Bang when, according to some physicists, an ultra-high energy particle inflated at an incomprehensible speed and scale. During this period matter or energy, such as it was, remained a cold dark formless mass. Then, less than a trillionth of a second later, came the Big Bang- an almost infinitely hot fireball which exploded ultimately forming all the matter and energy as now found in the universe. The theory fails to link the cold dark soup to the trigger of the explosion.

Now there is a new theory, by a team of physicists at the Massachusetts Institute, aided by teams from all over the world, that advances a linking theory, which they call a "reheating" phase. At a point gravity worked in reverse at the time of inflation to reheating period and at the same time gravity was modified by quantum effects – and it was this which allowed the hot Big Bang to emerge from the from the cold Cosmological Inflation period.

All this is not clear, but it shows that there was actually a presence of something before the Big Bang and an allusion of time before the Big Bang.

The Big Bang theory was proven by astronomical observations by Edwin Hubble and later confirmed in 1964 by the discovery of the cosmic background radiation by the Nobel Prize winners Arno Allan Penzias and Robert Woodrow. That radiation was predicted by the Big Bang theory. According to the current measurements, the universe came into being about 13.75 billion years ago. Physicists remain unsure about what preceded the Big Bang; the possibility of various multiverse is not excluded. The question is disturbing for theists, who are unable to situate God at the time preceding the Big Bang.

In 2007 the German physicist Martin Bojowald introduced a new mathematical model to derive new details about the properties of a quantum state as it travels through the Big Bounce (a mathematical time machine called loop quantum gravity, a state that initially has small fluctuations bounces and develops larger fluctuations), which replaces the classical idea of the Big Bang.[85] The research of Bojowald reveals that although it is possible to learn many properties of the earlier universe, it will always be uncertain about some of the properties because his calculations reveal a cosmic forgetfulness that results from the extreme quantum forces during the Big Bounce. He considers Einstein's theory of general relativity, as the basis of Lemâitre's Big Bang theory, a mathematical nonsensical state—a singularity of zero volume that nevertheless contained infinite density and infinitely large energy. Research in loop quantum cosmology purports to show that a previously existing universe collapsed not to the point of singularity, but to a point before that where the quantum effects of gravity become so strongly repulsive that the universe rebounds back out, forming a new branch. Throughout this collapse and bounce, the evolution of the universe is unitary. This model of the universe is highly speculative, has been extended, but knows no real breakthrough mainly because of the probability effects of some quantum mechanics and particle physics (scepticism evoked by Einstein, Dirac, Schrödinger, Penrose, and Feynman).[85] If there was a previous universe that collapsed, the discoveries that have actually been made would be probably totally different. However, further speculation on the universe and research is highly necessary for our evolution.

The initial hot, dense state of the universe is called the Planck epoch (cf. infra), a brief period extending from time zero to one Planck time unit of approximately 10^{-43} seconds.[80]

Thanks to the observations of satellites circling the earth, it was possible to establish the following.

- The oldest light was 379,000 years after the Big Bang
- The perception of the cosmic background radiation has, since the Big Bang, cooled to 2.73 kelvin.
- The stars have arisen earlier than thought—namely, 200 million years after the Big Bang.
- The age of the Earth indeed can be determined to 5 billion years ago (with a margin of +/- 1 per cent).
- The universe is composed of 4 per cent normal matter, 23 per cent dark matter, and 73 per cent dark energy.
- The universe is flat and not curved.
- The inflation theory is confirmed.
- The expansion continues forever, with a critical density equal to one.

The knowledge which we dispose of makes it very clear to what extent science has managed to unravel the secrets of the universe. The knowledge is such that rational man must be convinced that absolutely no deity has intervened in the creation of heaven and earth.

In the course of the Big Bang, different phases can be determined.[80–82] In the first phase, the very earliest universe was so hot, or energetic, that initially no matter particles existed or could exist, or perhaps only fleetingly. According to prevailing scientific theories, at this time the distinct forces we see around us today were joined in one unified force. Space-time itself expanded during an inflationary epoch due to the immensity of the energies involved. Gradually the immense energies cooled—still to a temperature inconceivably hot compared to any we see around us now, but sufficiently to allow forces to gradually undergo symmetry breaking, a kind of repeated condensation from one status quo to another, leading finally to the separation of the strong force from the electroweak force and the first particles.

In the second phase, the resulting quark-gluon plasma universe then cooled further, and the current fundamental forces we know now took their present forms through further symmetry breaking (notably the breaking of electroweak symmetry). The full range of complex and composite particles we see around us today became possible, leading to a gravitationally dominated universe, the first neutral atoms (80 per cent hydrogen), and the cosmic microwave background radiation we can detect today. Modern high-energy particle physics theories are satisfactory at these energy levels, and so physicists believe they have a good understanding of this and the subsequent development of the fundamental universe around us. Because of these changes, space had also become largely transparent to light and other electromagnetic energy, rather than "foggy", by the end of this phase.

The third phase started, after a short dark age, with a universe whose fundamental particles and forces were as we know them. This phase witnessed the emergence of large-scale stable structures, such as the earliest stars, quasars, galaxies, clusters of galaxies, and superclusters, and the development of these to create the kind of universe we see today. Some researchers call the development of all this physical structure over billions of years cosmic evolution. Others, such as more interdisciplinary researchers, refer to cosmic evolution as the entire scenario of growing complexity from the Big Bang to humankind, thereby incorporating biology and culture into a unified view of all complex systems in the universe to date.

Beyond the present day, scientists anticipate that Earth will cease to be able to support life in about a billion years, and it will be enveloped by a greatly expanded sun in about five billion years. On a far longer timescale, the stelliferous era will end as stars eventually die and fewer are born to replace them, leading to a darkening universe. Various theories suggest a number of subsequent possibilities. If particles such as protons are unstable, then eventually matter may evaporate into low-level energy in a kind of entropy-related heat death.

The ideas concerning the very early universe (cosmogony) are speculative. No accelerator (Hadron) experiments have yet probed energies of sufficient magnitude to provide any experimental insight into the behaviour of matter at the energy levels that prevailed during this period of the existence of the universe.

The Planck epoch—named after Max Planck,[1] who was the most respected German physicist of his time—is the era in traditional Big Bang cosmology wherein the temperature was so high that the four fundamental forces (electromagnetism, gravitation, weak nuclear interaction, and strong nuclear interaction) were one fundamental force. Little is understood about physics at this temperature, though different hypotheses propose different scenarios. Traditional Big Bang cosmology predicts a gravitational singularity before this time, but this theory relies on general relativity and could be hampered due to quantum effects; the hindrance was solved by physicist and mathematician Edward Witten.[80]

As the universe expanded and cooled, it crossed transition temperatures at which forces separated from each other. These are phase transitions much like condensation and freezing. The grand unification epoch began when gravitation separated from the other forces of nature, which are collectively known as gauge forces. The non-gravitational physics in this epoch would be described by a so-called grand unified theory (GUT). The grand unification epoch ended when the GUT forces further separated into the strong and electroweak forces.

According to traditional Big Bang cosmology, the electroweak epoch began 10^{-36} seconds after the Big Bang, when the temperature of the universe was low enough (1028 kelvin) to separate the strong force from the electroweak force (the name for the unified forces of electromagnetism and the weak interaction). In inflationary cosmology, the electroweak epoch ends when the inflationary epoch begins, at roughly 10^{-32} second.

After the Planck epoch and inflation came the epochs of the creation of particles, quark, hadron, and lepton.[1] Together, these epochs encompassed less than ten seconds of time following the Big Bang. As the universe expands, the energy density of electromagnetic radiation decreased more quickly than did that of matter because the energy of a photon decreases with its wavelength. As the universe expanded and cooled, elementary particles associated stably with ever larger combinations. Thus, in the early part of the matter-dominated era, stable protons and neutrons formed, which then formed atomic nuclei through nuclear reactions. This process, known as Big Bang nucleosynthesis, led to the present abundances of lighter nuclei, particularly hydrogen, deuterium, and helium. Big Bang nucleosynthesis ended about twenty minutes after the Big Bang, when the universe had cooled enough so that nuclear fusion could no longer occur. At this stage, matter in the universe was mainly a hot, dense plasma of negatively charged electrons, neutral neutrinos, and positive nuclei. This era, called the photon era, lasted about 380,000 years.

Nuclear reactions amongst nuclei led to the present abundances of lighter nuclei, particularly hydrogen, deuterium, and helium, through a process known as the Big Bang nucleosynthesis. Eventually, in the time known as recombination, electrons and nuclei formed stable atoms, which are transparent to most wavelengths of radiation. The universe entered with photons disconnected from the case, the matter-dominated era. Light from this period now can freely travel, and it can still be seen in the universe as the cosmic microwave background radiation (CMB).

After about 200 million years, the first stars formed. These were probably very massive, bright, and responsible for the reionisation of the universe. Containing no heavier elements than lithium, these stars produced the first heavy elements by stellar nucleosynthesis.

The universe also contains a mysterious energy called dark energy, which energy density does not change over time. After about 9.8 billion years, the universe expanded enough so that the density of the ordinary matter was less than the density of dark energy. It marks the beginning of the current dark energy–dominated era. In this age, dark energy accelerates the expansion of the universe.

Some argue that the chemistry of life may have begun shortly after the Big Bang, 13.75 billion years ago, during a habitable epoch when the universe was only 10^{-17} million years old.

Over a timescale of a billion years or more, Earth and the solar system will become unstable. Earth's existing biosphere is expected to vanish in about a billion years as the sun's heat production gradually increases to the point that liquid water and life are unlikely. Earth's magnetic fields, axial tilt, and atmosphere are subject to long-term change, and the solar system itself is chaotic over million- and billion-year timescales. Eventually, around 5.4 billion years from now, the core of the sun will become hot enough to trigger hydrogen fusion in its surrounding shell. This will cause the outer layers of the star to expand greatly, and the star will enter a phase of its life in which it is called a red giant. Within 7.5 billion years, the sun will have expanded to a radius of 1.2 astronomical units (AU)—256 times its current size. Studies announced in 2008 show that due to tidal interaction between the sun and Earth, Earth would actually fall back into a lower orbit and get engulfed and incorporated inside the sun before the sun reaches its largest size, despite the sun losing about 38 per cent of its mass. The sun itself will continue to exist for many billions of years, passing through a number of phases and eventually ending up as a long-lived white dwarf. Eventually, after billions of more years, the sun will finally cease to shine altogether, becoming a black dwarf.

This scenario is possible only if the energy density of dark energy actually increases without limit over time. Such dark energy is called phantom energy and is unlike any known kind of energy. In this case, the expansion rate of the universe will increase without limit. Gravitationally bound systems, such as clusters of galaxies, galaxies, and ultimately the solar system, will be torn apart. Eventually the expansion will be so rapid as to overcome the electromagnetic forces holding together molecules and atoms. Finally, even atomic nuclei will be torn apart, and the universe as we know it will end in an unusual kind of gravitational singularity. At the time of this singularity, the expansion rate of the universe will reach infinity so that any and all forces (no matter how strong) that hold composite objects together (no matter how closely) will be overcome by this expansion, literally tearing everything apart. Believers will have great difficulty digesting what will happen with God's creation.

Space is one of the few fundamental quantities in physics, meaning that it cannot be defined via other quantities because nothing more fundamental is known at the present. On the other hand, it can be related to other fundamental quantities. Thus, similar to other fundamental quantities (like time and mass), space can be explored via measurement and experiment.

The space-time of the universe is usually interpreted from a Euclidean perspective, with space consisting of three dimensions and time consisting of one dimension, the "fourth dimension". By combining space and time into a single manifold called space-time, physicists have simplified a large number of physical theories, as well as described in a more uniform way the workings of the universe at both the super galactic and subatomic levels.

The four dimensions of space-time consist of events that are not absolutely defined spatially and temporally, but rather are known relative to the motion of an observer. Minkowski-space first approximates the universe without gravity; the pseudo-Riemannian manifolds of general relativity describe space-time with matter and gravity. Georg Friedrich Bernhard Rieman was an influential German mathematician who made lasting contributions to analysis, number theory, and differential (non-Euclidian) geometry, which enabled the development of general relativity. Some areas of theoretical physics, such as string theory, postulate the existence of additional dimensions.

Of the four fundamental interactions, gravitation is dominant at cosmological length scales; that is, the other three forces play a negligible role in determining structures at the level of galaxies and larger-scale structures. Gravity's effects are cumulative; by contrast, the effects of positive and negative charges tend to cancel one another, making electromagnetism relatively insignificant on cosmological-length scales. The remaining two interactions, the weak and strong nuclear forces, decline very rapidly with distance.

The universe seems to have much more ordinary matter than antimatter, an asymmetry possibly related to the observations of CP-violation. In particle physics, CP violation (CP standing for charge parity) is a violation of the postulated CP-symmetry (or charge conjugation parity symmetry): the combination of C-symmetry (charge conjugation symmetry) and P-symmetry (parity symmetry). CP-symmetry states that the laws of the universe appear to have much more matter than antimatter. Physics should be the same if a particle is interchanged with its antiparticle (C symmetry) and when its spatial coordinates are inverted ("mirror" or P symmetry). The discovery of CP violation in 1964 in the decays of neutral kaons resulted in the Nobel Prize in physics in 1980 for its discoverers James Cronin and Val Fitch. It plays an important role in the attempts of cosmology to explain the dominance of matter over antimatter in the present universe, as well as in the study of weak interactions in particle physics.

The universe appears to have no net electric charge, and therefore gravity appears to be the dominant interaction on cosmological-length scales. The universe also appears to have neither net momentum nor angular momentum. The absence of net charge and momentum follows from accepted physical laws (Gauss's law and the non-divergence of the stress-energy-momentum pseudo-tensor, respectively), if the universe were finite.

The shape of the universe is related to general relativity, which describes how space-time is curved and bent by mass and energy. The particle horizon, also known as the light horizon or the cosmic light horizon, is the maximum distance from which particles can have travelled to the observer in the age of the universe. The horizon represents the boundary between the observable and the unobservable region of the universe. The existence, properties, and significance of a cosmological horizon depend on the particular cosmological model.

Observational data suggest the cosmological topological of the universe is infinite in extent of finite age, supported by the so-called Friedmann–Lemaître–Robertson–Walker (FLRW) models. These FLRW models of space are consistent with the Wilkinson Microwave Anisotropy Probe (WMAP) and Planck maps of cosmic background radiation, thus supporting inflationary models and the standard model of cosmology, describing a flat, homogeneous universe dominated by dark matter and dark energy.

According to a restrictive definition, the universe is everything within our connected space-time that could have a chance to interact with us and vice versa. According to the general theory of relativity, some regions of space may never interact with ours even in the lifetime of the universe, due to the finite speed of light and the ongoing expansion of space. For example, radio messages sent from

Earth may never reach some regions of space, even if the universe were to exist forever: space may expand faster than light can traverse it. Because we cannot observe space beyond the limitations of light or any electromagnetic radiation, it is unknown whether the size of the universe is finite or infinite.

Distant regions of space are taken to exist and be part of reality as much as we are, yet we can never interact with them. The spatial region within which we can affect and be affected is the observable universe. The observable universe depends on the location of the observer. By travelling, an observer can come into contact with a greater region of space-time than an observer who remains still. Nevertheless, even the most rapid traveller will not be able to interact with all of space. Typically, the observable universe is taken to mean the universe observable from our vantage point in the Milky Way Galaxy.

The proper distance—the distance as would be measured at a specific time, including the present—between Earth and the edge of the observable universe is 46 billion light years (14 × 109 parsecs), making the diameter of the observable universe about 91 billion light years (28 × 109 parsecs). The distance the light from the edge of the observable universe has travelled is very close to the age of the universe times the speed of light, 13.8 billion light years (4.2 × 109 parsecs), but this does not represent the distance at any given time because the edge of the universe and the Earth have since moved since farther apart. For comparison, the diameter of a typical galaxy is 30,000 light years, and the typical distance between two neighbouring galaxies is 3 million light years. As an example, the Milky Way Galaxy is roughly 100,000 light years in diameter, and the nearest sister galaxy to the Milky Way, the Andromeda Galaxy, is located roughly 2.5 million light years away.

Over time, the universe and its contents have evolved. For example, the relative population of quasars and galaxies has changed, and space itself has expanded. This expansion accounts for how it is that scientists on Earth can observe light from a galaxy 30 billion light years away, even if that light has travelled for only 13 billion years. The very space between them has expanded, and that is one of the tools used to calculate the age of the universe. This expansion is consistent with the observation that the light from distant galaxies has been red-shifted; the photons emitted have been stretched to longer wavelengths and lower frequency during their journey. Analyses of type Ia supernovae indicate that the spatial expansion is accelerating.

The more matter there is in the universe, the stronger will be the gravitational pull of the matter. If the universe were too dense, then it would re-collapse into a singularity. However, if the universe contained too little matter, then the expansion is accelerated greatly, thereby leaving no time for planets and planetary systems to form. After the Big Bang, the universe is continuously expanding. The rate of expansion is affected by the gravity amongst the matter present. Surprisingly, our universe has just the right mass density of about 5 protons per cubic metre, which has allowed the universe to expand for the last 13.75 billion years, giving time to form the universe as we see it today.

There are dynamical forces acting on the particles in the universe which affect the expansion rate. It was earlier expected that the Hubble Constant (the unit used to measure the expansion of the universe) would decrease as time went on due to the influence of gravitational interactions in the universe, and thus there is an additional observable quantity in the universe called the deceleration parameter, which cosmologists expected to be directly related to the matter density of the universe. Surprisingly, the deceleration parameter was measured by two different groups to be less than zero (actually, consistent with −1), which implied that today Hubble's Constant is increasing as time goes on.

Space and time are the arenas where all physical events occur. An event is a point in space-time specified by the time and place.

The universe appears to be a smooth space-time continuum consisting of three spatial dimensions and one temporal (time) dimension. On average, space is observed to be nearly flat (close to zero curvature) so that Euclidian geometry can be used throughout the universe with high accuracy.

The universe is composed of almost 100 per cent dark energy, dark matter, and ordinary matter. Other contents are electromagnetic radiation (estimated to be from 0.005 per cent to close to 0.01 per cent) and antimatter. Ordinary baryonic matter, which includes atoms, stars, galaxies, and life, is only 4.6 per cent of the contents. The present overall density of this type of matter is very low, roughly 4.5×10^{-31} grams per cubic centimetre, corresponding to a density of the order of only one proton for every four cubic metres of volume.

The nature of both dark energy and dark matter is unknown. Dark matter, a mysterious form of matter that has not yet been identified, is 26.8 per cent of the contents of all space. Dark energy, which is the energy of empty space and which is causing the expansion of the universe to accelerate, is the remaining 68.3 per cent of the contents of all space.

Matter, dark matter, and dark energy are distributed homogeneously throughout the universe over length scales longer than 300 million light years. However, on smaller length scales, matter is observed to form clump hierarchically. Many atoms are condensed into stars, most stars into galaxies, most galaxies into clusters, most clusters into superclusters, and finally, large-scale filments - the largest-scale structures such as the Sloan great wall. There are probably more than 100 billion galaxies in the observable universe. Typical galaxies range from dwarfs with as few as ten million stars up to giants with one trillion stars. A 2010 study by astronomers estimated that the observable universe contains 300 sextillion stars. Between the structures are voids, which are typically 10–150 MPC (33–490 million light years) in diameter. The Milky Way is in the local group of galaxies, which in turn is in the Lanikai Supercluster. This supercluster spans over 500 million light years, and the Local Group spans over 10 million light years. In April 2015, astronomers announced the discovery of a supervoid, the largest known structure in the universe. This big hole is 1.8 billion light years (550 MPC) across, characterised by its unusual emptiness.

The observable universe is isotropic on scales significantly larger than superclusters, meaning that the statistical properties of the universe are the same in all directions as observed from Earth. The universe is bathed in highly isotropic microwave radiation that corresponds to a thermal equilibrium blackbody spectrum of roughly

2.72548 kelvin. The hypothesis that the large-scale universe is homogeneous and isotropic is known as the cosmological principle.[1] A universe that is both homogeneous and isotropic looks the same from all vantage points and has no centre.

The explanation for why the expansion of the universe is accelerating remains elusive. It is often attributed to dark energy, an unknown form of energy that is hypothesised to permeate space. On a mass-energy equivalence basis, the density of dark energy (6.91×10^{-27} kg/m^3) is much less than the density of ordinary matter or dark matter within galaxies. However, in the present dark energy era, it dominates the mass-energy of the universe because it is uniform across space.

Dark matter is a hypothetical kind of matter that cannot be seen with telescopes but that accounts for most of the matter in the universe. The existence and properties of dark matter are inferred from its gravitational effects on visible matter, radiation, and the large-scale structure of the universe. Other than neutrinos, a form of hot dark matter, dark matter has not been detected directly, making it one of the greatest mysteries in modern astrophysics. Dark matter neither emits nor absorbs light or any other electromagnetic radiation at any significant level. Dark matter is estimated to constitute 26.8 per cent of the total mass-energy and 84.5 per cent of the total matter in the universe. The remaining 4.9 per cent of the mass-energy of the universe is composed of matter made up of ordinary matter, which is atoms, ions, electrons, and the objects they form. This matter includes stars, which produce nearly all of the light we see from galaxies, as well as interstellar gas in the interstellar and intergalactic media, planets, and all the objects from everyday life that we can bump into, touch, or squeeze.

Ordinary matter exists in four states or phases: solid, liquid, gas, and plasma. Advances in experimental techniques, however, have other theoretical phases, such as Bose-Einstein condensates and Fermionic condensates[1] revealed.

More fundamentally, matter is composed of two types of elementary particles: quarks and leptons. For example, the neutron is formed of two down quarks and one up quark, whereas the proton is formed of two up quarks and one down quark. Atoms are made up of several neutrons and protons (two types of baryons), which have several electrons (a type of lepton) orbiting them. Because most of the mass of the atom is concentrated in the atomic nucleus, which is made up of baryons, astronomers often use the term baryonic matter to describe ordinary matter, although a small fraction of this baryonic matter is also composed of electrons. A focus on an elementary-particle view of matter also leads to new phases of matter, such as the quark-gluon plasma.

The primordial protons and neutrons themselves were formed from the quark-gluon plasma during the Big Bang as it cooled below two trillion degrees. A few minutes afterwards, starting with only protons and neutrons, nuclei up to lithium and beryllium were formed, but the abundances of other elements dropped sharply with growing atomic mass. Some boron may have been formed at this time, but the process stopped before significant carbon could be formed. This process, known as Big Bang nucleosynthesis, essentially shut down after about twenty minutes due to drops in temperature and density as the universe continued to expand. The subsequent nucleosynthesis of heavier elements required the extreme temperatures and pressures found within stars and supernovas, in the processes of stellar nucleosynthesis and supernova nucleosynthesis.

Ordinary matter in the universe consists of particles which are the domain of particle physics. The Standard Model of particle physics suggests a universal set of physical laws and physical constants. It concerns the electromagnetic, weak, and strong nuclear interactions, as well as classifying all the subatomic particles known. It was developed throughout the latter half of the twentieth century as a collaborative effort of scientists around the world. The current formulation was finalised in the mid-1970s upon experimental confirmation of the existence of quarks. Since then, discoveries of the top quark (1995), the tau neutrino (2000), and more recently the Higgs boson (2013; this particle was discovered by the Belgian physicists Robert Brout and François Englert a fortnight before Peter Higgs did, but it is still coined the Higgs boson; Englert and Higgs received the Noble Prize for their achievements) and Penta quarks

(2015), have given further credence to the Standard Model. Because of its success in explaining a wide variety of experimental results, the Standard Model is sometimes regarded as a "theory of almost everything".[1]

Quantum mechanics is a branch of physics dealing with the behaviour of matter and energy at the microscopic level. Matter and antimatter are made up of atoms, which make up the basic units. An atom is unimaginably small. There are more atoms in a glass of water than there are glasses of water in all the oceans on Earth. But an atom itself consists of particles (subatomic particles) that are only observable by the vibrations they cause. An atom consists of an extremely small, positively charged nucleus (atomic nucleus) which is made up of positively charged protons and neutrally charged neutrons, surrounded by a cloud of negatively charged electrons. Further are protons and neutrons made up of quarks. Elementary particles possess no internal structure because they are not composed of even smaller particles. Electrons, neutrinos, and quarks are elementary particles. The subatomic particle of hydrogen, which consists only of one proton, has a mass of 0.000 000 000 000 000 000 000 000 001 672 kilogrammes.[1]

Molecules are the smallest amounts of matter. As a single molecule is further divided, it is no longer a molecule of that matter; a split water molecule is not water anymore.[1]

The fundamental laws of quantum mechanics, such as all laws of physics, apply to each individual atom and particle. Although the theory of relativity describes the four fundamental forces in physics (the electromagnetic force, the strong and weak nuclear forces, and gravity) on long distances and at high speeds, quantum mechanics describe the matter at the extremely small scale.

In particle physics, string theory is a theoretical framework in which the point-like particles of quantum mechanics are replaced by one dimensional objects coined as strings.[3] String theory states that the point-like particles are in fact vibrating strings, and so they are observable. In terms of string theory, a string can in turn produce different particles depending on the way they oscillate.[1]

Einstein's general relativity describes how gravity emerges and assumes that the universe is flat. This seems contradictory to quantum dynamics, and therefore in 1984 a string theory was proposed that could combine the two theories. The new string theory makes this possible by assuming that there are more than four dimensions. The string theory aims to provide an explanation of all observed elementary particles which is not possible with the standard quantum physics. The evolution of string theory (five super string theories) incorporated the application of gravity so that a conclusive hypothetical mathematical model was posited, in which all fundamental forces of physics play their roles. String theory is a theoretical tool that sheds light on many aspects of quantum field theory and quantum gravity. The theory requires the existence of extra spatial dimensions (ten or eleven) for her mathematical consistency, in contrast with the three tangible space dimensions plus the time dimension. Because the current particle accelerators are not able to reveal extra dimensions, the extra dimensions must be smaller than the length the particle accelerators can see, about 10^{15}. The objection to the string theory is its lack of providing new experimental predictions at accessible energy scales. Nevertheless, most theoretical physicists believe in it. The boson string theory was the original string theory developed at the end of 1960, but it was incomplete because it only referred to bosons, and protons also contain fermions. String theory evolved in the 1980s to superstring theory by mathematical approaches to symmetry (connection between bosons and fermions), open (thread-form) and closed (rubber band-form) strings, membranes as building blocks of particles, and multiverse leading finally to the M-theory, which in turn may constitute the physics unification theory of everything.

The term *multiverse* refers to the concept that many other universes may exist next to our visible universe and are referred to as parallel universes. Criticism of the concept is that it is little scientific and rather philosophical. The multiverse concept does allow application of the argued anthropic principle from which life can develop and evolve. The term *anthropic* in Anthropic principle has been argued to be a misnomer; although singling out our kind of carbon-based life, none of the finely tuned phenomena require human life or some kind of carbon chauvinism. Any form of life would do, seeing that nothing specifically human or anthropic is involved. The anthropic principle is the philosophical consideration that observations of the universe must be compatible with the conscious and sapient life that it observes.

The brane-theory (membranes) contributes to the existence of hyperspace in which multiverse are possible. A brane is a physical, dynamical object that generalises the notion of a point particle to higher dimensions.

It was the theoretical physicist and brilliant mathematician Edward Witten who posited the M-theory in 1995.[3] He found that the five different superstring theories are only distinguished by dualities and may be united by an overarching theory. In theoretical physics duality is the equivalence of two physical theories, which admits a theory that is difficult to approach with a theory in which it must be possible to make the calculations easier. The one-dimensional strings in any of the five ten-dimensional string theories are essentially two-dimensional cross-sections of membranes and form the eleven-dimensional M-theory. The higher dimensional objects are then called branes, which contain strings and membranes as 'diameter', and so in turn can carry all kinds of particles of matter in itself but are dimensionally locked up.

It is now by no means clear how exactly this M-theory should look, and a complete mathematical formulation (non-perturbative) is definitely not yet available. However, on the basis of existing formulations of superstring theories and the connections between them, it is already possible to derive certain results about this theory and prove certain properties.

There is no experimental evidence that supports string theory. The available particle accelerators are not able to produce the energy level necessary to retrieve the string theory and make it visible. The theory, failing to produce after so many years any experimental testability, runs up against violent criticism offered by Nobel Laureates Richard Feynman, Sheldon Glashow, and Gerard 'tHooft, as well by physicist Roger Penrose. Glashow stated that string theory was a tumour and compared the theory with medieval theology, relying more on faith and thoughts spinning than on observations and experiments of physics. The criticism is based by the lack of experimentally testable predictions.

Stephen Hawking was one of the many theoretical physicists who was convinced that the M-theory constitutes an important step towards the correct basic explanation of the universe. In the past, he had already cast heavy doubts on the existence of God.[4] He had never explicitly shown whether he was an atheist, although this turned out to be implied from his writings. His first wife, Jane Wilde, who is deeply religious and with whom he reconciled, confirmed during the divorce case that he had always been an atheist.[5] When he attended a cosmological congress in 1980 in the Vatican, he was not charmed at all when Pope John Paul II stated that the cosmologists were free to debate the Big Bang but that the creation of the universe belonged to the domain of God. In Hawking's popular scientific book *The Grand Design,*[6] written with his friend and physicist Leonard Mlodinow, he answered the question whether there is evidence that the universe was designed by a benevolent being, or whether science offers a better explanation. A similar reasoning follows from the brilliant book by the theoretical physicist Lawrence M. Krauss, *A Universe from Nothing.*[53] Evolutionary biologist and leading advocate of atheism Richard Dawkins welcomed the position of Hawking by stating, "Darwinism kicked God out of the biology, and now Hawking has done the same with a coup de grace in physics."[7]

The postulate by Hawking that the universe creates itself spontaneously is confirmed by the recent discovery of a new remote galaxy that was awarded the name z8GND_ 5296.[8] The new galaxy is calculated at being 30 billion light years away from earth. Because it takes light so long to travel from the outer edge of the universe to our planet, the galaxy appears as it was 13.1 billion light years ago, meaning that we are seeing this galaxy as it was 700 billion light years after the Big Bang. Its distance from the earth, 30 billion light years, is explained by the expansion of the universe, which is faster than the speed of light. The observable edge of the universe is actually 13.1 billion light years because the light outside this distance has not yet reached us. In the future, galaxies could enter the 13.1 billion light zone and bring us essential knowledge about the Big Bang. What is remarkable that this new galaxy, although small (only about 1–2 per cent the size of our galaxy), is able to transform gas and dust into new stars at a seed, hundreds of times faster than our own galaxy.

Something which comes spontaneously into being can have hardly a goal. Nevertheless, there are some, even atheists which is not understandable, who are of the opinion that there may be an occult cause behind the creation of the universe that provides purpose and meaning.

Most scientists are atheists. A study published in 1968 in a letter in the journal *Nature* shows that 93 per cent of the members of the American National Academy of Science are atheists or agnostics, without making any claim thereabouts, whereas 85 per cent of the American population are believers. (The United States is, after all, originally founded by migrants who left Europe for religious reasons.)

The Jewish faith precedes Christianity a long time. Christianity was founded by dissident Jews, who were disappointed that the promised arrival of the Messiahs was not forthcoming. It is indeed remarkable that many famous scientists are Jews who have renounced their faith.

Most people have a belief which can be organised, such as Judaism, Christianity, Islam, or Hinduism, and it could be a purely private personal conviction. However, a distinction is indicated. There are deep believers and others who believe only superficially. In both groups, there are intelligent and less intelligent people. The intelligent believers hold that everything goes back to the first cause as a start (creation) of the universe and relate it to the existence of a deity (cf. chapter XX, E, Considerations, infra).

Already now, it can be stated that if life makes no sense, many may be faced with a chaos syndrome.

CHAPTER 4

Origin of Life

The solar system began forming about 4.6 billion years ago, or about 9 billion years after the Big Bang. A fragment of a molecular cloud made mostly of hydrogen and traces of other elements began to collapse, forming a large sphere in the centre which would become the sun, as well as a surrounding disk. The surrounding accretion disk would coalesce into a multitude of smaller objects that would become planets, asteroids, and comets. The sun is a late-generation star, and the solar system incorporates matter created by previous generations of stars.

Life is a characteristic distinguishing physical entities having biological processes (such as signalling and self-sustaining processes) from those that do not, either because such functions have ceased or because they never had such functions and are classified as inanimate. Various forms of life exist such as plants, animals, fungi, protists, archaea, and bacteria. The criteria can at times be ambiguous and may or may not define viruses, viroids, or potential artificial life as living. Biology is the primary science concerned with the study of life, although many other sciences are involved.[81-86-88-87]

It is a challenge for scientists and philosophers to define life because life is a process and not substance. Any definition must be general enough to encompass all known life.[86]

The definition of life is controversial. The current definition is that organisms maintain homeostasis (regulation of the internal environment to maintain a constant state), are composed of cells, undergo metabolism, can grow, adapt to their environment, respond to stimuli, and reproduce. However, many other biological definitions have been proposed, and there are also some borderline cases, such as viruses. Biophysicists have also proposed some definitions, with many based on chemical systems. There are also some living systems theories, such as the Gaia hypothesis, the idea that the Earth is alive; this was first developed by the biologist James Grier Miller. Another one is that life is the property of ecological systems, and yet another is the complex systems biology, a branch or subfield of mathematical biology. Some other systemic definitions include the theory involving the Darwinian dynamic and the operator theory. However, throughout history there have been many other theories and definitions about life such as materialism, the belief that everything is made out of matter and that life is merely a complex form of it; hylomorphism, the belief that all things are a combination of matter and form, and that the form of a living thing is its soul; spontaneous generation, the belief that life repeatedly emerges from non-life; and vitalism, a discredited scientific hypothesis that living organisms possess a "life force" or "vital spark".

In May 2016, scientists reported that 1 trillion species were estimated to be on Earth currently, with only one-thousandth of 1 per cent described. Over 99 per cent of all species that ever lived on Earth are considered to be extinct. Abiogenesis is the natural process of life arising from non-living matter, such as simple organic compounds. Life on Earth arose 3.8–4.1 billion years ago. It is widely accepted that current life on Earth descended from an RNA world, but RNA-based life may not have been the first. The mechanism by which life began on Earth is unknown, although many hypotheses have been formulated, most based on the Miller-Urey experiment.

Living beings are thermodynamic systems with an organised structure that can reproduce itself and evolve as survival dictates.

Nature generates viruses which are a form of life which depends on a host. Viruses do not live in symbiosis with the host. On the contrary they feed on the host and eventually kill it. Viruses are combatted by organic or inorganic drugs administrated as a vaccine, which is an antigenic preparation used to stimulate the production of antibodies and procure immunity of the disease. Viruses are proof of the case of abiogenesis, which is the conviction of the scientific world.

Since appearing, life on Earth has changed its environment on a geologic time scale. To survive in most ecosystems, life can adapt and thrive in a wide range of conditions. Some organisms, called extremophiles, can thrive in physically or geochemically extreme conditions that are detrimental to most life on Earth. Properties common to all organisms are the need for certain core chemical elements needed for biochemical functioning. Aristotle was the first person to classify organisms. Later, Carl Linnaeus introduced his system of binomial nomenclature for the classification of species. He coined the term Homo *sapiens,* whether man or woman. Linnaus was a Swedish botanist, physician, and zoologist who formalised the modern system of naming organisms called binomial nomenclature. He is known by the epithet "father of modern taxonomy". The Swiss philosopher Jean-Jacques Rousseau sent him the message, "Tell him I know no greater man on earth." The German writer Johann Wolfgang von Goethe wrote, "With the exception of Shakespeare and Spinoza, I know no one among the no longer living who has influenced me more strongly." Swedish author August Strindberg wrote, "Linnaeus was in reality a poet who happened to become a naturalist." Among other compliments, Linnaeus has been called *Princeps botanicorum* (Prince of Botanists), the Pliny of the North, and the Second Adam. He is also considered as one of the founders of modern ecology.

Homo *sapiens* includes Homo *sapiens idaltu*, an archaic subspecies of Homo *sapiens.* Extant human populations have historically been divided into subspecies, but since the 1980s all extant groups tend to be subsumed into a single subspecies, Homo *sapiens sapiens.*

Some sources show Neanderthals (Homo *neanderthalensis*) as a subspecies (Homo *sapiens neanderthalensis*). Similarly, the discovered specimens of the Homo *rhodesiensis* species have been classified by some as a subspecies (Homo *sapiens rhodesiensis*), although it remains more common to treat these last two as separate species within the Homo genus rather than as subspecies within Homo *sapiens.*

Anatomically modern humans (Homo *sapiens sapiens*) evolved from archaic humans in the Middle Palaeolithic at least 300,000 years ago. The emergence of anatomically modern humans marks the dawn of the species Homo *sapiens*, the species to which all humans alive today belong.

The time frame for the human evolution of the genus Homo out of the chimpanzee's and human's last common ancestor is roughly 10 to 2 million years ago, and that of Homo *sapiens* out of Homo *erectus* roughly 1.8 to 0.2 million years ago.

Homo *sapiens idaltu*, the other known subspecies, is now extinct. Homo *neanderthalensis* became extinct 30,000 years ago and has sometimes been classified as a subspecies. Genetic studies suggest that the modern human diverged from neanderthalensis about 500,000 years ago.

Cells are the smallest units of life, often called the building blocks of life. There are two kinds of cells, prokaryotes and eukaryotes. Cells consist of cytoplasm enclosed within a membrane, which contains many biomolecules such as proteins and nucleic acids. Cells reproduce through a process of cell division in which the parent cell divides into two or more daughter cells.

Though only confirmed on Earth, many believe in the existence of extra-terrestrial life. Artificial life is a computer simulation of any aspect of life, which is used to examine systems related to life. Death is the permanent termination of all biological functions that sustain an organism, and as such it notes the end of its life. Extinction is the process by which a group of taxa, normally a species, dies out. Fossils are the preserved remains or traces of organisms.

There are hilarious fables of the Abrahamic religions left out of consideration (God created man), but there is no established theory in science about the origin of life, although the theory of Abiogenesis gains more ground.

Fossil recordings reveal that life on earth originated on earth between 4.4 billion years ago, when water vapour first liquefied, and 3.5 billion years ago. It is generally agreed that all life today evolved by common descent from a single primitive life form (Darwinism). We do not know how this early form came into being, but most scientists think it was a natural process which took place about 3.9 billion years ago. This process is in accord with the philosophy called naturalism, wherefore only natural causes are valid.[84]

What we also do not know is whether metabolism or genetics first happened. There are two important hypotheses. One is based on RNA (ribonucleic acid, later replaced by DNA, deoxyribonucleic acid) as first world hypothesis. The second is based on protein as world hypothesis. Then there is the problem of the cell formation because every living organism consists of cells.

DNA is the genetic code of humans. The molecule is a polymer of the deoxyribonucleic acid molecule in which all codes of the proteins have contained a person throughout his life needs.

Many modern theories of the origin of life take a primeval soup of organic molecules as a starting point of life. Earth's pre-biotic oceans were very different from what oceans are now. They were a soup containing the basic chemicals from which life is thought to have formed. In this soup, organic compounds, which are the building blocks of life, could have formed.[10] The idea is called biopoiesis or abiogenesis, the process of living matter evolving from self-replicating but non-living molecules.[10] Creation, especially creation of life, is considered by believers the prerogative of God. Today this is proven wrong. In the laboratories of the J. Craig Venter Institute in Rockville, Maryland, a team of scientists, using synthetic building blocks, created a living cell, a bacterium, from the basic chemicals of which DNA is composed. This first living organism with a completely synthetic gnome can only be seen under a microscope and is without a membrane, but its creation is a giant step forward for humanity. It is proof that genomes designed by computer and assembled in a lab can function in a donor cell, eventually reproducing fully functional living creatures and thereby establishing the reproducing creation of artificial life. This technology will fundamentally change the world by solving a variety of problems, from curing diseases to locking up greenhouse gases to consuming toxic waste. Most important, it will prolong human life.[11]

Evolution in biology is the process of change in all forms of life from generation to generation. The theory of evolution is the scientific explanation for life and for the variety of living species on Earth.

The theory of evolution describes the process by which genetic traits of life forms change from generation to generation on the basis of variation, reproduction, and natural selection. Charles Darwin and Albert Russell Wallace are the main founders of the theory of evolution, which is the generally accepted theory. A common misconception about evolution is that it's optimising for the survival of organisms, whereas evolution is the survival of the most fitted. Evolution seems to be optimising for the replication of genes. Once you have reproduced, it can be considered that you are not any further use to evolution.

Earth came into existence approximately 4.5 billion years ago, and living forms appeared on the surface a billion years later. The similarities between the current life forms admit assuming that there has been a common ancestor from which all currently living species by evolution are descended. Life is suspected to have originated during the first 600 million years of Earth's history. The first known organisms were bacteria that lived approximately 3.5 billion years ago in an aqueous environment. Microbes appeared 2.9 billion years ago. The first plant life 1 billion years ago consisted of a covering of Earth's crust with algae. Higher plants date to 450 million years ago, and insects date to 400 million years ago. Although life was present for most of Earth's history, it took until between 600 and 500 million years ago before animals appeared, and from which almost all present animals descend. Around 1.7 billion years ago, the first multicellular organisms appeared, but the organisms that multiply by sexual reproduction must have existed previously. The first fish appeared about 500 million years ago. Approximately 350 million years ago, the first amphibians appeared, which could live both on land and in water. Amphibians are both the ancestors of the dinosaurs as the therapsids (reptile mammals) and the ancestors of mammals.

Because the therapsids were duly affected during a major mass extinction 251 million years ago, the dinosaurs became the dominant species during the Mesozoic and could keep the upper hand ecologically over the remaining mammals. The dinosaurs (except birds) disappeared by a mass extinction event 65 million years ago.

Apart from mutations of genes, genetic drift is the factor for genetic change. However, sexual reproduction is the essential requirement for life and its evolution.

In 1944, Austrian scientist Erwin Schrödinger, a 1933 Nobel Prize laureate, a pioneer of quantum physics, and an atheist, wrote a non-fiction science book for the lay reader, *What Is Life*.[88] The book was based on a course of public lectures delivered by Schrödinger in February 1943, under the auspices of the Dublin Institute for Advanced Studies at Trinity College, Dublin. The lectures attracted an audience of about four hundred, who were warned "that the subject-matter was a difficult one and that the lectures could not be termed popular, even though the physicist's most dreaded weapon, mathematical deduction, would hardly be utilised". Schrödinger's lecture focused on one important question: "How can the events in space and time which take place within the spatial boundary of a living organism be accounted for by physics and chemistry?"

In the book, Schrödinger introduced the idea of an "aperiodic crystal" that contained genetic information in its configuration of covalent chemical bonds. In the 1950s, this idea stimulated enthusiasm for discovering the genetic molecule. Although the existence of DNA had been known since 1869, its role in reproduction and its helical shape were still unknown at the time of Schrödinger's lecture. In retrospect, Schrödinger's aperiodic crystal can be viewed as a well-reasoned theoretical prediction of what biologists should have been looking for during their search for genetic material. James D. Watson and Francis Crick, independent co-discoverers of the structure of DNA, credited Schrödinger's book with presenting an early theoretical description of how the storage of genetic information would work, and they acknowledged the book as a source of inspiration for their initial researches.

In chapter 1, Schrödinger explains that most physical laws on a large scale are due to chaos on a small scale. He calls this principle "order-from-disorder". As an example, he mentions diffusion, which can be modelled as a highly ordered process but which is caused by random movement of atoms or molecules. If the number of atoms is reduced, the behaviour of a system becomes more and more random. He states that life greatly depends on order and that a naïve physicist may assume that the master code of a living organism has to consist of a large number of atoms. What Schrôdinger suggests is that out of chaos, which is a disorder, comes order.

In chapters 2 and 3, he summarises what was known at this time about the hereditary mechanism. Most important, he elaborates the important role mutations play in evolution. He concludes that the carrier of hereditary information has to be both small in size and permanent in time, contradicting the naïve physicist's expectation. This contradiction cannot be resolved by classical physics.

In chapter 4, Schrödinger presents molecules (which are indeed stable even if they consist of only a few atoms) as the solution. Even though molecules were known before, their stability could not be explained by classical physics, but it was due to the discrete nature of quantum mechanics. Furthermore, mutations are directly linked to quantum leaps.

He continues to explain, in chapter 5, that true solids, which are also permanent, are crystals. The stability of molecules and crystals is due to the same principles, and a molecule might be called "the germ of a solid". On the other hand, an amorphous solid without crystalline structure should be regarded as a liquid with a very high viscosity. Schrödinger believes the heredity material to be a molecule, which (unlike a crystal) does not repeat itself. He calls this an aperiodic crystal. Its aperiodic nature allows it to encode an almost infinite number of possibilities with a small number of atoms. He finally compares this picture with the known facts and finds it in accordance with them.

In chapter 6 Schrödinger states,

> Living matter, while not eluding the "laws of physics" as established up to date, is likely to involve "other laws of physics" hitherto unknown, which however, once they have been revealed, will form just as integral a part of science as the

> former (Are these not the laws of the universe? Out the chaos of the Big Bang came order from disorder, which order pervades the universe).

He knows that this statement is open to misconception and tries to clarify it. The main principle involved with "order-from-disorder" is the second law of thermodynamics, according to which entropy only increases in a closed system (such as the universe). Schrödinger explains that living matter evades the decay to thermodynamically by homeostatic maintaining negative entropy (today, this quantity is called information) in an open system.[88]

In chapter 7, he maintains that "order-from-order" is not absolutely new to physics; in fact, it is even simpler and more plausible. Nature follows "order-from-disorder", with some exceptions, as the movement of the celestial bodies and the behaviour of mechanical devices such as clocks. But even those are influenced by thermal and frictional forces. The degree to which a system functions mechanically or statistically depends on the temperature. If heated, a clock ceases to function because it melts. Conversely, if the temperature approaches absolute zero, any system behaves more and more mechanically. Some systems approach this mechanical behaviour rather fast, with room temperature already being practically equivalent to absolute zero.

Schrödinger concludes this chapter and the book with philosophical speculations on determinism, free will, and the mystery of human consciousness. He believes he must reconcile two premises: (1) the body fully obeys the laws of quantum mechanics, where quantum indeterminacy plays no important role except to increase randomness at the quantum scale, and (2) there is "incontrovertible direct experience" that we freely direct our bodies, can predict outcomes, and take responsibility for our choice of action. Schrödinger rejects the idea that the source of consciousness should perish with the body because he finds the idea "distasteful". He also rejects the idea that there are multiple immortal souls that can exist without the body because he believes that consciousness is highly dependent on the body.

The only possible alternative is simply to keep to the immediate experience that consciousness is a singular of which the plural is unknown, that there is only one thing, and that what seems to be a plurality is merely a series of different aspects of this one thing.

Any intuitions that consciousness is plural, he says, are illusions. Schrödinger is sympathetic to the Hindu concept of Brahman, by which each individual's consciousness is only a manifestation of a unitary consciousness pervading the universe—which corresponds to the Hindu concept of God. Schrödinger concludes, "'I' am the person, if any, who controls the 'motion of the atoms' according to the Laws of Nature." However, he also qualifies the conclusion as "necessarily subjective" in its "philosophical implications". In the final paragraph, he points out that what is meant by "I (me)" is not the collection of experienced events but "namely the canvas upon which they are collected". If a hypnotist succeeds in blotting out all earlier reminiscences, he writes, there would be no loss of personal existence_"Nor will there ever be".

In a world governed by the second law of thermodynamics, all isolated systems are expected to approach a state of maximum disorder. Because life approaches and maintains a highly ordered state, some argue that this seems to violate the aforementioned Second Law, implying that there is a paradox. However, because the biosphere is not an isolated system, there is no paradox. The increase of order inside an organism is more than paid for by an increase in disorder outside this organism by the loss of heat into the environment. By this mechanism, the Second Law is obeyed, and life maintains a highly ordered state, which it sustains by causing a net increase in disorder in the universe. In order to increase the complexity of Earth—as life does—free energy is needed. Free energy for life here on Earth is provided by the sun.

Schrödinger wrote about his cat paradox thought experiment in "The Present Situation in Quantum Mechanics" (translated by John D. Trimmer in *Proceedings of the American Philosophical Society*. One can even set up quite ridiculous cases. A cat is penned up in a steel chamber, along with the following device (which must be secured against direct interference by the cat): in a Geiger counter, there is a tiny bit of radioactive substance so small that perhaps in the course of the hour, one of the atoms decays—but also with equal probability, perhaps none. If it happens, the counter tube discharges and, through a relay, releases a hammer that shatters a small flask of hydrocyanic acid. If one has left this entire system to itself for an hour, one would say that the cat still lives if no atom has decayed. The psi-function of the entire system would express this by having in it the living and dead cat mixed or smeared out in equal parts.

It is typical of these cases that an indeterminacy originally restricted to the atomic domain becomes transformed into macroscopic indeterminacy, which can then be resolved by direct observation. That prevents us from naively accepting as valid a "blurred model" for representing reality. In itself, it would not embody anything unclear or contradictory. There is a difference between a shaky or out-of-focus photograph and a snapshot of clouds and fog banks.

Schrödinger's famous thought experiment poses the question, "When does a quantum system stop existing as a superposition of states and become one or the other?" If the cat survives, it remembers only being alive.

Schrödinger was a highly gifted scientist but a controversial figure. He cohabited with his wife and with his mistress. He called himself an atheist but favoured pantheism and loved to dabble in metaphysics. He contributed greatly to quantum mechanics but was not entirely comfortable with the implications of quantum mechanics, saying, "I don't like it, and I am sorry I ever had anything to do with it."

In January 1926, Schrödinger published in *Annalen der Physik* the paper "Quantisation as an Eigenvalue Problem". It was on wave mechanics and presented what is now known as the Schrödinger equation. In this paper, he gave a "derivation" of the wave equation for time-independent systems and showed that it gave the correct energy eigenvalues for a hydrogen-like atom. This paper has been universally celebrated as one of the most important achievements of the twentieth century, and it created a revolution in most areas of quantum mechanics and indeed of all physics and chemistry. A second paper was submitted just four weeks later that solved the quantum harmonic oscillator, rigid rotor, and diatomic molecule problems and that gave a new derivation of the Schrödinger equation. A third paper, published in May, showed the equivalence of his approach to that of Heisenberg and gave the treatment of the Stark effect. The fourth paper in this series showed how to treat problems in which the system changes with time, as in scattering problems. In this paper, he introduced a complex solution to the Wave equation in order to prevent the occurrence of a fourth order differential equation. This was arguably the moment when quantum mechanics switched from real to complex numbers, never to return. These papers were his central achievement and were at once recognised as having great significance by the physics community. The Stark effect is the shifting and splitting of spectral lines of atoms and molecules due to the presence of an external electric field. The amount of splitting or shifting is called the Stark Splitting or Stark Shift. In general, one distinguishes first- and second-order Stark effects. The first-order effect is linear in the applied electric field, whereas the second-order effect is quadratic in the field. The Stark effect can be explained with fully quantum-mechanical approaches, but it has also been a fertile testing ground for semi-classical methods. The effect is named after the Nazi scientist and Nobel Prize laureate Johannes Stark, who discovered it in 1913. It was independently discovered in the same year by Italian physicist Antonino Lo Surdo, and in Italy it is sometimes called the Stark–Lo Surdo effect. The discovery of this effect contributed the development of quantum theory.

In 1953 James Watson and Francis Crick, using experimental data collected mainly by chemist Rosalind Franklin without her permission, and molecular biologist Maurits Wilkins, Nobel Prize laureate with Watson and Crick (Franklin had died in 1958 and was therefore ineligible for nomination), deduced the double helix structure of DNA,[72] which was the most important scientific discovery of the twentieth century. Human understanding of life was fundamentally changed, and the modern era of biology began.

Watson is a brilliant scientist and earned his PhD at the age of twenty-two. However, he has often expressed provocative concepts and disparaging opinions of others within the realm of genetic research.[131]

He has been quoted in *The Sunday Telegraph* in 1997 as stating, "If you could find the gene which determines sexuality and a woman decides she doesn't want a homosexual child, well, let her." The biologist Richard Dawkins wrote a letter to *The Independent* claiming that Watson's position was misrepresented by *The Sunday Telegraph* article, and that Watson would equally consider the possibility of having a heterosexual child to be just as valid as any other reason for abortion, to emphasise that Watson is in favour of allowing choice.

- On the issue of obesity, Watson has also been quoted as saying in 2000, "Whenever you interview fat people, you feel bad, because you know you're not going to hire them."
- While speaking at a conference in 2000, Watson had suggested a link between skin colour and sex drive, hypothesising that dark-skinned people have stronger libidos. His lecture argued that extracts of melanin—which gives skin its colour—had been found to boost subjects' sex drive. "That's why you have Latin lovers," he said, according to people who attended the lecture. "You've never heard of an English lover. Only an English patient."
- Watson has repeatedly supported genetic screening and genetic engineering in public lectures and interviews, arguing that stupidity is a disease and the "really stupid" bottom 10 per cent of people should be cured. He has also suggested that beauty could be genetically engineered, saying in 2003, "People say it would be terrible if we made all girls pretty. I think it would be great."
- Watson has had quite a few disagreements with the experiments of biochemist Craig Venter, creator of synthetic life.[1] He was even quoted as calling Venter "Hitler".
- On 25 October 2007, Watson was compelled to retire as chancellor of the Cold Spring Harbor Laboratory on New York's Long Island and from its board of directors, after he had been quoted in *The Times* the previous week

> as saying, "I am inherently gloomy about the prospect of Africa [because] all our social policies are based on the fact that their intelligence is the same as ours—whereas all the testing says not really." He went on to say that despite the desire that all human beings should be equal, "people who have to deal with black employees find this not true". In a 2008 BBC documentary, Watson said, "I have never thought of myself as a racist. I don't see myself as a racist. I am mortified by it." Before, in a *Sunday Times* magazine, he said that that "you should not discriminate on the basis of colour, because there are many people of colour who are very talented, but you cannot promote them when they have not succeeded at the lower level". Rightly, he added that there is no firm reason to anticipate that the intellectual capacities of people geographically separated in their evolution should prove to have evolved identically.

Watson, as all great scientists, is a humanist and an atheist. The question arises as to whether believers are as intelligent as non-believers. To be a top scientist, you have to be very intelligent and have amassed a great amount of knowledge which the ordinary man does not have—and that the common intelligent man who does not need a vast knowledge to fulfil his job, and who does not take the trouble to increase his knowledge. A blatant example is the Jews, who are considered an intelligent race. A lot of top scientists are Jews, yet nearly all of them have forsaken their religion for atheism. All believers should reflect on this. Politicians who misuse religion to get elected are evil men. They exploit the ignorance of the people. Belief is contrary to truth. People who believe are susceptible to fanaticism and do not have an open mind. Modern science has shown why God does not exist. People, however, must have the intelligence and the effort to seek knowledge and the truth. Intelligence is the ability to perceive or infer information, and to retain it as knowledge towards adaptive behaviors within an environment or context. General knowledge demands education, but intelligence requires an open mind capable of assimilating the knowledge and allowing objective reasoning. The western civilisation can call on many educated people of some sort but unfortunately few have an open mind. This is caused by their religious nature. They are the victims of the context of their faith.

The anthropic principle (from the Greek *anthropos*, meaning "human") is the philosophical consideration that observations of the universe must be compatible with the conscious and sapient life that observes it. Some proponents of the anthropic principle reason that it explains why the universe has the age and the conscious life. As a result, they believe it is unremarkable that the universe's fundamental constants happen to fall within the narrow range thought to be compatible with life.[90] All that pertains to the universe is completely normal and can hardly be used as an argument.

The principle was formulated as a response to a series of observations that the laws of nature and parameters of the universe take on values that are consistent with conditions for life as we know it rather than a set of values that would not be consistent with life on Earth. The anthropic principle states that this is a necessity because if life were impossible, no living entity would be there to observe it and thus would not be known. That is, it must be possible to observe *some* universe, and hence the laws and constants of any such universe must accommodate that possibility. The anthropic principle concerns humans and not all living entities who are also observers and are less intelligent. Building a hypothesis on the fact of observance by humans seems farfetched. The nature of the universe is such that it has allowed on earth, and perhaps on other places in the universe, the creation of living forms.

The term *anthropic* in anthropic principle has been argued to be a misnomer. While singling out our kind of carbon-based life, none of the finely tuned phenomena require human life or some kind of carbon chauvinism. Any form of life or any form of a heavy atom, stone, star, or galaxy would do; nothing specifically human or anthropic is involved.

The anthropic principle has given rise to some confusion and controversy, partly because the phrase has been applied to several distinct ideas. All versions of the principle have been accused of discouraging the search for a deeper physical understanding of the universe. The anthropic principle is often criticised for lacking falsifiability, and therefore critics of the anthropic principle may point out that the anthropic principle is a non-scientific concept, even though the weak anthropic principle *"conditions that are observed in the universe must allow the observer to exist"* is "easy" to support in mathematics and philosophy (i.e., it is a tautology or truism). However, building a substantive argument based on a tautological foundation is problematic. Stronger variants of the anthropic principle are not tautologies and thus make claims that are considered controversial by some and that are contingent upon empirical verification.

In 1961, theoretical astrophysicist Robert Dicke noted that the age of the universe, as seen by living observers, cannot be random. Instead, biological factors constrain the universe to be more or less in a "golden age", neither too young nor too old (the Goldilocks state). If the universe were one-tenth as old as its present age, there would not have been sufficient time to build up appreciable levels of metallicity (levels of elements besides hydrogen and helium), especially carbon, by nucleosynthesis. Small rocky planets did not yet exist. If the universe were ten times older than it actually is, most stars would be too old to remain on the main sequence and would have turned into white dwarfs, aside from the dimmest red dwarfs, and stable planetary systems would have already come to an end. Thus, Dicke explained the coincidence between large, dimensionless numbers constructed from the constants of physics and the age of the universe—a coincidence which had inspired Dirac's Varying-G theory.[1]

Dicke later reasoned that the density of matter in the universe must be almost exactly the critical density needed to prevent the Big Crunch (the "Dicke coincidences" argument). The most recent measurements may suggest that the observed density of baryonic matter, and some theoretical predictions of the amount of dark matter, account for about 30 per cent of this critical density, with the rest contributed by a cosmological constant.

The phrase "anthropic principle" first appeared in Brandon Carter's contribution to a 1973 Kraków symposium honouring Copernicus's five hundredth birthday. Carter articulated the anthropic principle in reaction to the Copernican principle, which states that humans do not occupy a privileged position in the universe. Indeed, Carter said, "Although our situation is not necessarily in disagreement with using the Copernican principle to justify the 'Perfect central', it is inevitably privileged to some extent." Specifically, Carter's Cosmological Principle states that all large regions *and times* in the universe must be statistically identical. The latter principle underlays the steady-state theory, which had recently been falsified by the 1965 discovery of the cosmic microwave background radiation. This discovery was unequivocal evidence that the universe has changed radically over time (for example, via the Big Bang).

Carter defined two forms of the anthropic principle, a "weak" one which referred only to the anthropic selection of privileged locations in the universe, and a more controversial "strong" form which addressed the values of the fundamental constants of physics space.[132] How can a coincidence provoke a privileged position? Einstein argued the same.

The mathematical physicist Roger Penrose explained the weak anthropic principle as follows.

> The argument can be used to explain why the conditions happen to be just right for the existence of (intelligent) life on the Earth at the present time. For if they were not exactly right, and then we should not have found ourselves to be here now, but somewhere else, at some other appropriate time.

This principle was used very effectively by Brandon Carter and Robert Dicke to resolve an issue that had puzzled physicists a good many years. The issue concerned various striking numerical relations that are observed to hold between the physical constants (the gravitational constant, the mass of the proton, the age of the universe, etc.). A puzzling aspect of this was that some of the relations hold only at the present epoch in Earth's history, so we appear to coincidentally be living at a very special time (give or take a few million years). Carter and Dicke later explained this by the fact that this epoch coincided with the lifetime of what are called main-sequence stars, such as the sun. At any other epoch, or so the argument ran, there would be no intelligent life around in order to measure the physical constants in question—so the coincidence had to hold, simply because there would be intelligent life around only at the particular time that the coincidence did hold!

One reason this is plausible is that there are many other places and times in which we can imagine finding ourselves. But when applying the strong principle, we only have one universe, with one set of fundamental parameters. So, what exactly is the point being made? Carter offers two possibilities: First, we can use our own existence to make predictions about the parameters. But second, "as a last resort", we can convert these predictions into *explanations* by assuming that there *is* more than one universe, in fact a large and possibly infinite collection of universes—something that is now called the multiverse ("world ensemble" was Carter's term), in which the parameters (and perhaps the laws of physics) vary across universes. The strong principle then becomes an example of a selection effect, exactly analogous to the weak principle. Postulating a multiverse is certainly a radical step, but taking it could provide at least a partial answer to a question which had seemed to be out of the reach of normal science: Why do the fundamental laws of physics take the particular form we observe and not another?

Since Carter's 1973 paper, the term "anthropic principle" has been extended to cover a number of ideas which differ in important ways from those he espoused. Particular confusion was caused in 1986 by the book *The Anthropic Cosmological Principle* by John D. Barrow and Frank Tipler, which distinguished between "weak" and "strong" anthropic principle in a way different from Carter.

Carter's weak anthropic principle states that we must be prepared to take account of the fact that our location in the universe, in time as in space, is *necessarily* privileged to the extent of being compatible with our existence as observers.

Carter's strong anthropic principle states that the universe (and hence the fundamental parameters on which it depends on) must be such as to admit the creation of observers within it at some stage. To paraphrase Descartes, *Cogito ergo mundus talis est* (I think, therefore the world is such as it is). That makes it clear that "must" indicates a deduction from the fact of our existence; the statement is thus a truism.

The strong anthropic principle (SAP) as explained by John D. Barrow and Frank Tipler state that this is the case because the universe is compelled to eventually have conscious and sapient life emerge within it.

John Barrow and Frank Tipler depart from Carter and define the WAP and SAP as follows.

> WAP: The observed values of all physical and cosmological quantities are not equally probable, but they take on values restricted by the requirement that there exist sites where carbon-based life can evolve and by the requirements that the universe is old enough for it to have already done so.

Unlike Carter they restrict the principle to carbon-based life rather than just "observers". A more important difference is that they apply the WAP to the fundamental physical constants, such as the fine structure constant, the number of space-time dimensions, and the cosmological constant—topics that fall under Carter's SAP.

> SAP: "The universe must have those properties which allow life to develop within it at some stage in its history."

This looks very similar to Carter's SAP, but unlike the case with Carter's SAP, the "must" is an imperative, as shown by the following three possible elaborations of the SAP, each proposed by Barrow and Tipler:

- "There exists one possible Universe 'designed' with the goal of generating and sustaining 'observers'."

This can be seen as simply the classic design argument restated in the garb of contemporary cosmology. It implies that the purpose of the universe is to give rise to intelligent life, with the laws of nature and their fundamental physical constants set to ensure that life as we know it will emerge and evolve.

- "Observers are necessary to bring the universe into being."

Barrow and Tipler believe that this is a valid conclusion from quantum physics.

- "An ensemble of other different universes is necessary for the existence of our Universe."

By contrast, Carter merely says that an ensemble of universes is necessary for the SAP to count as an explanation.

The "problem" of existence is only relevant to a species capable of formulating the question. Prior to Homo *sapiens'* intellectual evolution to the point where the nature of the observed universe—and humans' place within the same—spawned deep inquiry into its origins, the problem did not exist.

> Many 'anthropic principles' are simply confused. Some, especially those drawing inspirations from Brandon Carter's seminal papers, look sound, but … they are too weak to do any real scientific work. In particular, existing methodology does not permit any observational consequences to be derived from contemporary cosmological theories, though these theories quite plainly

> can be and are being tested empirically by astronomers. What is needed to bridge this methodological gap is an adequate formulation of how observation selection effects are to be taken into account.

Carter chose to focus on a tautological aspect of his ideas, which has resulted in much confusion. In fact, anthropic reasoning interests scientists because of something that is only implicit in the above formal definitions: namely, that we should give serious consideration to there being other universes with different values of the "fundamental parameters"—that is, the dimensionless physical constants and initial conditions for the Big Bang. Carter and others have argued that life as we know it would not be possible in most such universes. In other words, the universe we are in is fine-tuned to permit life. The physicists Collins and Hawking characterised Carter's then-unpublished big idea as the postulate that "there is not one universe but a whole infinite ensemble of universes with all possible initial conditions".[75] If this is granted, the anthropic principle provides a plausible explanation but is not realistic for the fine-tuning of our universe: the "typical" universe is not fine-tuned, but given enough universes, a small fraction thereof will be capable of fine-tuning should be no cause for wonder.

Although philosophers have discussed related concepts for centuries, in the early 1970s the only genuine physical theory yielding a multiverse of sorts was the many-worlds interpretation of quantum mechanics. This would allow variation in initial conditions, but not in the truly fundamental constants. Since that time, a number of mechanisms for producing a multiverse have been suggested. An important development in the 1980s was the combination of inflation theory with the hypothesis that some parameters are determined by symmetry breaking[1] in the early universe, which allows parameters previously thought of as "fundamental constants" to vary over very large distances, thus eroding the distinction between Carter's weak and strong principles. At the beginning of the twenty-first century, the string landscape emerged as a mechanism for varying essentially all the constants, including the number of spatial dimensions.

The anthropic idea that fundamental parameters are selected from a multitude of different possibilities (each actual in some universe or other) contrasts with the traditional hope of physicists for a theory of everything having no free parameters; as Einstein said, "What really interests me is whether God had any choice in the creation of the world." In 2002, proponents of the leading candidate for a "theory of everything" string theory proclaimed "the end of the anthropic principle" because there would be no free parameters to select. Ironically, string theory now seems to offer no hope of predicting fundamental parameters, and now some who advocate it invoke the anthropic principle as well.

The modern form of a design argument is put forth by intelligent design. Intelligent design proponents[167] seek to change this fundamental basis of science by eliminating "methodological naturalism" from science and replacing it with what the leader of the intelligent design movement, Phillip E. Johnson, calls theistic realism. Intelligent design proponents argue that naturalistic explanations fail to explain certain phenomena and that supernatural explanations provide a very simple and intuitive explanation for the origins of life and the universe. Many intelligent design followers believe that scientism is itself a religion that promotes secularism and materialism in an attempt to erase theism from public life. They view their work in the promotion of intelligent design as a way to return religion to a central role in education and other public spheres.

Proponents of intelligent design often cite the fine-tuning observations that (in part) preceded the formulation of the anthropic principle by Carter as a proof of an intelligent designer. Opponents of intelligent design are not limited to those who hypothesise that other universes exist; they may also argue, anti-anthropically, that the universe is less fine-tuned than often claimed, or that accepting fine tuning as a brute fact is less astonishing than the idea of an intelligent creator.

No possible observational evidence bears on Carter's WAP because it is merely advice to the scientist and asserts nothing debatable. The obvious test of Barrow's SAP, which says that the universe is "required" to support life, is to find evidence of life in universes other than ours. Any other universe is, by most definitions, unobservable; otherwise, it would be included in *our* portion of *this* universe. Thus, in principle Barrow's SAP cannot be falsified by observing a universe in which an observer cannot exist.

One thing that would *not* count as evidence for the anthropic principle is evidence that Earth or the solar system occupied a privileged position in the universe, in violation of the Copernican principle (no favoured universe, or privileged observers of the universe, unless there was some reason to think that that position was a necessary condition for our existence as observers).

Physicist Don Page, a student and collaborator of Hawking, criticised the entire theory of cosmic inflation.[76] He emphasised that initial conditions which made possible a thermodynamic arrow of time in a universe with a Big Bang origin must include the assumption that at the initial singularity, the entropy of the universe was low and therefore extremely improbable. Physicist Paul Davies rebutted this criticism by invoking an inflationary version of the anthropic principle. Although Davies accepted the premise that the initial state of the visible universe (which filled a microscopic amount of space before inflating) had to possess a very low entropy value—due to random quantum fluctuations—to account for the observed thermodynamic arrow of time, he deemed this fact an advantage for the theory. That the tiny patch of space from which our observable universe grew had to be extremely orderly in order to allow the post-inflation universe to have an arrow of time makes it unnecessary to adopt any ad hoc hypotheses about the initial entropy state—hypotheses other Big Bang theories require. Davies is a controversial scientist who mixes faith and science, and he is praised by the fundamental conservative foundation Templeton but is heavily criticised by most of his colleagues. There are serious concerns about his responsibility as one of Wolfe-Simon's co-authors of the article "A Bacterium That Can Grow by Using Arsenic Instead of Phosphorous" (*Science* 332, pp. 1163–1166; rebutted in *Science* 337, pp. 467–477). Later it was proved that the DNA of said organism contained no arsenic at all.

String theory predicts a large number of possible universes, called the backgrounds or vacua. The set of these vacua is often called the multiverse, anthropic landscape, or string landscape. Theoretical physicist and string theory pioneer Leonard Susskind has argued that the existence of a large number of vacua puts anthropic reasoning on firm ground: only universes whose properties are such as to allow observers to exist are observed, whereas a possibly much larger set of universes lacking such properties go unnoticed.

On the other hand, theoretical physicist Lee Smolin, coined the new Einstein, disagrees with Susskind. Smolin is best known for his contributions to quantum gravity theory, in particular the approach known as loop quantum gravity. He advocates that the two primary approaches to quantum gravity, loop quantum gravity and string theory, can be reconciled with different aspects of the same underlying theory. His research interests also include cosmology, elementary particle theory, the foundations of quantum mechanics, and theoretical biology.[91]

Smolin is amongst those theorists who have proposed that the effects of quantum gravity can be experimentally probed by searching for modifications in special relativity detected in observations of high-energy astrophysical phenomena. These include very high-energy cosmic rays and photons and neutrinos from gamma ray bursts. Amongst Smolin's contributions are the co-invention of doubly special relativity (with João Magueijo, independently of work done by Giovanni Amelino-Camelia) and of relative locality (with Amelino-Camelia, Laurent Freidel, and Jerzy Kowalski-Glikman). Smolin has worked since the early 1980s on a series of proposals for hidden variables theories, which would be non-local deterministic theories that would give a precise description of individual quantum phenomena. In recent years, he has pioneered two new approaches to the interpretation of quantum mechanics suggested by his work on the reality of time, called the real ensemble formulation and the principle of precedence.

Smolin's hypothesis of cosmological natural selection, also called the fecund universes theory, suggests that a process analogous to biological natural selection applies at the grandest of scales. Smolin published the idea in 1992 and summarised it in a book aimed at a lay audience called *The Life of the Cosmos.*

Black holes have a role in natural selection. Black holes of stellar mass are expected to form when very massive stars collapse at the end of their life cycle. In fecund theory, a collapsing black hole causes the emergence of a new universe on the "other side", whose fundamental constant parameters (masses of elementary particles, Planck constant, elementary charge, and so forth) may differ slightly from those of the universe where the black hole collapsed. Each universe thus gives rise to as many new universes as it has black holes. The theory contains the evolutionary ideas of "reproduction" and "mutation" of universes, and so it is formally analogous to models of population biology. After a black hole has formed, it can continue to grow by absorbing mass from its surroundings. By absorbing other stars and merging with other black holes, supermassive black holes of millions of solar masses ($M_{\odot}$) may form. There is general consensus that supermassive black holes exist in the centres of most galaxies.

Alternatively, black holes play a role in cosmological natural selection by reshuffling only some matter affecting the distribution of elementary quark universes. The resulting population of universes can be represented as a distribution of a landscape of parameters where the height of the landscape is proportional to the numbers of black holes that a universe with those parameters will have. Applying reasoning borrowed from the study of fitness landscapes in population biology, one can conclude that the population is dominated by universes whose parameters drive the production of black holes to a local peak in the landscape. This was the first use of the notion of a landscape of parameters in physics.

Leonard Susskind,[94] who later promoted a similar string theory landscape, stated, "I'm not sure why Smolin's idea didn't attract much attention. I actually think it deserved far more than it got."

However, Susskind also argued that because Smolin's theory relies on information transfer from the parent universe to the baby universe through a black hole, it ultimately makes no sense as a theory of cosmological natural selection. According to Susskind and many other physicists, the last decade of black hole physics has shown us that no information that goes into a black hole can be lost. Indeed, the debate over this issue has been resolved with Stephen Hawking, the largest proponent of the idea that information is lost in a black hole, reversing his position. In this light, information transfer from the parent universe into the baby universe through a black hole is not conceivable.

Smolin has noted that the string theory landscape is not falsifiable if other universes are not observable. This is the subject of the Smolin-Susskind debate concerning Smolin's argument: "The Anthropic principle cannot be a part of science." There are then only two ways out: traversable wormholes connecting the different parallel universes and "signal non-locality", as described by the theoretical physicist Antony Valentini.

When Smolin published the theory in 1992, he proposed as a prediction of his theory that no neutron star should exist with a mass of more than 1.6 times the mass of the sun. Later, this figure was raised to two solar masses following more precise modelling of neutron star interiors by nuclear astrophysicists. If a more massive neutron star was ever observed, it would show that our universe's natural laws were not tuned for maximal black hole production because the mass of the strange quark could be re-tuned to lower the mass threshold for production of a black hole. A two-solar-mass pulsar was discovered in 2010.

In 1992 Smolin also predicted that inflation, if true, must only be in its simplest form, governed by a single field and parameter. Both predictions have held up, and they demonstrate Smolin's main thesis: that the theory of cosmological natural selection is Popper falsifiable. Karl Popper is the greatest philosopher of science of the twentieth century, and he rejected the classical inductivist views on the scientific in favour of empirical falsification (a theory in the empirical sciences can never be proved, but it can be falsified, meaning that it can and should be scrutinised by decisive experiments).

A book-length exposition of Smolin's philosophical views appeared in April 2013. In his book *Time Reborn: From a Crisis in Physics to the Future of Physics,* he argues that physical science has made time unreal while, as Smolin insists, it is the most fundamental feature of reality: "Space may be an illusion, but time must be real" (p. 179). An adequate description, according to him, would give a Leibnizian universe: indiscernibles would not be admitted, and every difference should correspond to some other difference, as the principle of sufficient reason would have it. A few months later, a more concise text has been made available in a paper with the title "Temporal Naturalism".

Smolin's 2006 book *The Trouble with Physics* explored the role of controversy and disagreement in the progress of science. It argued that science progresses fastest if the scientific community encourages the widest possible disagreement amongst trained and accredited professionals prior to the formation of consensus brought about by experimental confirmation of predictions of falsifiable theories. He proposed that this meant the fostering of diverse competing research programs, and that premature formation of paradigms not forced by experimental facts can slow the progress of science.

As a case study, *The Trouble with Physics* focused on the issue of the falsifiability of string theory due to the proposals that the anthropic principle is used to explain the properties of our universe in the context of the string landscape.

Falsifiability or refutability of a statement, hypothesis, or theory is the inherent possibility that it can be proven false. A statement is called falsifiable if it is possible to conceive of an observation or an argument which negates the statement in question. In this sense, *falsify* is synonymous with *nullifying*, meaning to invalidate or show to be false. The concern with falsifiability gained attention by way of the philosopher of science Karl Popper's scientific epistemology falsificationism. Popper stresses the problem of demarcation—distinguishing the scientific from the unscientific—and makes *falsifiability* the demarcation criterion, such that what is unfalsifiable is classified as unscientific, and the practise of declaring an unfalsifiable theory to be scientifically true is pseudoscience.

In his earlier book *Three Roads to Quantum Gravity* (2002), Smolin stated that loop quantum gravity and string theory were essentially the same concepts seen from different perspectives. In that book, he also favoured the holographic principle. *The Trouble with*

Physics, on the other hand, was strongly critical of the prominence of string theory in contemporary theoretical physics, which he believes has suppressed research in other promising approaches. Smolin suggests that string theory suffers from serious deficiencies and has an unhealthy near monopoly in the particle theory community. He called for a diversity of approaches to quantum gravity and argued that more attention should be paid to loop quantum gravity, an approach Smolin has devised. Finally, *The Trouble with Physics* is also broadly concerned with the role of controversy and the value of diverse approaches in the ethics and process of science. On the nature of time, he stated, "More and more, I have the feeling that quantum theory and general relativity are both deeply wrong about the nature of time. It is not enough to combine them. There is a deeper problem, perhaps going back to the beginning of physics."

Smolin does not believe that quantum mechanics is a "final theory".

> I am convinced that quantum mechanics is not a final theory. I believe this because I have never encountered an interpretation of the present formulation of quantum mechanics that makes sense to me. I have studied most of them in depth and thought hard about them, and in the end I still can't make real sense of quantum theory as it stands.

In a 2009 article, Smolin articulated the following philosophical views.

> There is only one universe. There are no others, nor is there anything isomorphic to it. Smolin denies the existence of a "timeless" multiverse. Neither other universes nor copies of our universe—within or outside— exist. No copies can exist within the universe, because no subsystem can model precisely the larger system

> it is a part of. No copies can exist outside the universe because the universe is by definition all there is. This principle also rules out the notion of a mathematical object isomorphic in every respect to the history of the entire universe, a notion more metaphysical than scientific.

All that is real is real in a moment, which is a succession of moments. Anything that is true is true of the present moment. Not only is time real, but everything that is real is situated in time. Nothing exists timelessly.

Everything that is real in a moment is a process of change leading to the next or future moments. Anything that is true is then a feature of a process in this process, causing or implying future moments. This principle incorporates the notion that time is an aspect of causal relations. The reason for asserting it is that anything that existed for just one moment, without causing or implying some aspect of the world at a future moment, would be gone in the next moment. Things that persist must be thought of as processes leading to newly changed processes. An atom at one moment is a process leading to a different or a changed atom at the next moment.

Mathematics is derived from experience as a generalisation of observed regularities, when time and particularity are removed.

Smolin views rejecting the idea of a creator as essential to cosmology. He opposes the anthropic principle, which he claims "cannot help us to do science". He also advocates "principles for an open future", which he claims underlie the work of both healthy scientific communities and democratic societies.

> When rational argument from public evidence suffices to decide a question, it must be considered to be so decided. When rational argument from the public evidence does not suffice to decide a question, the community must encourage a diverse range of viewpoints and hypotheses consistent

> with a good-faith attempt to develop convincing public evidence. (*Time Reborn*, p. 265)

Steven Weinberg is an American theoretical physicist and Nobel laureate in physics for his contributions with Abdus Salam and Sheldon Glashow regarding the unification of the weak force and electromagnetic interaction between elementary particles.

Weinberg is an atheist who stated his views on religion in 1999 in *A Designer Universe.*[128] He believes the anthropic principle may be appropriated by cosmologists committed to non-theism, and he refers to that principle as a "turning point" in modern science because applying it to the string landscape "may explain how the constants of nature that we observe can take values suitable for life without being fine-tuned by a benevolent creator". Others, such as Lee Smolin, argue that this is not predictive.

Weinberg states that some physicists have argued that certain constants of nature have values that seem to have been mysteriously fine-tuned to just the values that allow for the possibility of life, in a way that could only be explained by the intervention of a designer with some special concern for life. He rightly states that he is not impressed with these supposed instances of fine-tuning. For instance, one of the most frequently quoted examples of fine-tuning has to do with a property of the nucleus of the carbon atom. The matter left over from the first few minutes of the universe was almost entirely hydrogen and helium, with virtually none of the heavier elements like carbon, nitrogen, and oxygen that seem to be necessary for life. The heavy elements that we find on earth were built up hundreds of millions of years later in the first generation of stars and then spewed out into the interstellar gas out of which our solar system eventually formed. The first step in the sequence of nuclear reactions that created the heavy elements in early stars is usually the formation of a carbon nucleus out of three helium nuclei. There is a negligible chance of producing a carbon nucleus in its normal state (the state of lowest energy) in collisions of three helium nuclei, but it would be possible to produce appreciable amounts of carbon in stars if the carbon nucleus could exist in a radioactive state with an energy of roughly

7 million electron volts (MeV) above the energy of the normal state, matching the energy of three helium nuclei, but (for reasons I'll come to presently) not more than 7.7 MeV above the normal state. This radioactive state of a carbon nucleus could be easily formed in stars from three helium nuclei. After that, there would be no problem in producing ordinary carbon; the carbon nucleus in its radioactive state would spontaneously emit light and turn into carbon in its normal, nonradioactive state (the state found on earth). The critical point in producing carbon is the existence of a radioactive state that can be produced in collisions of three helium nuclei. In fact, the carbon nucleus is known experimentally to have just such a radioactive state, with an energy 7.65 MeV above the normal state. At first sight this may seem like a pretty close call; the energy of this radioactive state of carbon misses being too high to allow the formation of carbon (and hence of us) by only 0.05 MeV, which is less than 1 per cent of 7.65 MeV. It may appear that the constants of nature on which the properties of all nuclei depend on have been carefully fine-tuned to make life possible. Looked at more closely, the fine-tuning of the constants of nature here does not seem so fine. We must consider the reason why the formation of carbon in stars requires the existence of a radioactive state of carbon with energy not more than 7.7 MeV above the energy of the normal state. The reason is that the carbon nuclei in this state are actually formed in a two-step process. First, two helium nuclei combine to form the unstable nucleus of a beryllium isotope, beryllium 8, which before it falls apart occasionally captures another helium nucleus, forming a carbon nucleus in its radioactive state, which then decays into normal carbon. The total energy of the beryllium 8 nucleus and a helium nucleus at rest is 7.4 MeV above the energy of the normal state of the carbon nucleus. Therefore if the energy of the radioactive state of carbon were more than 7.7 MeV, it could only be formed in a collision of a helium nucleus and a beryllium 8 nucleus if the energy of motion of these two nuclei were at least 0.3 MeV—an energy which is extremely unlikely at the temperatures found in stars. The crucial thing that affects the production of carbon in stars is not the 7.65 MeV energy of the radioactive state of carbon in its

normal state, but the 0.25 MeV energy of the radioactive state, an unstable composite of a beryllium 8 nucleus and a helium nucleus, above the energy of those nuclei at rest. This energy misses being too high to produce of carbon by a fractional amount of 0.05 MeV / 0.25 MeV, or 20 per cent, which is not such a close call after all. This conclusion about the lessons to be learned from carbon synthesis is somewhat controversial. In any case, there is one constant whose value does seem remarkably well adjusted. It is the energy density of empty space, also known as the cosmological constant. It could have any value, but from first principles one would guess that this constant should be very large and could be positive or negative. If large and positive, the cosmological constant would act as a repulsive force that increases with distance, a force that would prevent matter from clumping together in the early universe—the process that was the first step in forming galaxies and stars and planets and people. If large and negative, the cosmological constant would act as an attractive force increasing with distance, a force that would almost immediately reverse the expansion of the universe and cause it to recollapse, leaving no time for the evolution of life. In fact, astronomical observations show that the cosmological constant is quite small, much smaller than would have been guessed from first principles. It is still too early to tell whether there is some fundamental principle that can explain why the cosmological constant must be this small. But even if there is no such principle, recent developments in cosmology offer the possibility of an explanation of why the measured values of the cosmological constant and other physical constants are incidentally favourable for the appearance of intelligent life.

According to the chaotic inflation theories of Andrei Linde and others, the expanding cloud of billions of galaxies that we call the Big Bang may be just one fragment of a much larger universe in which big bangs go off all the time, each one with different values for the fundamental constants.

Carter has frequently regretted his own choice of the word *anthropic* because it conveys the misleading impression that the principle involves humans specifically, rather than intelligent observers in general. Others have criticised the word *principle* as being too grandiose to describe straightforward applications of selection effects.

A common criticism of Carter's SAP is that it is an easy "*deus ex machina*" which discourages searches for physical explanations. To quote Penrose, "It tends to be invoked by theorists whenever they do not have a good enough theory to explain the observed facts."

Carter's SAP and Barrow and Tipler's WAP have been dismissed as truisms (obvious truths that state nothing beyond what is applied in any of its terms) or trivial tautologies—that is, statements true solely by virtue of their logical form (the conclusion is identical to the premise), and not because of a substantive claim is made and supported by the observation of reality. As such, they are criticised as an elaborate way of saying, "If things were different, they would be different," which is a valid statement but does not make a claim of some factual alternative over another.

Critics of the Barrow and Tipler SAP claim that it is neither testable nor falsifiable, and thus it is not a scientific statement but rather a philosophical one. It seems a metaphysical theory based on pseudoscientific data to defend intelligence design. The same criticism has been levelled against the hypothesis of a multiverse, although some argue that it does make falsifiable predictions. A modified version of this criticism is that we understand so little about the emergence of life, especially intelligent life, that it is effectively impossible to calculate the number of observers in each universe. Also, the prior distribution of universes as a function of the fundamental constants is easily modified to get any desired result.[62]

Many criticisms focus on versions of the strong anthropic principle, such as Barrow and Tipler's *anthropic cosmological principle*, which are teleological notions that tend to describe the existence of life as a *necessary prerequisite* for the observable constants of physics. Others claim that the stronger versions of the anthropic principle seem to reverse known causes and affects the claim that the universe is fine-tuned for the benefit of our kind of life to saying that sausages were made long and narrow so that they could fit into modern hotdog buns, or saying that ships had been invented to house barnacles. These critics cite the vast physical, fossil, genetic, and other biological evidence consistent with life having been fine-tuned through natural selection to adapt to the physical and geophysical environment in which life exists. Life appears to have adapted to the universe and not vice versa.

Some applications of the anthropic principle have been criticised as an argument by lack of imagination, for tacitly assuming that carbon compounds and water are the only possible chemistry of life (sometimes called carbon chauvinism; see also alternative biochemistry). The range of fundamental physical constants consistent with the evolution of carbon-based life may also be wider than those who advocate a fine-tuned universe have argued.

Lee Smolin has offered a theory designed to improve on the lack of imagination that anthropic principles have been accused of. He puts forth his fecund universes theory, which assumes universes have "offspring" through the creation of black holes, whose offspring universes have values of physical constants that depend on those of the mother universe.

Some versions of the anthropic principle are only interesting if the range of physical constants that allow certain kinds of life are unlikely in a landscape of possible universes. But Lee Smolin assumes that conditions for carbon-based life are similar to conditions for black hole creation, which would change the a priori distribution of universes such that universes containing life would be likely. In *Smolin vs. Susskind: The Anthropic Principle,* the string theorist Leonard Susskind disagrees about some assumptions in Lee Smolin's theory, whereas Smolin defends his theory.

In his book *The Physics of Immortality,* Frank Tipler advances the term *omega point* to describe a cosmological state in the distant proper-time future of the universe that he maintains is required by the known physical laws. According to this cosmology, it is required for the known laws of physics to be mutually consistent that intelligent life takes over all matter in the universe and eventually forces its collapse. During that collapse, the computational capacity of the universe diverges to infinity and environments emulated with that computational capacity last for an infinite duration as the universe attains a solitary-point cosmological singularity. This singularity is

Tipler's omega point. With computational resources diverging to infinity, Tipler states that a society far in the future would be able to resurrect the dead by emulating all alternative universes of our universe from its start at the Big Bang. Tipler identifies the omega point with God because, in his view, the omega point has all the properties claimed for gods by most of the traditional religions. Tipler offered the omega point cosmology as a hypothesis while still claiming to confine the analysis to the known laws of physics. Intelligent information processing must come into existence in the universe, and once it comes into existence, it will never die out. Critics of the final omega point principle say its arguments violate the Copernican principle, that it incorrectly applies the laws of probability, and that it is really a theology or metaphysics principle made to sound plausible to laypeople by using the esoteric language of physics. Oxford-based philosopher Nick Bostrom writes that the final anthropic principle has no claim on any special methodological status; it is "pure speculation", despite attempts to elevate it by calling it a principle. Philosopher Rem B. Edwards called it "futuristic, pseudoscientific eschatology" that is "highly conjectural, unverified, and improbable". The physicist Lawrence Krauss described the book as the most "extreme example of uncritical and unsubstantiated arguments put into print by an intelligent professional scientist".

Martin Gardner, the American popular mathematics and science writer, delivered a death blow to the anthropic principle by quoting the last two sentences of Barrow and Tipler's book as defining a Completely Ridiculous Anthropic Principle (CRAP).

> At the instant the Omega Point is reached, life will have gained ground of all matter and forces not only in a single universe, but in all universes whose existence is logically possible; life will have spread into all spatial regions in all universes which could possible exist, and will have stored an infinite amount of information, including all bits of knowledge which is logically possible to know. And this is the end.

Indeed, there is nothing logical possible nor logical possible existence. The constraint of Barrow and Tipler that the universe would end in a big crunch is unlikely in view of the tentative conclusions drawn since 1998 about dark energy, based on observations of very distant supernovas.

The anthropic principle is a beautiful item of philosophy without any real scientific value. It is an invention of intelligent but rather conceited people who stand in awe of humankind as the most important life form in the universe, while not realising that it took humans several million years to evolve from the genus ape and hominids and that it will take lots of more time to achieve real wisdom. We must not forget the sorry state of humankind at the present time. The anthropic principle can be compared to string theory (threadlike concentration of energy *hypothesised* to exist within the structure of space-time), a theory of possibilities and probabilities.

Preceding scientific comments which I have expounded are complicated and difficult to understand for us laymen. However, we can distil from it how the cosmos was created (cosmogony), which allows us to approach scientifically the purpose and meaning of life, and life is part of the universe. Scientific explanation is necessary to justify the facts on which the essay is based, however it will hurt the feelings of the people who are believers and do not have open minds.

The anthropic principle, whatever its scientific value, does not allow one to conclude that there has been a supernatural creator of the universe, although this presents a purpose and meaning to life. Man, descended from animal, cannot deny his animal instinct and is still no Homo *sapiens*, in such a way that we still do not possess the ability to fix the world conflicts and contentions. Our rationality is limited and, in many populations, even minimal. Religions have created a "rational animal", a being in imitation of their deity, an exaggerated being. More rationality and reflection remain necessary.

The presence of life on Earth must be considered as the result of an accidental process which excludes any purpose or meaning. To proclaim the opposite and claim the intervention of a supernatural being defies all reason and can only be described to a sick mind.

Man, in nature plays a momentary role. In its short-lived existence it is important that it is as pleasant as possible, which humans can undertake. The realisation that life has neither purpose nor meaning is indeed a doomsday syndrome which may lead to destruction of life if *homo sapiens* cannot react upon it. The fear of death with which man is afflicted is often the determent of suicide.

The Universal Declaration of the Rights of Man decreed by the United Nations declares that the right upon living the most fundamental value (the highest good) of human is. The Global Compact for Migration is the first ever Global UN agreement for a common approach to international migration in all its dimensions. It is not legally binding, therefore called a "compact" and regretfully remains a dead letter. States will not adjust to it and it is unenforceable, so it won't work. The basic principles are state sovereignty, international responsibility, non-discrimination and human rights. The cause of migration is the urge of a better standard of living and even more the escape of warzones. No civilisation can master massive immigration. Immigrants once settled return to the customs of their homeland and inevitable undermine the prosperity they sought. This does not mean at all that we do not have to help our fellowman. It is our duty to bring help and relief to the zones where it is needed and even more so to all undeveloped countries of the third world. Warlords must be eliminated before aid is possible. It is a very costly intervention which can only achieved by a far-reaching solidarity and where the western world should take the initiative. The Unite Nations fails to unite the world on many matters, being an assembly of all talk and no action.

Europe is an example of where migration went mostly wrong. After the second world war France and England lost their colonies. They opened their frontiers to welcome their former colonised subjects. Few of the immigrants integrated, the rest returned to the customs of their homeland. One would have thought that different cultures could live together but it was not to be. Mainly the Moslems were the culprits. They radicalised which led to terrorism. The aftermath is that second generation teenagers of allochthonous origin are dropouts at school, have no jobs, linger at the corner of the streets and are always at the lookout for rioting and plundering. Authorities, incompetent or acting out of humanitarian feelings, fail to take effective measures. One day the indigenous populations will have enough; they will grant power to the extreme right to curb the troubles at the expense, however, of democracy.

CHAPTER 5

Evolution of Life

Evolution in biology is the process of change in all forms of life from generation to generation. The theory of evolution is the scientific explanation for life and for the variety of living species on Earth. The theory of evolution describes the process by which genetic traits of life forms change from generation to generation on the basis of variation, reproduction, and natural selection. Charles Darwin and Albert Russel are the main founders of the theory of evolution, which is generally accepted theory. The Earth came about 4.5 billion years ago, and living forms appeared on the surface a billion years later. The similarities between the current life forms allow stating that there has been a common ancestor from which all currently living species by evolution are descended. Life is suspected to have originated during the first 600 million years of Earth's history.[9-11]

As stated before, the first known organisms were bacteria about 3.5 billion years ago, and they lived in an aqueous environment. Microbes appeared 2.9 billion years ago. The first vegetable life one billion years ago consisted of a covering of Earth's crust with algae. Higher plants date to 450 million years ago, and insects date to 400 million years ago. Although for most of the terrestrial history life was present, it wasn't until between 500 and 600 million years ago that animals appeared, which currently represent almost all stems within the animal kingdom. Around 1.7 billion years ago, the first multicellular organisms appeared, but the organisms that multiplied by sexual reproduction must have existed earlier.

The first fish appeared about 500 million years ago, and amphibians came about 150 million years later. From amphibians developed the first amphibians that could live both on land and in the water. From these amphibians developed both the ancestors of the dinosaurs as the therapsida (reptile mammals) and the ancestors of mammals. Because the therapsids were heavily affected during a major mass extinction 251 million years ago, the dinosaurs could become dominant during the Mesozoic ecological period and keep the upper hand over the remaining mammals. The dinosaurs (except birds) disappeared in turn by the mass extinction event 65 million years ago.

Why do living beings have an urge to reproduce? If the only intention is to survive, why haven't the organisms learned to be immortals? Is it not that organisms have not evolved for any purpose, but that organisms that do not feel compelled to reproduce swiftly get crowded out by those that do? It is a fact that a lot of single-celled organisms are nearly immortal unless they meet with an accident. Senescence is really a feature of complex organisms such as humans. In big organisms, the individual cells suffer damage and start malfunctioning. It is in the interest of the genes that death occurs.

Apart from mutations of genes, genetic drift is the factor for genetic change. Sexual reproduction is the essential requirement for life and its evolution.

CHAPTER 6

Evolution of Humans

Humans, taxonomically[9] known as Homo *sapiens* (Latin for a wise or developed man), are the only living extant beings of the bipedal hominid clade, a branch of great apes. Homo *sapiens* is the only extant human species. Homo is the human genus, which also includes Neanderthals and many other extinct species of hominids. Homo *sapiens* is the only surviving species of the genus Homo. Modern humans are the subspecies Homo *sapiens sapiens*, which differentiates from their direct ancestor Homo *sapiens idaltu* (the name given to an extinct subspecies of Homo *sapiens* that lived approximately 160,000 years ago in Pleistocene Africa and had certain cranial traits). The ingenuity and adaptability of Homo *sapiens* have led to its becoming the most influential species on Earth.[151]

Homo *sapiens* emerged in Africa around 300,000 ago and began their modern behaviour change between 40,000 and 50,000 years ago when they came to Europe. Studies show that over a period of time, Cro-Magnons and Neanderthals may have existed side by side. It is contested whether both species, by interbreeding, may have contributed to the existence of Homo *sapiens*.[93]

The human belongs to the vertebrates and disposes of top and bottom limbs and head with a complex brain, with which he is able to manipulate tools. His brain allows him to think, communicate, and develop technologies to promote his welfare.

The human sees himself as the most intelligent life form on Earth. Mammals like elephants, whales, dolphins, and killer whales have a high intelligence that most people do not realise. At the beginning of the tradition of Western philosophy, the human being was defined as "animal rationale", the animal endowed with reason. Since then, reason has become an absolute value which through education brings gradual transformation of all spheres of human life. On the other hand, Martin Heidegger, a Roman Catholic and founder of existentialism (Dasein), posits that we do not need more reason but more openness and reflection.

Man is spread all over the world. At the end of October 2014, seven billion living people populated the Earth, which ultimately can mean danger for humanity. Overpopulation inevitably leads to suffocation in the absence of living space, and it is one of the main reasons that poverty occurs.

Human evolution is the evolutionary process leading to the existence of the modern human (Homo *sapiens*). It started with the last common ancestor of all life but covers mainly the evolutionary history of primates, in particular the genus Homo, and the emergence of modern man as a distinct species of the great apes, the hominids. The timeline of human evolution spans some 7 million years, from the separation of the Pan Genus until the emergence of behaviour modernity 50,000 years ago. Of this timeline, the first 3 million years concern Sahelanthropos, the following 2 million years' concern Australopithecus, and the final 2 million years span the actual Homo species (the Palaeolithic). Many traits of human intelligence, such as empathy, mourning, ritual, and the use of symbols and tools, are already apparent in great apes, although in lesser sophistication than in humans.

Human beings are the result of natural selection acting over millions of tears of breeding and eating. When Darwin published his book *Origin of Species*, the believers published caricatures of Darwin with an ape or monkey body to symbolise his evolution theory. Christianity is, after all, hard to find in believers who cannot overcome their bigotry.

The studies of human evolution involve many scientific disciplines such as physical anthropology, archaeology, genetics, and more.

Together with the gibbon (small arboreal ape), the chimpanzee, the gorilla, and the orangutan, the human forms the hominids, which are the descendants of a common ancestor. The fossils allow establishing the evolutionary history of the primates to 60 million years ago. Except for America and South Asia, the first primates died by climate fluctuations about 40 million years ago. Genetic studies have shown that the primates diverged from other mammals about 85 million years ago. The first fossils date of approximately 55 million years ago. The family Hominids deflected from the gibbon about 15–20 million years ago, from the orangutans approximately 14 million years ago, and from the chimpanzee and the gorilla about 4–5 million years ago. The early bipedal primates eventually developed to the genus Homo.

The bonobo is the primate that sexually behaves the most like humans. They have genital sex facing each other, do tongue kissing, and have oral sex. The females have a clitoris that is three times as large as that of the human female, and they indulge in self-gratification.

The human female is fertile throughout the year. She shows no external sign of fertility, such as swelling during oestrus. With the exception of the bonobos, humans are the only primates that approach each other sexually face-to-face. Sex by humans is very sophisticated and refined, usually carried out without any urge for reproduction.

Man is the only surviving species of the genus Homo. The species Cro-Magnon and Neanderthal became extinct 40,000 years ago. It's still a search for the roots of man. The species that is actually our ancestor remains unknown. What we do know is that there is a line going from Homo *habilis* (handy man) to Homo *erectus* (erect) to Homo *sapiens*. The use of tools characteristically marks humans and has greatly contributed to their evolution. During the last 2–3 million years, the human brain has become three times as big. This was mainly due to the switch from eating plants to eating meat obtained by hunting large animals. Meat has a greater nutritional value than plants. By the manufacture of tools, the human brain became larger and more complex. The old Stone Age started somewhere between 2 and 5 million years in East Africa, when Homo *habilis* made tools from stone. In the period 700,000–300,000 years ago, Homo *erectus* made stone artefacts which became more and more sophisticated. About 50,000 years ago, the extinct Homo *Neanderthal* was also able to produce knives and blades. Man is the only animal species that is capable of making fire. It made a dramatic change in the habits of early humans. Traces of cooked food date from 1.9 million years ago. However, the invention of the wheel is a very recent invention of man and dates to only about 3,500 years ago. Before the wheel, the transport of heavy loads took place by the rolling of logs.

Hunting and gathering were the ancestral subsistence mode for modern humans until around 10,000 years ago. They moved from campsite to campsite, following game and wild fruits and vegetables. The nomadic life ended when human settled down and cultivated the soil. There are still nomads in Mongolia, Manchuria, and Siberia. The man knew an extraordinary development in the twentieth century. The Earth is very old, and the existence of Homo *sapiens* is a rather recent thing. It can be expected that further development will occur extremely rapidly. Unfortunately, there are many regions of the world whose populations do not profit from the development of man, and that is the reason there is so much dissension in the world.

The emancipation of women in the twentieth century has created a metamorphosis of society. The man is no longer the head of the family, and neither is he still the sole provider (the former hunter who provided food). The emancipation of women has resulted in an equivalent role in the family and no longer a subordinate role of caring for the children and running the household. The woman has often become the breadwinner so that the child care and the burden of the household must be carried and distributed by both parents. However, the advancement of women is a phenomenon which is limited to Western civilisation and has not occurred in Africa, Asia, and parts of South America, where religion exerts a brake.

Nearly all scientists are atheists and are calling for humanism to replace religion. Humanism is a philosophical and ethical stance that emphasises the value and agency of human beings, individually and collectively, while imposing critical thinking and evidence (rationalism and empiricism) over the acceptance of dogma or superstition. The philosopher A. C. Crayling defines humanism in his book *The God Argument: The Case Against Religion and for Humanism* as a powerful alternative to religion. It is an approach to life for those who wish to live with intellectual integrity based on reason, evidence, and a desire to do and be good, and one which does not interfere with people's rights to their own beliefs and freedom of expression. It is an ethics of sympathy and tolerance based on the best endeavour to try to make sense of human nature and the human condition. As of 2015, humanism typically refers to a non-theistic life stance centred on human agency and looking to science rather than revelation from a supernatural source to understand the world. Nobel Prize laureate and molecular biologist Francis Crick defined humanism as the belief that human problems can and must be faced in terms of human moral and intellectual resources without invoking supernatural authority. The simple fables of the religions of the world have come to seem like tales narrated to children. Even if the theologians pretend that the Bible should be read allegorically, it remains often perverse and full of barbarous atrocities. Some of the Bible is so manifestly wrong and stupid; why, then, should any of the rest of it be accepted?[134]

Consciousness (cognition) is the state or quality of awareness that is more advanced than the primitive awareness that insects have. Being conscious is also being aware of something within oneself, such as ideas and thoughts. It has been defined as sentience, awareness, subjectivity, the ability to experience or to feel, wakefulness, having a sense of selfhood, and the executive control system of the mind. Despite the difficulty in definition, many philosophers believe that there is a broadly shared, underlying intuition about what consciousness is.

Western philosophers since the time of Descartes and Locke have struggled to comprehend the nature of consciousness and pin down its essential properties. Issues of concern in the philosophy of consciousness include whether the concept is fundamentally coherent, whether consciousness can ever be explained mechanistically, whether non-human consciousness exists (and if so, how can it be recognised), how consciousness relates to language, whether consciousness can be understood in a way that does not require a dualistic distinction between mental and physical states or properties, and whether it may ever be possible for computing machines like computers or robots to be conscious—a topic studied in the field of artificial intelligence.

Thanks to recent developments in technology, consciousness has become a significant topic of research in psychology, neuropsychology, and neuroscience within the past few decades. The primary focus is on understanding what it means biologically and psychologically for information to be present in consciousness—that is, on determining the neural and psychological correlates of consciousness. The majority of experimental studies assess consciousness by asking human subjects for a verbal report of their experiences (e.g., "Tell me if you notice anything when I do this"). Issues of interest include phenomena such as subliminal perception, blind sight, denial of impairment, and altered states of consciousness produced by alcohol and other drugs or by spiritual or meditative techniques.[77]

Motivation is the driving force of desire behind all deliberate actions of humans. It is based on emotion, especially on the search of for satisfaction and the avoidance of conflict. Emotion has a significant influence on human behaviour, and it can lead to social disorder and crime.

Man considers himself a superior being and grants himself the title of "homo sapiens". Man is indeed the most developed being of the hominid species but is far from being a wise being. Man is at most a developed animal with all its faults that entails. In a world population of nearly eight billion people, less than 10% can be considered as developed with sufficient knowledge that can be expected from a rational being. Only a small fraction of educated people has an open mind which allows them to reason objectively.

CHAPTER 7

Human Nature

Human nature refers to the distinguishing characteristics of the human, including ways of thinking, feeling, and acting, which humans tend to have naturally and independent of the influence of culture. The questions of what these characteristics are, how fixed they are, and what causes them are amongst the oldest, dating from Greek philosophy and Western philosophy.[95]

In the school of Socrates, later adopted by Plato and Aristoteles, the concept of human nature was approached in two ways: first from the metaphysical aspect (namely, the soul of man), and then from the teleological aspect (namely, the purpose of living to live in accordance with nature).

Aristotle, Plato's most famous student, made some of the most famous and influential statements about human nature. In his works, apart from using a similar scheme of a divided human soul, some clear statements about human nature are made.

- Man is a conjugal animal, meaning an animal which is born to couple when an adult, thus building a household (*oikos*) and, in more successful cases, a clan or small village still run upon patriarchal lines.
- Human is a political animal, meaning an animal with an innate propensity to develop more complex communities the size of a city or town, with a division of labour and

> law-making. This type of community is different in kind from a large family and requires the special use of human reason (rules).

Humans are mimetic animals. They love to use their imagination (and not only to make laws and run town councils). They say, "We enjoy looking at accurate likenesses of things which are themselves painful to see—obscene beasts, for instance, and corpses. And the reason why we enjoy seeing likenesses is that as we look, we learn and infer what each is—for instance, 'That is so-and-so.'"

Almost all classical philosophers accepted that a good human life is a life in accordance with nature.

One of the defining changes that occurred at the end of the Middle Ages was the end of the dominance of Aristotelian philosophy, and its replacement by a new approach to the study of nature, including human nature. In this approach, all attempts at conjecture about formal and final causes were rejected as useless speculation. Also, the term "law of nature" now applied to any regular and predictable pattern in nature, not literally a law made by a divine lawmaker. In the same way, "human nature" became not a special metaphysical cause but simply whatever can be said to be typical tendencies of humans.

Although this new realism applied to the study of human life from the beginning—for example, in Machiavelli's works—the definitive argument for the final rejection of Aristotle was associated especially with the scientist and philosopher Francis Bacon and then René Descartes, whose new approach returned philosophy or science to its pre-Socratic focus upon non-human things. Thomas Hobbes, Giambattista Vico, and David Hume all claimed to be the first to properly use a modern Baconian scientific approach to human things.

Hobbes famously followed Descartes in describing humanity as matter in motion, just like machines. He also very influentially described man's natural state (without science and artifice) as one where life would be "solitary, poor, nasty, brutish and short". Following him, John Locke's *Philosophy of Empiricism* also saw human nature as a *tabula rasa*. In this view, the mind is at birth a blank slate without rules, and so data are added and rules for processing them are formed solely by our sensory experiences.

Jean-Jacques Rousseau pushed the approach of Hobbes to an extreme and criticised it at the same time. He was a contemporary and acquaintance of Hume, writing before the French Revolution and long before Darwin and Freud. He shocked Western civilisation with his *Second Discourse* by proposing that humans had once been solitary animals, without reason or language or communities, and had developed these things due to accidents of prehistory. This proposal was also less famously made by Giambattista Vico. In other words, Rousseau argued that human nature was not only not fixed but was not even approximately fixed compared to what had been assumed before him. Humans are political and rational and have language now, but originally they had none of these things. This in turn implied that living under the management of human reason might not be a happy way to live at all, and perhaps there is no ideal way to live. Rousseau is also unusual in the extent to which he took the approach of Hobbes, asserting that primitive humans were not even naturally social. A civilised human is therefore imbalanced and unhappy because of the mismatch between civilised life and human nature. Unlike Hobbes, Rousseau also became well-known for the suggestion that primitive humans had been happier, noble savages.

Rousseau's conception of human nature has been seen as the origin of many intellectual and political developments of the nineteenth and twentieth centuries. He was an important influence upon the idealist Kant, the absolute idealist Hegel (absolute knowledge), and Marx, as well as the development of German idealism, historicism, and romanticism.

What human nature did entail, according to Rousseau and the other modernists of the seventeenth and eighteenth centuries, were animal-like passions that led humanity to develop language and reasoning, as well as more complex communities (or communities of any kind).

In contrast to Rousseau, David Hume was a critic of the oversimplifying and systematic approach of Hobbes, Rousseau, and some others whereby, for example, all human nature is assumed to be driven by variations of selfishness. Influenced by Hutcheson and Earl Shaftesbury, he argued against oversimplification. On the one hand, he accepted that for many political and economic subjects, people could be assumed to be driven by such simple selfishness, and he also wrote of some of the more social aspects of human nature as something which could be destroyed—for example if people did not associate in just societies. On the other hand, he rejected what he called the "paradox of the sceptics", saying that no politician could have invented words like honourable and shameful, lovely and odious, noble and despicable, unless there was not some natural "original constitution of the mind".[14]

Hume, like Rousseau, was controversial in his own time for his modernist approach, following the example of Bacon and Hobbes of avoiding consideration of metaphysical explanations for any type of cause and effect. He was accused of being an atheist. He wrote,

> We needn't push our research so far as to ask "Why do we have humanity, i.e. a fellow-feeling with others?" It's enough that we experience this as a force in human nature. Our examination of causes must stop somewhere.

After Rousseau and Hume, the nature of philosophy and science changed, branching into different disciplines and approaches, and the study of human nature changed accordingly. Rousseau's proposal that human nature is malleable became a major influence upon international revolutionary movements of various kinds, whereas Hume's approach has been more typical in Anglo-Saxon countries, including the United States.

As the sciences then concerned with humanity split up into more specialised branches, many of the key figures of this evolution expressed influential understandings about human nature.

Charles Darwin gave a widely accepted scientific argument for what Rousseau had already argued from a different direction: that humans and other animal species have no truly fixed nature, at least in the very long term. However, he also gave modern biology a new way of understanding how human nature does exist in a normal human time frame, and how it is caused. Unavoidably, humans endure the nature of the universe of which they are a part.

Sigmund Freud, the founder of psychoanalysis, famously referred to the hidden pathological character of typical human behaviour. He believed that the Marxists were right to focus on what he called "the decisive influence which the economic circumstances of men have upon their intellectual, ethical and artistic attitudes". But he thought that the Marxist view of the class struggle was too shallow, assigning to recent centuries conflicts that were actually primordial. Behind the class struggle, according to Freud, there stands the struggle between father and son, between established clan leader and rebellious challenger. Freud also popularised his notions of the id and the desires associated with each supposed aspect of personality.

E. O. Wilson's socio-biology and closely related theory of evolutionary psychology give scientific arguments against the *tabula rasa* hypotheses of Hobbes, Locke, and Rousseau. In his book *Consilience: The Unity of Knowledge*, Wilson claimed that it was time for a cooperation of all the sciences to explore human nature. He defined human nature as a collection of epigenetic rules. (In the science of genetics, epigenetics is the study of cellular and physiological phenotypic trait variations that result from external or environmental factors that switch genes on and off and affect how cells express genes), specifically the genetic patterns of mental development. Cultural phenomena, rituals, and more are products, not part of human nature. For example, artworks are not part of human nature, but our appreciation of art is. This art appreciation, or our fear of snakes, or incest taboo (Westermarck effect, reverse sexual imprinting) can be studied by the methods of reductionism. Until now, these phenomena were only part of psychological, sociological, and anthropological studies. Wilson proposes that they can be part of interdisciplinary research.

In Christian theology, there are two ways of conceiving human nature.

(1) Spiritual, biblical, and theistic
(2) Natural, cosmically, and anti-theistic

Various views of human nature have been held by theologians. However, there are some "basic assertions" in all "biblical anthropology", which are invoked to still the minds of the simple people.

(1) Humankind has its origin in God, its creator
(2) Humans bear the "image of God"
(3) Humans are "to rule the rest of creation"
(4) Humans have the "ability to transcend" themselves

The Bible contains no single "doctrine of human nature". Rather, it provides material for more philosophical descriptions of human nature. For example, Creation as found in the Book of Genesis provides a theory of human nature. As originally created, the Bible describes "two elements" in human nature: "the body and the breath or spirit of life breathed into it by God". By this was created a "living soul" that is a "living person". According to Genesis 1:27, this living person was made in the "image of God". From the biblical perspective, "to be human is to bear the image of God".

Genesis does not elaborate the meaning of "the image of God", but scholars find suggestions. One is that being created in the image of God distinguishes human nature from that of the beasts. Another is that as God is "able to make decisions and rule", so are humans made in God's image "able to make decisions and rule". A third is that mankind possesses an inherent ability to "to set goals" and move towards them. That God denoted creation as good suggests that Adam was "created in the image of God, in righteousness".

Adam was created with the ability to make "right choices", but also with the ability to choose sin, by which he fell from righteousness into a state of "sin and depravity". Thus, according to the Bible "humankind is not as God wished to create it". God is thus not faultless!

By Adam's fall into sin, human nature became corrupt, although it still bears God's image. The Bible, both the Old Testament and the New Testament, teaches that "sin is universal". For example, "I was sinful at birth," says Psalm 51:5. Jesus taught that everyone is a "sinner naturally" because it is mankind's "nature and disposition of sin". Paul, in Romans 7:18, speaks of his "sinful nature".

Such a "recognition that there is something wrong with the moral nature of man is found in all religions". Augustine of Hippo coined a term for the assessment that all humans are born sinful: original sin. Original sin means "the tendency to sin innate in all human beings".

"The corruption of original sin extends to every aspect of human nature: to reason and will" as well as to "appetites and impulses". This condition is sometimes called total depravity, but that does not mean that humanity is as "thoroughly depraved" as it could become. Commenting on Romans 2:14, John Calvin writes that all people have "some notions of justice and rectitude ... which are implanted by nature". Of course, there can be no natural implantation of sin!

Adam embodied the "whole of human nature' so when Adam sinned 'all of human nature sinned", though he was alone. The Old Testament does not explicitly link the 'corruption of human nature' to Adam's sin. However, the universality of sin implies a link to Adam. In the New Testament, Paul, the persecutor of sin, concurs with the universality of sin. He also makes explicit what the Old Testament implied: the link between humanity's "sinful nature" and Adam's sin. In Romans 5:19, Paul writes, "Through [Adam's] disobedience humanity became sinful." Paul also applied humanity's sinful nature to himself: "there is nothing good in my sinful nature."

The theological doctrine of original sin as an inherent element of human nature is not only based on the Bible, theological writings, and Christian philosophers but also constitutes a reasoning for the existence of sin in the world and defence of the necessity of religion. The stain of original sin is a denigration of humankind to justify the importance of God. Rational people, who do not believe, have no need of the fables of the Bible to conform to ethics.

Long before the monotheism of the Abrahamic religions, humanity had created gods to appease their state of mind. Every civilisation in the world had its specific gods. The Abrahamic religions rejected pantheism. They were more sophisticated and better organised, which allowed them to form a dominant culture that, only after two thousand years, began to waver due to the progress of science.

People tend to forget that the human was originally a wandering hunter who later settled and tilled the soil. From that moment, he started to live in community and had to adhere to rules. He had to forsake his innate selfishness (cf. Richard Dawkins, *The Selfish Gene*). A selfish trait is also found in children.[70]

CHAPTER 8

Instinct

Instinct or innate behaviour is the inherent inclination of a living organism towards a particular complex behaviour. The description of instinct is rather vague and little scientific. It is usually described as a pattern of behaviour of a living organism that is specific and hereditary, in which experience and learning do not play a role. The instinct feeling is genetically recorded and handed down from generation to generation, and so it is innate. In the literature, where opinions vary, instinct is referred to as stimulus-response processes. When talking about the nature of man we are talking about his behaviour, his innate tendencies. In this purpose, of course, is behaviour a certain innate pattern that distinguishes man. Human nature refers to the distinguishing characteristics of the human, including ways of thinking, feeling, and acting, which humans tend to have naturally, independent of the influence of culture. The questions of what these characteristics are, how fixed they are, and what causes them are amongst the oldest, dating from Greek philosophy, and most important questions of Western philosophy.[95]

In social psychology, socio-biology, and behavioural biology in humans, it is disputed whether there is such a thing in humans as an instinct. The man is, after all, able to break through the instinct pattern. The survival instinct of the living organisms is the strongest instinct and dominates over all other instincts. When a man is in jeopardy, he doesn't think any more but reacts to impulses to survive. Science is not even a certified statement in that respect. The instinct is stronger than the human will, although certain events have shown that one is able to break the urge. It can mean an act of desperation, but it can also be an act of self-sacrifice, in which the will is expressed to prove something rational and the desire to dodge the impulse wilfully. Instincts in humans are not reflexes because they are not controlled by the brain and neither are such character traits as aggression, introversion, and extraversion, instincts which are dispositions to be classified.

Now proven is that man in some instances is able to break through or to neglect instincts, not only in terms of self-preservation but also in terms of childcare, child abuse, and infanticide. Some doubt whether there is such a thing as instinct in humans. However, childcare by the mother must be classified as a very strong drive which cannot be overlooked, and which is common to all living forms. Harvard professor in cognitive science and experimental psychology Steven Pinker, a Jewish atheist, popularised Noam Chomsky's theory that language is an innate faculty of mind. But unlike Chomsky and others who believe the human language instinct is a by-product of other adaptations, Pinker is of the opinion that a language instinct is a biological adaptation shaped by natural selection as an adaptation of communication.

In modern psychology, the connection with instinct completely is ignored. A movement in psychology is behaviourism. It is defined as the scientific study (experimental and empirical) of human behaviour. It speaks out about the research domain and the research methods of psychology. It's actually the philosophy behind the psychology, as B. F. Skinner defines it: "Behaviourism is not the science of human behaviour; it is the philosophy of that science."[12] In the behavioural psychology there is also no link established with the instinct. J. B. Watson was the behaviourist who propagated, "Give me a dozen healthy infants, well-formed, and my own specified world to educate them, and I guarantee that they become chosen by me a specialist: doctor, lawyer, artist, merchant and, yes, even beggar and thief, regardless of his talents, inclinations, trends, vocations and race of his ancestors."[13]

The flow of instinct was formed at the beginning of the twentieth century but now has little influence.

CHAPTER 9

Innatism, Nativism, and Nurture

Innatism is a philosophical (epistemological) doctrine that holds that the mind is born with ideas/knowledge, and that therefore the mind is not a *tabula rasa (*blank state) at birth, as early empiricists such as John Locke and David Hume claimed. Innatism asserts that not all knowledge is gained from experience and the senses.[117]

Since the early nineteenth century, thinkers such as G. W. Friedrich Hegel, the Christian Soren Kierkegaard, the atheist Friedrich Nietzsche, and the atheistic existentialist Jean-Paul Sartre have sometimes argued against a fixed or innate nature.

In general terms, the terms *innatism* and *nativism* are synonymous because they both refer to notions of pre-existing knowledge present in the mind at childbirth. However, more correctly, innatism refers to the philosophy of rationalism posited by such as Plato, René Descartes, and Gottfried Leibniz, who assumed that a deity or process placed innate ideas and principles in the human mind. On the other hand, nativism is a modern adaption of innatism, rooted in innatism but grounded in the fields of genetics, cognitive psychology, and psycholinguistics. Nativists hold that innate knowledge is genetically programmed to arise in the mind and is shared by all humans in common.

Nativism is an understanding of the philosophy of which there is no consensus. The nativist's general objection against empiricism is still the same as was raised by the rationalists such as Plato and his student Aristotle (although they had conflicting views), Descartes,

Spinoza, and Leibniz: the human mind of a new born child is not a *tabula rasa* but is equipped with an inborn structure. The leading protagonist of the nativists is Avram N. Chomsky, an atheistic Jew, liberalistic socialist, and linguistic philosopher considered a universal genius, as was Leibniz. According to Chomsky, to explain the extraordinary ability to learn complex concepts possessed by young children, he posits that human linguistic systems contain a systemic complexity which supposedly could not be empirically derived because the environment seems too poor, variable, and indeterminate. It follows that humans must be born with a universal innate grammar, which is determinate and has highly organised directive component, and which enables the language learner to ascertain and categorise language heard into a system. If Chomsky is correct, then at least a part of human knowledge consists in cognitive dispositions, which are triggered and developed by the environment but not determined by it. It would mean that if the earth is struck by a nuclear catastrophe and the human population becomes deaf/mute except for a few families, the children born into the not-stricken families would also be deaf/mute because their environment would not allow their cognitive predispositions to be triggered. Chomsky's ideas allow a parallel to draw with moral faculties exerted by humans, such as stated by the socio-biologist E. O. Wilson and the evolutionary psychologist Steven Pinker.

In the psychological nature (in the sense of innatism and nativism) versus nurture (in the sense of empiricism and behaviourism) debate is the discussion on the origin of the properties of an individual. The debate includes many views that extremely vary, ranging from

- nature, in which the properties of the individual are determined due to genetic material,

to

- nurture, in which all the properties of the individual are determined by education and environment.

The debate is situated also in terms of morality.

Both Hobbes and Jean-Jacques Rousseau assumed that morality is not a social construction but rather "natural" in the sense of innate, an outgrowth of humankind's inclination to behold suffering from which emotion, compassion, or empathy emerge. However, Rousseau disagreed with Hobbes when the latter asserted that because man in the state of nature has no idea of goodness, he must obviously be bad and common as he is ignorant about virtue (cf. chapter VII, *Human Nature*, supra).

The notions of nature and nurture were coined by the polymath Francis Galton in the discussion of the influence of heredity and environment on social advancement. Galton was influenced by the book *Origin of Species* written by his half cousin Charles Darwin.[14]

It is a philosophical debate conducted by the rationalists (the ratio as non-sensory ability) versus the empiricists (sensory experience). The contemporary psychological debate consists in what role the genes and environment play in the development of man. There is now agreement that both factors play an important role in the final intelligence and personality of an individual, but without agreeing which factor is dominant. About the vital functions, like breathing, eating, drinking, thinking, and moving, there is obviously no dispute. J. B. Watson,[13] in his research on babies, concluded that there were three innate emotions, love, anger, and fear, which constituted their character, but which could be developed by conditioning.

All believers assume that the existence of God is innate.

If the knowledge of God is innate, then many questions are raised. How did God create such imperfect beings? The profound innate knowledge of God makes it exceedingly difficult to exercise evil, or the innate knowledge is superficial and imagined! In fact, God is an entity invented by man and thus cannot be innate.

What is the difference between instinct and innatism? Many psychologists revoke instinct, inborn behaviour, yet the influent evolutionary psychologist Steve Pinker, an agnostic Jew leaning towards atheism, bases all his studies on instinctive innatism and inborn knowledge. The nuance must be indeed very slight. He also stated, "We're learning more and more about what makes us tick, including our moral sense, without needing the assumption of a deity or a soul."[79]

We are as we are, and we live as we do because of the interplay of our inherent natures and the world around us. This much is uncontroversial. However, one cannot ignore wondering about the extent of the contributions of the two broad factors and about the nature of the interactions.

Does our inherent nature include a priori knowledge, or do we start with a blank cognitive slate (tabula rasa) and get all our information and knowledge from perception? Until recently, the empiricists seemed to have carried the day, but prompted by Noam Chomsky's claim that findings in linguistics vindicate nativism against empiricism, innateness has made a strong comeback. Contemporary research in cognitive development, genetics, and evolutionary psychology has extended Chomsky nativist thinking to the very concepts of morality and to the principles that were at the heart of the historical philosophical debate concerning God, personhood/ mind, causality, mathematics, ontology, and more. Finally, both factors cannot be ignored. Evolution of humankind has done away with the exclusion of some cognition and made it possible that some knowledge is carried forward. The more humankind evolves, the more cognition will prevail. Morality is a domain where debate remains intense. Believers should not have a problem in distinguishing good from evil because they are convinced that a deity has planted the difference in the mind. However, they should bear in mind that they are born with original sin. Ethics (the reasoning and philosophy of morality) is a necessary invention of human to establish law and order in a community to prevent chaos and anarchy.

Even Saul of Tarsus (Saint Paul) admits that those who do not believe in God still often follow God's laws as given in the Ten Commandments. "When that is, Centiles, which have not the law, the law of nature, then they are themselves into law, even though they have him. They prove by their actions that what the law requires is written on their hearts; and their conscience confirms this, because they accuse or absolve themselves with their thoughts" (Romans 2:14–15). It is interpreted by believers that those who do not believe in God remain behind, with the only possible conclusion that the unbelievers find that the divine decisions are just based on the need to survive. In this case, that would be what the unbelievers call conscience, based on learned behaviour, instead of a part of divine design.

In his theory of knowledge, Immanuel Kant instituted a new (third) meaning for the term *transcendental.* The first and original meaning, as part of the concept pair transcendence (beyond knowledge) and immanence (divine omnipresent), is primarily used with reference to God's relation to the world. In this meaning, God is completely outside of and beyond the world, as contrasted with the notion that God is manifested in the world, being an immanent presence as maintained by the pantheism (God is nature) of Baruch Spinoza. The meaning originated with the Aristotelian view of God as the prime mover, a nonmaterial self-consciousness that is outside of the world. The second (medieval) meaning is that concepts are transcendental if they are broader than what falls within the Aristotelian categories that were used to organise reality conceptually (unity, truth, and goodness).

Kant opposed the term *transcendental* to the term *transcendent,* the latter meaning "that, which goes beyond" (transcends) any possible knowledge of a human being.[68] For him, transcendental meant knowledge about human cognition with regards to knowing how objects are possible *a priori.*

CHAPTER 10

Empathy

Empathy is the ability to live in the feelings of others. It exists both in animals and in humans. Empathy in humans is not the same thing as altruism, although it can be a breeding ground for altruistic behaviour by providing assistance to his fellow man.[123]

Empathy denotes a deep emotional understanding of another's feelings or problems, whereas sympathy is more general and implying pity or sorrow for others' misfortunes.

Empathy is the property that is embedded in the emotional and cognitive development of man, but it is by no means innate. Research has shown that empathy develops about the nursery age. One distinguishes two components of empathy: effective, or emotional empathy, the capacity to respond with appropriate emotion to the mental state of his fellow man; and cognitive empathy, the capacity to understand another's perspective and mental state. It leans to the theory of the mind (intellect).

The use of the magnetic resonance imaging (MRI) scanner has shown that different parts of the brain are activated by both components of empathy. Empathy, as introspection of oneself and of his fellow man, fosters inevitably the goodness (morality) of man and contributes towards the welfare of man as a whole.

Empathy has many definitions that encompass a broad range of emotional states varying from caring for other people, experiencing emotional emotions that match another person's emotions, discerning what another person is thinking, and feeling to distinct the difference between oneself and another.

The terms cognitive empathy and theory of mind are used synonymously, but it is unclear whether these are equivalent.

Psychopathy is a personality disorder partly characterised by antisocial and aggressive behaviours, as well as emotional and interpersonal deficits, including shallow emotions and a lack of remorse and empathy.

The capacity of empathy, which can be learned, is a revered trait in society, motivating unselfishness and altruism. Empathy for others is the route to value morality in life, the essence of right and wrong.[67]

CHAPTER 11

Morality and Ethics

Morality is the disjunction between right and wrong. It is a set of rules, essential and indispensable for humans living in community, derived from a code of conduct from a particular philosophy, religion, or culture. It can also be derived from a standard that a person believes should be universal. A universal rule is the golden rule, which states, "One should treat others as one would like others to treat oneself."[118]

Moral philosophy includes moral ontology, or the origin of morals, as well as moral epistemology, or what is known about morals.

Immorality is the active neglect of morality, whereas amorality is the unawareness, indifference, or disbelief in any set of moral standards or principles.

In neuroscience, the brain areas involved when humans reason are consistently investigated. In fact, the neural network underlying moral decisions overlaps with the network pertaining to representing others' intentions (i.e., the theory of mind) and the network pertaining to representing others' emotional states (i.e., empathy). It is doubtful if there is such a thing as "moral module". The explicit making of morally right and wrong judgements coincides with activation in the ventromedial prefrontal cortex, while intuitive reactions to situations containing explicit moral issues activate the temporoparietal junction area.

If morality is the answer to the question of how we ought to live at the individual level, politics can be seen *mutatis mutandis* as addressing the same question at the social level.

Religion and morality are not synonymous, although most religions claim it as an automatic assumption. Denmark and Sweden belong to the least religious countries in the world, yet they enjoy the lowest violent crime rates in the world and the lowest level of corruption in the world.[70] The United States, with a high religiosity level, has a high crime and corruption rate.[71]

Ethics or moral philosophy is the branch of philosophy that involves systematising, defending, and recommending concepts of right and wrong conduct.

The ancient Greek philosophers, led by Socrates, were the first philosophers to encourage both scholars and common citizens to turn their attention from the outside world to the condition of humankind. In this view, knowledge bearing on human life was placed highest, and all other knowledge was secondary. Self-knowledge was considered necessary for success and an inherently essential good. A self-aware person will act completely within his capabilities to his pinnacle, whereas an ignorant person will flounder and encounter difficulty. To Socrates, a person must become aware of every fact (and its context) relevant to his existence if he wishes to attain self-knowledge. He posited that people would naturally do what is good if they knew what was right. Evil or bad actions are the result of ignorance. If a criminal was truly aware of the intellectual and spiritual consequences of his actions, he would neither commit nor even consider committing those actions. According to Socrates, any person who knows what is truly right will automatically do it. While he correlated knowledge with virtue, he similarly equated virtue with joy. The truly wise man will know what is right, do what is good, and therefore be happy.

Aristotle posited an ethical system that may be termed self-realisationism. In Aristotle's view, when a person acts in accordance with his nature and realises his full potential, he will do good and be content. At birth, a baby is not a person but a potential person. To become a "real" person, the child's inherent potential must be realised. Unhappiness and frustration are caused by the unrealised potential of a person, leading to failed goals and a poor life. Aristotle said, "Nature does nothing in vain." Therefore, it is imperative for people to act in accordance with their nature and develop their latent talents in order to be content and complete. Happiness was held to be the ultimate goal (cf. chapter XXIII, infra). All other things, such as civic life or wealth, are merely a means to an end. Self-realisation, the awareness of one's nature, and the development of one's talents are the surest path to happiness.

The Stoic philosopher Epictetus posited that the greatest good was contentment and serenity. Peace of mind (*Apatheia)* was of the highest value; self-mastery over one's desires and emotions leads to spiritual peace. The "unconquerable will" is central to this philosophy. The individual's will should be independent and inviolate. Death is not feared. People do not "lose" their life but instead "return", for they are returning to God (who initially gave what the person is as a person). Epictetus said difficult problems in life should not be avoided but rather embraced. They are spiritual exercises needed for the health of the spirit, just as physical exercise is required for the health of the body. He also stated that sex and sexual desire are to be avoided as the greatest threat to the integrity and equilibrium of a man's mind. Abstinence is highly desirable. Epictetus said remaining abstinent in the face of temptation was a victory for which a man could be proud, which is a proverb often cited by Catholic clerics.

Hedonism posits that the principal ethic is maximising pleasure and minimising pain. There are several schools of Hedonist thought ranging from those advocating the indulgence of even momentary desires to those teaching a pursuit of spiritual bliss. In their consideration of consequences, they range from those advocating self-gratification regardless of the pain and expense to others to those stating that the most ethical pursuit maximises pleasure and happiness for the most people. Aristippus of Cyrene, a pupil of Socrates, supported immediate gratification or pleasure: "Eat, drink and be merry, for tomorrow we die." Even fleeting desires should be indulged, for fear the opportunity should be forever lost. There was little to no concern with the future; the present dominated the pursuit of immediate pleasure. Cyrenaic hedonism encouraged the pursuit of enjoyment and indulgence without hesitation, believing pleasure to be the only good.

Epicurus was the founder of the school of philosophy called Epicureanism, which is a hedonist form of virtue ethics. Epicurus "presented a sustained argument that pleasure, correctly understood, will coincide with virtue". He rejected the extremism of Cyrenaicism, believing some pleasures and indulgences to be detrimental to human beings. Epicureans observed that indiscriminate indulgence sometimes resulted in negative consequences. Some experiences were therefore rejected out of hand, and some unpleasant experiences endured in the present to ensure a better life in the future. To Epicurus, the *summum bonum*, or greatest good, was prudence exercised with moderation and caution. Excessive indulgence can be destructive to pleasure and can even lead to pain. For example, eating one food too often will cause a person to lose the taste for it. Eating too much food at once will lead to discomfort and ill health. Pain and fear were to be avoided. Living was essentially good, barring pain and illness. Death was not to be feared. Fear was considered the source of most unhappiness. Conquering the fear of death would naturally lead to a happier life. Epicurus reasoned if there were an afterlife and immortality, the fear of death was irrational. If there was no life after death, then the person would not be alive to suffer, fear, or worry; he would be non-existent in death. It is irrational to fret over circumstances that do not exist, such as one's state of death in the absence of an afterlife.

Mohism or Monism was a Chinese philosophy developed by the followers of Mozi (Mo Tzu). It evolved about the same time as Confucianism and Taoism. Mohism promotes a philosophy of impartial caring; that is, a person should care equally for all other individuals, regardless of their relationship to him or her. The expression of this thought is indiscriminate caring, which results in making man a righteous being.

Modern virtue ethics was popularised during the late twentieth century in large part as a response to Elisabeth Anscombe's *Modern Moral Philosophy.* Anscombe was a Roman Catholic and the favourite student of the famous philosopher Ludwig Wittgenstein, who argued that consequentialism and deontological ethics are only feasible as universal theories if the two schools ground themselves in divine law.[119] Consequentialism, coined by Elizabeth Anscombe in her essay "Modern Moral Philosophy" in 1958 in criticism of the utilitarists J. S. Mill and Sidgwickold, holds that the consequences of one's conduct are the ultimate basis for any judgements about the rightness and wrongness of that conduct. The extreme aphorism "the end justifies the means" means that if a goal is morally important enough then any method of achieving it is acceptable. Consequentialism contrasts with deontological ethics in that deontology, in which rules and moral duty are central, derives the rightness or wrongness of one's conduct from the character of the behaviour itself rather than the outcomes of the conduct. It also contrasts with virtue ethics, which focusses on the character of the agent rather than on the nature or consequences of the act. Finally, it contrasts also with pragmatic ethics, propagated by such as Charles Sanders Peirce, William James, and especially John Dewey, which hold that moral correctness evolves similarly to scientific knowledge: socially and over the course of many lifetimes. Social reform should be preferred above attempts to account for consequences, individual virtue, or duty, notwithstanding their worthwhile attempts. Pragmatism contends that most philosophical topics—such as the nature of knowledge, language, concepts, meaning, belief, and science—are all best served in terms of their practical uses and success.

State consequentialism, also known as Mohist consequentialism, is an ethical theory that evaluates the moral worth of an action based on how much it contributes to the basic goods of a state. The *Stanford Encyclopaedia of Philosophy* describes Mohist consequentialism, dating back to the fifth century BC, as "a remarkably sophisticated version based on a plurality of intrinsic goods taken as constitutive of human welfare". Unlike utilitarianism, which views pleasure as a moral good, "the basic goods in Mohist consequentialist thinking are order, material wealth, and an increase in population". During Mozi's era, war and famines were common, and population growth was seen as a moral necessity for a harmonious society. The "material wealth" of Mohist consequentialism refers to basic needs like shelter and clothing, and the "order" of Mohist consequentialism refers to Mozi's stance against warfare and violence, which he viewed as pointless and a threat to social stability. Stanford sinologist David Shepherd Nivison, in *The Cambridge History of Ancient China*, writes that the moral goods of Mohism "are interrelated: more basic wealth, then more reproduction; more people, then more production and wealth ... if people have plenty, they would be good, filial, kind, and so on unproblematically". The Mohists believed that morality is based on "promoting the benefit of all under heaven and eliminating harm to all under heaven". In contrast to Jeremy Bentham's views, state consequentialism is not utilitarian because it is not hedonistic or individualistic.

Utilitarianism is an ethical theory that argues the proper course of action is one that maximises a positive effect, such as happiness, welfare, or the ability to live according to personal preferences. Jeremy Bentham, liberalistic social reformer, and John Stuart Mill, nephew of Bentham, are influential proponents of this school of thought. In *A Fragment on Government,* Bentham says that "the best moral action is the one that maximises utility" and that "it is the greatest happiness of the greatest number that is the measure of right and wrong"; he describes this as a fundamental axiom. In his *An Introduction to the Principles of Morals and Legislation,* he talks of "the principle of utility' but later prefers 'the greatest happiness principle".

Utilitarianism is the paradigmatic example of a consequentialist moral theory. This form of utilitarianism holds that what matters is the aggregate positive effect on everyone and not only for any one person. John Stuart Mill, in his exposition of utilitarianism, proposed a hierarchy of pleasures, meaning that the pursuit of certain kinds of pleasure is more highly valued than the pursuit of other pleasures.

Contemporary noteworthy proponents of utilitarism are Sam Harris and Peter Singer.

Samuel Benjamin Harris is an atheist American philosopher and neuroscientist who advocates the separation of church and state, as well as the liberty to criticise religion (especially Islam). He has empirical insights about the nature of consciousness that do not depend on faith. His book *The End of Faith,* published in 2004, appeared in *The New York Times* bestseller list for thirty-three weeks. In 2010 he published his book *The Moral Landscape*, in which he argues that science can help answer moral problems and can aid the facilitation of human well-being.

Peter Singer is an Australian atheistic moral philosopher, considered the best-known and almost the most widely read of all contemporary philosophers. Singer's *Practical Ethics* analyses why and how a living being's interests should be weighed. His principle of equal consideration of interests does not dictate equal treatment of all those with interests because different interests warrant different treatment. All have an interest in avoiding pain, for instance, but relatively few have an interest in cultivating their abilities. Not only does his principle justify different treatment for different interests, but it allows different treatment for the same interest when diminishing marginal utility is a factor. For example, this approach would privilege a starving person's interest in food over the same interest of someone who is only slightly hungry. Amongst the more important human interests are those in avoiding pain, in developing one's abilities, in satisfying basic needs for food and shelter, in enjoying warm personal relationships, in being free to pursue one's projects without interference, and many others. The fundamental interest that entitles a being to equal consideration is the capacity for suffering and/or enjoyment or happiness. Singer holds that a being's interests should always be weighed according to that being's concrete properties. He favours a journey model of life, which measures the wrongness of taking the life of the degree to which doing so frustrates a life journey's goals. The journey model is tolerant of some frustrated desire and explains why persons who have embarked on their journeys are not replaceable. Only a personal interest in continuing to live brings the journey model into play. This model also explains the priority that Singer attaches to interests over trivial desires and pleasures. Ethical conduct is justifiable for reasons that go beyond prudence to "something bigger than the individual," addressing a larger audience. Singer thinks this going beyond identifies moral reasons as "somehow universal", specifically in the injunction to "love thy neighbour as thyself", interpreted by him as demanding that one gives the same weight to the interests of others as one gives to one's own interests. This universalizing step, which Singer traces from Kant to Robert Hare, is crucial and sets him apart from moral theorists such as Hobbes and David Gauthier, who are known for their constrained maximisation and who tie morality to prudence. Universalisation leads directly to utilitarianism, Singer argues, on the strength of the thought that one's own interests cannot count for more than the interests of others. Taking these into account, one must weigh them up and adopt the course of action that is most likely to maximise the interests of those affected; utilitarianism has been arrived at. Singer's universalising step applies to interests without reference to who has them, whereas a Kantian's approach applies to the judgements of rational agents (in Kant's *Kingdom of Ends*, or Rawls's *Original Position, Political Liberalism*). Singer regards Kantian universalisation as unjust to animals. As for the Hobbesians, Singer attempts a response in the final chapter of *Practical Ethics,* arguing that self-interested reasons support adoption of the moral point of view, such as "the paradox of hedonism", which counsels that happiness is best found by not looking for it, and the need most people feel to relate to something larger than their own concerns.

Singer holds that the right to life is essentially tied to a being's capacity to hold preferences, which in turn is essentially tied to a being's capacity to feel pain and pleasure.

In *Practical Ethics,* Singer argues in favour of abortion on the grounds that foetuses are neither rational nor self-aware and can therefore hold no preferences. As a result, he argues that the preference for a mother to have an abortion automatically takes precedence. In sum, Singer argues that a foetus lacks personhood.

Similar to his argument for abortion, Singer argues that newborns lack the essential characteristics of personhood—"rationality, autonomy, and self-consciousness"—and therefore "killing a new born baby are never equivalent to killing a rational person, that is, a being who wants to go on living".

Singer classifies euthanasia as voluntary, involuntary, or non-voluntary. Voluntary euthanasia is that to which the subject consents. He argues in favour of voluntary euthanasia and some forms of non-voluntary euthanasia, including infanticide in certain instances, but he opposes involuntary euthanasia.

Religious critics have argued that Singer's ethic ignores and undermines the traditional notion of the sanctity of life. Such a thing as sanctity of life does not really exist. It is called traditional by theists, but it has no basis. Singer agrees and believes the notion of the sanctity of life ought to be discarded as outdated, unscientific, and irrelevant to understanding problems in contemporary bioethics. Bioethicists associated with the disability rights and disability studies communities have argued that his epistemology is based on ablest conceptions of disability.

Bioethics is the study of the typically controversial ethical issues emerging from new situations and possibilities brought about by advances in biology and medicine. It is also moral discernment as it relates to medical policy and practise. Bioethicists are concerned with the ethical questions that arise in the relationships amongst life sciences, biotechnology, medicine, politics, law, and philosophy. It also includes the study of the most commonplace questions of values ("the ethics of the ordinary") which arise in primary care and other branches of medicine.

Singer has experienced the complexities of some of these questions in his own life. His mother had Alzheimer's disease. He said, "I think this has made me see how the issues of someone with these kinds of problems are really very difficult. In an interview with the scientific journalist Ronald Bailey published in December 2000, he explained that his sister shares the responsibility of making decisions about his mother. He did say that if he were solely responsible, his mother might not continue to live.

Singer is an advocate of effective altruism. He argues that people should not only try to reduce suffering but reduce it in the most effective manner possible. While Singer has previously written at length about the moral imperative to eliminate the suffering of nonhuman animals, particularly in the meat industry, and end world poverty, he writes about how the effective altruism movement is doing these things more effectively in his 2015 book *The Most Good You Can Do Do.*[120] He is a board member of Animal Charity Evaluators, a charity evaluator used by many members of the effective altruism community which recommends the most cost-effective animal advocacy charities and interventions.

His own organisation, The Life You Can Save, also recommends a selection of charities deemed by charity evaluators to "Give to be the most effective when it comes to helping those in extreme poverty"[120] The organisation was founded after Singer released his 2009 book *The Life You Can Save*, in which he argues more generally in favour of giving to charities that help to end global poverty. In particular, he expands upon some of the arguments made in his 1972 essay "Famine, Affluence and Morality", in which he posits that citizens of rich nations are morally obligated to give at least some of their disposable income to charities that help the global poor. He supports this using the drowning child analogy, which states that most people would rescue a drowning child from a pond even if it meant that their expensive clothes were ruined, so we clearly value a human life more than the value of our material possessions. As a result, we should take a significant portion of the money that we spend on our possessions and instead donate it to charity.

Altruism comes from Auguste Comte's injunction "*Vivre pour autrui*" (live for others). The positivism of Comte led to an atheistic cult, *Religion of Humanity*, which influenced the Christian Victorian novelists even though they rejected the austere world of Comte.

Deontological ethics or deontology (from Greek δέον, *deon*, "obligation, duty"; and -λογία, *-logia*) is an approach to ethics that determines goodness or rightness from examining acts, or the rules and duties that the person doing the act strove to fulfil. This is in contrast to consequentialism, in which rightness is based on the consequences of an act and not the act by itself. In deontology, an act may be considered right even if the act produces a bad consequence, if it follows the rule that "one should do unto others as they would have done unto them", and even if the person who does the act lacked virtue and had a bad intention in doing the act. According to deontology, we have a duty to act in a way that does those things that are inherently good as acts (truth telling, for example) or that follow an objectively obligatory rule (as in rule utilitarianism). For deontologists, the ends or consequences of our actions are not important in and of themselves, and our intentions are not important in and of themselves. Immanuel Kant's theory of ethics is considered deontological for several different reasons. First, Kant argues that to act in the morally right way, people must act from duty (*deon*). Second, Kant argued that it was not the consequences of actions that make them right or wrong but the motives (Maxime) of the person who carries out the action. Kant's argument that to act Mn the morally right way, one must act from duty begins with an argument that the highest good must be both good in itself and good without qualification. Something is "good in itself" when it is intrinsically good, and it is "good without qualification" when the addition of that thing never makes a situation ethically worse. Kant then argues that those things that are usually thought to be good, such as intelligence, perseverance, and pleasure, fail to be either intrinsically good or good without qualification. Pleasure, for example, appears to not be good without qualification because when people take pleasure in watching someone suffer, they make the situation ethically worse. He concludes that there is only one thing that is truly good: nothing in the world—indeed, nothing even beyond the world—can possibly be conceived which could be called good without qualification except a good will.

An axiom or postulate, as defined in classical philosophy, is a statement (in mathematics often shown in symbolic form) that is so evident or well established that it is accepted without controversy or question. Thus, the axiom is the promise or starting point for further reasoning or arguments, usually in logic or mathematics.

CHAPTER 12

Mind

The mind is a product of physical brain activity, and the mind has evolved by natural means over a period of millions of years.[114]

The concept of mind is understood in many different ways by many different cultural and religious traditions. Broadly speaking, a mind is the set of cognitive faculties that enables consciousness, perception, thinking, judgement, and memory as characteristics of a human, but it may also apply to other life forms. During the ages, enquiries in philosophy, religion, psychology, and cognitive science have been made in order to understand the mind and what its distinguishing properties are in regards to the body and the nervous system.

The nature and origin of consciousness and the mind itself are also widely debated in science. The explanatory gap is generally equated with the hard problem of consciousness, and the question of free will is also considered to be of fundamental importance.

Consciousness in humans (this includes mammals) is an aspect of the mind generally thought to comprise qualities such as subjectivity and sentience, as well as the ability to perceive the relationship between oneself and one's environment.[122] It is a subject of much research in philosophy of mind, psychology, neuroscience, and cognitive science. Some philosophers divide consciousness into phenomenal consciousness, which is the subjective experience itself, and access consciousness, which refers to the global availability of information to processing systems in the brain. Phenomenal consciousness has many different experienced qualities, often referred to as qualia. Phenomenal consciousness is usually consciousness *of* something or *about* something, a property known as intentionality in the "philosophy of mind".

Thought is a mental act that allows humans to make sense of things in the world, and to represent and interpret them in ways that are significant that accord with their needs, attachments, goals, commitments, plans, ends, and desires. Thinking involves the symbolic or semiotic mediation of ideas or data, such as when we form concepts or engage in problem-solving, reasoning, and making decisions. Words that refer to similar concepts and processes include deliberation, cognition, ideation, discourse, and imagination.

Thinking is sometimes described as a "higher" cognitive function, and the analysis of thinking processes is a part of cognitive psychology. It is also deeply connected with our capacity to make and use tools, to understand cause and effect, to recognise patterns of significance, to comprehend and disclose unique contexts of experience or activity, and to respond to the world in a meaningful way.

Memory is the ability to preserve, retain, and subsequently recall knowledge, information, or experience. Although memory has traditionally been a persistent theme in philosophy, the late nineteenth and early twentieth centuries also saw the study of memory emerge as a subject of inquiry within the paradigms of cognitive psychology. In recent decades, it has become one of the pillars of a new branch of science called cognitive neuroscience, a marriage between cognitive psychology and neuroscience.

Imagination is the activity of generating or evoking novel situations, images, ideas, or other qualia in the mind. It is a characteristically subjective activity rather than a direct or passive experience. The term is technically used in psychology for the process of reviving in the mind of perceptions objects formerly given in sense perception. Since this use of the term conflicts with that of ordinary language, some psychologists have preferred to describe this process as imaging or imagery, or to speak of it as reproductive as opposed to productive or constructive imagination. Things imagined are said to be seen in the mind's eye. Amongst the many practical functions of imagination are the ability to project possible futures (or histories), to see things from another's perspective, and to change the way something is perceived, including to make decisions to respond to or enact what is imagined.

Memetic is a theory of mental content based on an analogy with Darwinian evolution, which was originated by Richard Dawkins and Douglas Hofstadter in the 1980s. It is an evolutionary model of cultural information transfer. A meme, analogous to a gene, is an idea, belief, or pattern of behaviour "hosted" in one or more individual minds, and it can reproduce itself from mind to mind. Thus, what would otherwise be regarded as one individual influencing another to adopt a belief is seen memetic ally as a meme reproducing itself.

Understanding the relationship between the brain and the mind, or the mind-body problem, is one of the central issues in the history of philosophy. It is a challenging problem both philosophically and scientifically. There are three major philosophical schools of thought concerning the answer: dualism, materialism, and idealism. Dualism holds that the mind exists independently of the brain, materialism holds that mental phenomena are identical to neuronal phenomena, and idealism holds that only mental phenomena exist.

Throughout most of history, many philosophers found it inconceivable that cognition could be implemented by a physical substance such as brain tissue (that is neurons and synapses). Descartes, who thought extensively about mind-brain relationships, found it possible to explain reflexes and other simple behaviours in mechanistic terms, although he did not believe that complex thought, and language in particular, could be explained by reference to the physical brain alone.

The most straightforward scientific evidence of a strong relationship between the physical brain matter and the mind is the impact physical alterations to the brain have on the mind, such as with traumatic brain injury and psychoactive drug use.

In addition to the philosophical questions, the relationship between mind and brain involves a number of scientific questions, including understanding the relationship between mental activity and brain activity, the exact mechanisms by which drugs influence cognition, and the neural correlates of consciousness.

The evolution of human intelligence refers to a set of theories that attempt to explain how human intelligence has evolved, closely tied to the evolution of the human brain and to the origin of language. The timeline of human evolution spans some 7 million years, from the separation of the Pan genus until the emergence of behavioural modernity by 50,000 years ago. Of this timeline, the first 3 million years concern *Sahelanthropus*, the following 2 million concern *Australopithecus*, and the final 2 million span the history of actual *Homo* species (the Palaeolithic).

Cognition is "the mental action or process of acquiring knowledge and understanding through thought, experience, and the senses". It encompasses processes such as knowledge, attention, memory and working memory, judgment and evaluation, reasoning and computation, problem-solving and decision-making, comprehension, and production of language. Human cognition is conscious and unconscious, concrete or abstract, as well as intuitive (like knowledge of a language) and conceptual (like a model of a language). Cognitive processes use existing knowledge and generate new knowledge.[78]

Many traits of human intelligence, such as empathy, the theory of mind, mourning, ritual, and the use of symbols and tools, are already apparent in great apes, although in lesser sophistication than in humans. There is a debate between supporters of the idea of a sudden emergence of intelligence, or "great leap forward", and those of a gradual or continuum hypothesis.

Philosophy of mind is the branch of philosophy that studies the nature of the mind, mental events, mental functions, mental properties, and consciousness, as well as their relationship to the physical body. The mind-body problem (i.e., the relationship of the mind to the body) is commonly seen as the central issue in philosophy of mind, although there are other issues concerning the nature of the mind that do not involve its relation to the physical body.

Dualism and monism are the two major schools of thought that attempt to resolve the mind-body problem. Dualism is the position that mind and body are in some way separate from each other. It can be traced back to Plato, Aristotle, and the Samkhya and Yoga schools of Hindu philosophy, but it was most precisely formulated by René Descartes in the seventeenth century. Substance dualists argue that the mind is an independently existing substance, whereas property dualists maintain that the mind is a group of independent properties that emerge from and cannot be reduced to the brain, but that it is not a distinct substance. Twentieth-century philosopher Martin Heidegger suggested that subjective experience and activity (i.e., the "mind") cannot be made sense of in terms of Cartesian "substances" that bear "properties" at all (whether the mind itself is thought of as a distinct, separate kind of substance or not). This is because the nature of subjective, *qualitative* experience is incoherent in terms of—or semantically incommensurable with the concept of—substances that bear properties. This is a fundamentally ontological and not an existentialism argument.

Monism is the position that mind and body are not physiologically and ontologically distinct kinds of entities. This view was first advocated in Western philosophy by Parmenides in the fifth century BC and was later espoused by the seventeenth-century rationalist Baruch Spinoza. According to Spinoza's dual-aspect theory, mind and body are two aspects of an underlying reality which he variously described as "Nature" or "God".

- Physicalists argue that only the entities postulated by physical theory exist, and that the mind will eventually be explained in terms of these entities as physical theory continues to evolve.
- Idealists maintain that the mind is all that exists, and that the external world is either mental itself or an illusion created by the mind.
- Neutral monists adhere to the position that perceived things in the world can be regarded as either physical or mental depending on whether one is interested in their relationship to other things in the world or their relationship to the perceiver. For example, a red spot on

> a wall is physical in its dependence on the wall and the pigment of which it is made, but it is mental in so far as its perceived redness depends on the workings of the visual system. Unlike a dual-aspect theory, neutral monism does not posit a more fundamental substance of which mind and body are aspects.

The most common monisms in the twentieth and twenty-first centuries have all been variations of physicalism; these positions include behaviourism, the type identity theory, anomalous monism, and functionalism.

Many modern philosophers of mind adopt either a reductive or non-reductive physicalist position, maintaining in their different ways that the mind is not something separate from the body. These approaches have been particularly influential in the sciences, such as in the fields of socio-biology, computer science, evolutionary psychology and the various neurosciences. Other philosophers, however, adopt a non-physicalist position which challenges the notion that the mind is a purely physical construct.

- Reductive physicalists assert that all mental states and properties will eventually be explained by scientific accounts of physiological processes and states.
- Non-reductive physicalists argue that although the brain is all there is to the mind, the predicates and vocabulary used in mental descriptions and explanations are indispensable and cannot be reduced to the language and lower-level explanations of physical science.

Continued progress in neuroscience has helped to clarify many of these issues, and its findings strongly support physicalists' assertions. Nevertheless, our knowledge is incomplete, and modern philosophers of mind continue to discuss how subjective qualia and the intentional can be naturally explained.

Neuroscience studies the nervous system, the physical basis of the mind. At the systems level, neuroscientists investigate how biological neural networks form and physiologically interact to produce mental functions and content such as reflexes, multisensory integration, motor coordination, circadian rhythms, emotional responses, learning, and memory. At a larger scale, efforts in computational neuroscience have developed large-scale models that simulate simple, functioning brains. As of 2012, such models include the thalamus, basal ganglia, prefrontal cortex, motor cortex, and occipital cortex. Consequentially, simulated brains can learn, respond to visual stimuli, coordinate motor responses, form short-term memories, and learn to respond to patterns. Currently, researchers aim to program the hippocampus and limbic system, hypothetically imbuing the simulated mind with long-term memory and crude emotions.

By contrast, affective neuroscience studies the neural mechanisms of personality, emotion, and mood primarily through experimental tasks.

Cognitive science examines the mental functions that give rise to information processing, termed cognition. These include attention, memory, producing and understanding language, learning, reasoning, problem-solving, and decision-making. Cognitive science seeks to understand thinking "in terms of representational structures in the mind and computational procedures that operate on those structures".

Psychology is the scientific study of human behaviour, mental functioning, and experience. As both an academic and applied discipline, Psychology involves the scientific study of mental processes such as perception, cognition, emotion, personality, environmental influences such as social and cultural influences, and interpersonal relationships in order to devise theories of human behaviour. Psychological patterns can be understood as low-cost ways of information processing. Psychology also refers to the application of such knowledge to various spheres of human activity, including problems of individuals' daily lives and the treatment of mental health problems.

Psychology differs from the other social sciences (e.g., anthropology, economics, political science, and sociology) due to its focus on experimentation at the scale of the individual, or individuals in small groups as opposed to large groups, institutions, or societies. Historically, psychology differed from biology and neuroscience in that it was primarily concerned with the mind rather than the brain. Modern psychological science incorporates physiological and neurological processes into its conceptions of perception, cognition, behaviour, and mental disorders.

Psychotherapy is an interpersonal, relational intervention used by trained psychotherapists to aid clients in problems of living. This usually includes increasing individual sense of well-being and reducing subjective discomforting experience. Psychotherapists employ a range of techniques based on experiential relationship building, dialogue, communication, and behaviour change, which are designed to improve the mental health of a client or patient or to improve group relationships (such as in a family). Most forms of psychotherapy use only spoken conversation, though some also use various other forms of communication such as the written word, art, drama, narrative story, or therapeutic touch. Psychotherapy occurs within a structured encounter between a trained therapist and the client. Purposeful, theoretically based psychotherapy began in the nineteenth century with psychoanalysis; since then, scores of other approaches have been developed and continue to be created.

Many religions associate spiritual qualities to the human mind, which are often tightly connected to mythology and afterlife.

The philosophy of mind is totally different from the theory of mind. Theory of mind is the human ability to read and attribute the feelings, thoughts, and intentions of others, as well as make a perspective of oneself. One is aware of the mental state of others or of oneself. The theory cannot be otherwise than a more elaborate application of empathy. Theory of mind, in so far as that it is not possible to observe the mind, is the subject of much research and theory in philosophy, psychiatry, and psychology, in particular in the field of autism.

One of the most important milestones (if not the most important) in the theory of mind developments is gaining the ability to attribute false beliefs—that is, to recognise that others can have beliefs that are wrong or diverging. To do this, one must have knowledge that is superior to the knowledge of the other. Mental states can differ from reality so that other people's behaviour can be predicted by their mental state.

The theory was employed by the cognitive and evolutionary psychologist Jesse Bering when writing his book, *The God Instinct.*[15] Bering is a highly successful popular author who advances his argumentation in a bright and witty style. In his book, he examines how the daily thoughts, behaviours, and emotions of man involve a reasoning in which God is part of life. This is without prejudice to his atheism, but he considers that God is no delusion such as Richard Dawkins[16] sets but is a useful illusion that has fostered the well-being of humans. His view that man needs illusions to be happy seems to denigrate a rational being who is not able to live with the truth and needs placebos. In any case, his analysis of the human mind shows that the current development of man is rather modest.

CHAPTER 13

Sexuality

Concupiscence or fornication consists of the corporeal union of male and female. The coupling generates extreme pleasure and is exercised by human even when he finds himself in the most miserable circumstances. The male spouts his seed in a frenzy of passion, regardless of the consequences. Children are born without the prospect of a decent life. Religions estimate that fornication is a gift of god that ensures reproduction; it is also the drama of overpopulation entailing great misery.

For humans, sexuality is the capacity of humans to have erotic experiences and responses. Physical and emotional aspects of sexuality, besides ensuring biological reproduction, include bonds between individuals that are expressed through profound feelings or physical manifestations of love, trust, and care. Social aspects deal with the effects of human society on one's sexuality, whereas spirituality concerns an individual's spiritual connection with others. Sexuality also affects and is affected by cultural, political, legal, philosophical, moral, ethical, and religious aspects of life.[125]

Sexual desire, or libido, is experienced as a bodily urge, often accompanied by strong emotions such as love, ecstasy, and even jealousy. The biological and physical aspects of sexuality mainly relate to the basic biological reproductive functions of the humans and the driving force that is present in all species. Sex also creates an emotional bond of love between the sexes. Sexual acts are many and the need varies from person to person: the caress of yourself or of another, kissing, masturbation, oral sex (cunnilingus and fellatio), vaginal sex, anal sex, and exhibitionism (mere display of the genitals). Genitals, intended for reproduction, are the organs that provide pleasure and erogenous stimuli and in consequence are of decisive nature in sexual acts. The forming of hormones at ovulation contributes to the sexual drive.[125]

Libido, or sex drive, is the greatest instinct of all, a human's overall sexual drive or desire for sexual activity.

People who are sexually attracted to the opposite sex are heterosexual. People who must contend with a deviation and who do not possess the genes of reproduction are usually attracted to the same sex. They are called homosexuals. There are also bisexual people, who are attracted to both sexes. The pleasure associated with sexual behaviour can lead to extreme acts that are grouped under the heading of paraphilia such as bondage (sexual stimulation by means of tying up and being at the mercy of the sex partner by movement restriction), efeboly (sexual preference for adolescents), masochism (enjoying undergoing pain and humiliation), necrophilia (attraction to acts with a deceased person), nymphomania (excessive sexual drive of the woman), paedophilia (sexual attraction to children who are not yet sexually mature), promiscuity (contacting many sexual encounters), sadomasochism (sexual expressions where power, humiliation and pain play an important role), satyriasis (excessive sexual drive of the man), voyeurism (watching sexual acts of another), and strangle sex (sexual pleasure by squeezing the throat). These extreme acts show to what man is able to comply with his sexual pleasure. But it does remain the exceptions on healthy sex. Cunnilingus and fellatio were formerly classified as extreme sexual acts but belong now to the normal habits. These acts with various partners of unknown health status can lead to the contraction of sexually transmitted infections.

Throughout the centuries, the reflections on sex varied greatly. In ancient Rome and even during the papacy of Borgia, there was much promiscuity. Still, there have always been religious and ethnic concerns about sex. The Bible and the Koran are extremely strict about certain sexual acts that they consider as unchaste and sinful. In fact, speaking openly about sexuality is still a taboo in many cultures with surrounding feelings of shame on sexuality, which is pure hypocrisy because sexuality is an important part of human life. Formerly there were certain cultures in Asia where prostitution was part of religious customs. Sexuality turns up the debate on nature versus nurture. Some assume that sexual orientation or behaviour is genetically determined, whereas others claim that the environment is of decisive nature. It cannot be denied that the sex is an innate ability, but sexual behaviour can be determined by the environment.

Thomas of Aquino, the medieval and conservative philosopher of the Roman Catholic Church, suggested in accordance with the teachings of Aristotle that with sex, the virtue of temperance tempers excess in acts and habits, where the aim is not necessarily total abstinence. He condemned lust and sex practise outside reproduction as deadly sins.[17] His predecessor, Augustine, Bishop of Hippo, had a broader view and stated that such as food is necessary for the good of man, sexual intercourse is for the good of the body (*Bono Conjugalis*).

The sense of shame about sexual intercourse began to disappear in the early twentieth century when scientists such as neurologist Sigmund Freud started to examine this important branch of human life. Freud argued that sexual behaviour is biologically innate. He suggested that the instincts are the principal motivating forces in the mental realm and that notwithstanding the very many branches, they can be subdivided into two groups. In one group, the life instinct *eros,* which covers all the self-preserving and erotic instincts, and in the other group, the death instinct *thanatos*, which covers instincts toward aggression, self-destruction, and cruelty.[18] Freud gave sexual drives a centrality in human life, actions, and behaviours that had not been accepted before his proposal. His instinct theory suggested that humans are driven from birth by the desire to acquire and enhance bodily pleasures, thus supporting the nature debate. Freud successfully redefined the term sexuality to make it cover any form of pleasure that can be derived from the human body.[18] He raised the notion that the pre-genital zones are primitive areas of preliminary enjoyment preceding sexual intercourse and orgasm.[19] He reasoned that pleasure lowers tension and displeasure raises it, influencing the sexual drive in humans. His mentalist perspective of development mentality was dictated by innate powers, especially biological drives and maturation. The fact that humans are biologically inclined to seek pleasure by sexual gratification demonstrates the nature side of the nature debate. Freud had the merit to eliminate the taboos around sexuality. Since his death in 1939, numerous physiological investigations have taken place that confirmed sexuality is an innate need of man stretching to his well-being.

For man, the greatest pleasure on earth is sex. The urge for sex is so great that sometimes barbaric manners are involved. The large relaxation that resides in sex is at the disposal of everybody, poor or rich. Often sex is the only relaxation and pleasure at the disposal of the poor. Consequently, the sole disposal of sex results in overpopulation and the suffocation of the habitat, the sex act being done without the concern of preventing the conception of a child, which proves the general stupidity of average human.

Religions have the tendency to associate sex with sin because it can lead to excesses. In particular, the Catholics preach that sex mainly aims to ensure the creation of offspring, which is inconsistent with the nature of man because it is a natural need. However, to conclude that we live to practise sex is a bridge too far.

Only in the beginning of the thirteenth century did the Catholic Church formally recognize that marriage was a sacrament, an outward sign communicating a special gift of god's love. In the Bible there is no precedent of clergy performing marriage ceremonies.

Marriage was stated as a relief of concupiscence as well as holding a spiritual purpose. It is a scenario depicted to circumvent the shame and taboo of sex.

The sex act, the orgasm, is a discharge of sexual energy, by which a pleasure feeling is experienced that stirs the body and creates gooseflesh. After the discharge, the body relaxes and there is created a satisfied feeling. Sex is an act that promotes health. Excessive desire for sex gratification, however, creates a disorder that hinders not only the health but also has social consequences.

Orgasms are so all-consuming. In his book *The Science of Orgasms*, neuroscientist Barry Komisar of the Rutgers-State University of Newark states that when the whole forest is blazing, it's difficult to discriminate between the different campfires that were there at the start. At orgasms, if everything gets activated simultaneously, this can obliterate the fine discriminations between activities, and that is why you can't think about anything else.

CHAPTER 14

Existence and Existentialism

Existence is commonly held to be that which objectively persists independently of one's presence.[97]

Ontology is the philosophical study of the nature of being, existence, or reality in general, as well as of the basic categories of being and their relations. Traditionally listed as a part of the major branch of philosophy known as metaphysics, ontology deals with questions concerning what entities exist or can be said to exist, and how such entities can be grouped, related within a hierarchy, and subdivided according to similarities and differences. A lively debate continues about the existence of God. Ontology, as part of metaphysics, is highly theoretical and obscure, and apart from the original proposal of Parmenides (cf., infra), it became highly hypothetical, having little use for humankind.

Epistemology is the branch of philosophy concerned with the nature and scope of knowledge; it is also referred to as "theory of knowledge". Usually, it is limited to the study of the classical components of justified true belief. Epistemology also investigates how knowledge can be taught or acquired, and the conditions and extent to which any given subject or entity can be known.

Materialism holds that the only things that exist are matter and energy, that all things are composed of material, that all actions require energy, and that all phenomena (including consciousness) are the result of material interactions. The laws of nature are what they are so that we can exist without further explanation.

Life is a characteristic that distinguishes objects that have self-sustaining biological processes from those that do not—either because such functions have ceased (death), or else because they lack such functions and are classified as inanimate.

In mathematics, existence is asserted by a quantifier, the existential quantifier (one of two quantifiers, the other being the universal quantifier). The properties of the existential quantifier are established by axioms.

Parmenides of Elea was a pre-Socratic Greek philosopher from Elea in Magna Graecia (Greater Greece, which included southern Italy). He was the founder of the Eleatic school of philosophy and was acclaimed by Socrates, Aristotle, and Plato as having an influence on all Grecian thought. Thought and being are the same. The single known work of Parmenides is a poem, "On Nature", which has survived only in fragmentary form. In this poem, Parmenides describes two views of reality. In "the way of truth" (a part of the poem), he explains how reality (coined as "what-is") is one, change is impossible, and existence is timeless, uniform, necessary, and unchanging. In "the way of opinion," he explains the world of appearances, in which one's sensory faculties lead to conceptions which are false and deceitful. These ideas had a strong effect on Plato and in turn influenced the whole of Western philosophy.

In the Western tradition of philosophy, the earliest known comprehensive treatments of the subject are from Plato's *Phaedo*, *Republic*, and *Statesman* and Aristotle's *Metaphysics*, though earlier fragmentary writing exists. Aristotle developed a comprehensive theory of being, according to which only individual things, called substances, fully have being; other things such as relations, quantity, time, and place (called the categories) have a derivative kind of being, dependent on individual things. In Aristotle's *Metaphysics*, there are four causes of existence or change in nature: the material cause, the formal cause, the efficient cause, and the final cause.

The Neo-Platonists and some early Christian philosophers argued about whether existence had any reality except in the mind of

God. Some taught that existence was a snare and a delusion, that the world, the flesh, and the devil existed only to tempt weak humankind away from God.

The medieval philosopher Thomas Aquinas argued that God is pure being, and that in God essence and existence are the same.[7] At about the same time, the nominalist philosopher William of Ockham, a friar but a critic of Aquinas, argued in Book I of his *Summa Totius Logicae* (*Treatise on All Logic*) that categories are not a form of being in their own right, but derivative on the existence of individuals. The principle of simplicity is the central theme of Ockham's philosophy, so much that this principle has come to be known Ockham's Razor. Ockham uses the razor to eliminate unnecessary hypotheses. In metaphysics, Ockham champions nominalism, the view that universal essences, such as humanity or whiteness, are nothing more than concepts in the mind.

David Hume argued that the claim that a thing exists, when added to our notion of a thing, does not add anything to the concept. For example, if we form a complete notion of Moses and super add to that notion the claim that Moses existed, we are not adding anything to the notion of Moses.

Immanuel Kant also argued that existence is not a "real" predicate but gave no explanation of how this is possible. Indeed, his famous discussion of the subject is merely a restatement of the theologian Arnauld's doctrine that in the proposition "God is omnipotent", the verb *is* signifies the joining or separating of two concepts such as God and omnipotence.

Arthur Schopenhauer claimed that "everything that exists for knowledge, and hence the whole of this world, is only object in relation to the subject, the perception of the perceiver, in a word, representation". According to him, there can be "no object without a subject" because "everything objective is already conditioned as such in manifold ways by the knowing subject with the forms of its knowing and presupposes these forms". He is best known for his 1818 work *The World as Will and Representation,* in which he characterises the phenomenal world, and consequently all human action, as the blind, insatiable, and malignant metaphysical will. A key focus of

Schopenhauer was his investigation of individual motivation. Before Schopenhauer, Hegel had popularised the concept of zeitgeist, the idea that society consisted of a collective consciousness which moved in a distinct direction, dictating the actions of its members. Schopenhauer, a reader of both Kant and Hegel, criticised their logical optimism and the belief that individual morality could be determined by society and reason. Schopenhauer believed that humans were motivated by only their own basic desires, or *Wille zum Leben* ("Will to Live"), which directed all of mankind. The malignant will an evil to be terminated via mankind's duties: asceticism and chastity. He is credited with one of the most famous opening lines of philosophy: "The world is my representation." Will, for Schopenhauer, is what Kant called the "thing-in-itself". Nietzsche was greatly influenced by this idea of will, while developing it in a different direction. Bertrand Russell considered Schopenhauer shallow and insincere because he advanced asceticism and chastity while dining continuously in good restaurants and having many trivial love affairs, which were sensual but not passionate (Russell himself had many love affairs). Schopenhauer failed to garner substantial attention during his life, and his criticism of his contemporary Hegel was badly taken. But he had a profound posthumous impact on many following philosophers and scientists, such as Friedrich Nietzsche, Ludwig Wittgenstein, Albert Einstein, and Erwin Schrödinger.

The most famous statement in being philosophy is René Descartes' statement "*Cogito ergo sum* (I think thus I am)". Jean Paul Sartre believed that human existence is not an abstract matter but is always situated ("*en situation*").[98]

Existentialism is a term applied to the work of certain late nineteenth- and twentieth-century European philosophers who, despite profound doctrinal differences (theists opposed to atheists), shared the belief that philosophical thinking begins with the human subject—not merely the thinking subject, but the acting, feeling, living human individual. Although the supreme value of existentialist thought is commonly acknowledged to be freedom, its primary virtue is authenticity. In the view of the existentialist, the individual's starting point is characterised by what has been called "the existential attitude", or a sense of disorientation and confusion in the face of an apparently meaningless or absurd world. Many existentialists have also regarded traditional systematic or academic philosophies, in both style and content, as too abstract and remote from concrete human experience.

The Christian Søren Kierkegaard[154] is generally considered to have been the first existentialist philosopher, though he did not use the term existentialism. He proposed that each individual—not society or religion—is solely responsible for giving meaning to life and living it passionately and sincerely (authentically). Existentialism became popular in the years following World War II, and it strongly influenced many disciplines besides philosophy, including theology, drama, art, literature, and psychology.

A central proposition of existentialism is that existence precedes essence,[98] which means that the most important consideration for individuals is that they are individuals—independently acting and responsible, conscious beings ("existence")—rather than what labels, roles, stereotypes, definitions, or other preconceived categories the individuals fit ("essence"). The actual life of the individuals is what constitutes what could be called their "true essence" instead of there being an arbitrarily attributed essence other use to define them. Thus, human beings, through their own consciousness, create their own values and determine a meaning to their lives.[22] Although it was Jean Paul Sartre who explicitly coined the phrase, similar notions can be found in the thought of existentialist philosophers such as Heidegger and Kierkegaard.

> The subjective thinker's form, the form of his communication, is his style. His form must be just as manifold as are the opposites that he holds together. The systematic eins, zwei, drei is an abstract form that also must inevitably run into trouble whenever it is to be applied to the concrete. To the same degree as the subjective thinker is concrete, to the same degree his form must also be concretely dialectical. But just as

> he himself is not a poet, not an ethicist, not a dialectician, so also his form is none of these directly. His form must first and last be related to existence, and in this regard, he must have at his disposal the poetic, the ethical, the dialectical, the religious. Subordinate character, setting, etc., which belong to the well-balanced character of the aesthetic production, are in themselves breadth; the subjective thinker has only one setting—existence—and has nothing to do with localities and such things. The setting is not the fairyland of the imagination, where poetry produces consummation, nor is the setting laid in England, and historical accuracy is not a concern. The setting is inwardness in existing as a human being; the concretion is the relation of the existence-categories to one another. Historical accuracy and historical actuality are breadths. —Søren Kierkegaard (Concluding Postscript, Hong p. 357–358)
>
> It is often claimed in this context that people define themselves, which is often perceived as stating that they can wish to be something, anything—a bird, for instance—and then be it. According to most existentialist philosophers, however, this would constitute an inauthentic existence. Instead, the phrase should be taken to say that people are:
>
> (1) defined only insofar as they act
> (2) responsible for their actions

For example, someone who acts cruelly towards other people is, by that act, defined as a cruel person. Furthermore, by this action of cruelty, such persons are themselves responsible for their new identity (cruel persons). This is as opposed to their genes, or human nature, bearing the blame.

As Sartre writes in his work *Existentialism Is a Humanism*, "Man first of all exists, encounters himself, surges up in the world—and defines himself afterwards." Of course, the more positive, therapeutic aspect of this is also implied: A person can choose to act in a different way, and to be a good person instead of a cruel person. Here, it is also clear that because humans can choose to be either cruel or good, they are in fact neither of these things essentially.

The notion of the absurd contains the idea that there is no meaning in the world beyond what meaning we give it. This meaninglessness also encompasses the amorality or "unfairness" of the world. This contrasts with the notion that "bad things don't happen to good people". To the world, metaphorically speaking, there is no such thing as a good person or a bad person; what happens happens, and it may just as well happen to a "good" person as to a "bad" person.

Because of the world's absurdity, at any point in time, anything can happen to anyone, and a tragic event could plummet someone into direct confrontation with the absurd. The notion of the absurd has been prominent in literature throughout history. Many of the literary works of Søren Kierkegaard, Samuel Beckett, Franz Kafka, Fyodor Dostoyevsky, Eugène Ionesco, Luigi Pirandello, Jean-Paul Sartre, Joseph Heller, and Albert Camus contain descriptions of people who encounter the absurdity of the world.

It is in relation to the concept of the devastating awareness of meaninglessness that Albert Camus claimed in his book *The Myth of Sisyphus*, "There is only one truly serious philosophical problem, and that is suicide." Although "prescriptions" against the possibly deleterious consequences of these kinds of encounters vary, from Kierkegaard's religious "stage" to Camus' insistence on persevering in spite of absurdity, the concern with helping people avoid living their lives in ways that put them in the perpetual danger of having everything meaningful break down is common to most existentialist philosophers. The possibility of having everything meaningful break down poses a threat of quietism, which is inherently against the existentialist philosophy.[29] It has been said that the possibility of suicide makes all humans existentialists.

Facticity is a concept defined by Sartre in *Being and Nothingness* as the "in-itself", of which humans are in the mode of not being. This can be more easily understood when considering it in relation to the temporal dimension of past: one's past is what one is, in the sense that it co-constitutes oneself. However, to say that one is only one's past would be to ignore a significant part of reality (the present and the future), while saying that one's past is only what one was would entirely detach it from oneself now. A denial of one's own concrete past constitutes an inauthentic lifestyle, and the same goes for all other kinds of facticity (having a body, identity, values, etc.).

Facticity is both a limitation and a condition of freedom. It is a limitation in that a large part of one's facticity consists of things one couldn't have chosen (birthplace, etc.), but a condition in the sense that one's values most likely depend on it. However, even though one's facticity is "set in stone" (as being the past, for instance), it cannot determine a person. The value ascribed to one's facticity is still ascribed to it freely by that person. As an example, consider two men, one who has no memory of his past and another who remembers everything. They have both committed many crimes, but the first man, knowing nothing about this, leads a rather normal life. The second man, feeling trapped by his own past, continues a life of crime, blaming his own past for "trapping" him in this life. There is nothing essential about his committing crimes, but he ascribes this meaning to his past.

However, to disregard one's facticity when, in the continual process of self-making, one projects oneself into the future would be to put oneself in denial of oneself, and that would thus be inauthentic. In other words, the origin of one's projection must still be one's facticity, though in the mode of not being it (essentially). Another aspect of facticity is that it entails angst, both in the sense that freedom "produces" angst when limited by facticity, and in the sense that the lack of the possibility of having facticity to "step in" for one to take responsibility for something one has done also produces angst.

Angst means fear or anxiety. In existentialist philosophy, the term means dread or anxiety to describe a profound and deep-seated condition. While Kierkegaard's angst referred mainly to ambiguous feelings about moral freedom within a religious personal belief system, later existentialists discussed conflicts of personal principles, cultural notions, and existential despair.

Another aspect of existential freedom is that one can change one's values. Thus, one is responsible for one's values regardless of society's values. The focus on freedom in existentialism is related to the limits of the responsibility one bears as a result of one's freedom: the relationship between freedom and responsibility is one of interdependency, and a clarification of freedom also clarifies that for which one is responsible.

Many noted existentialist writers consider the theme of authentic existence important. Authentic existence involves the idea that one has to "create oneself" and then live in accordance with this self. What is meant by authenticity is that in acting, one should act as oneself, not as one acts or as one's genes or any other essence requires. The authentic act is one that is in accordance with one's freedom. Of course, as a condition of freedom is facticity, and this includes one's facticity—but not to the degree that this facticity can in any way determine one's choices (in the sense that one could then blame one's background for making the choice one made). The role of facticity in relation to authenticity involves letting one's actual values come into play when one makes a choice (instead of, like Kierkegaard's *Aesthete*, "choosing" randomly), so that one also takes responsibility for the act instead of choosing either/or without allowing the options to have different values.

In contrast to this, the inauthentic is the denial to live in accordance with one's freedom. This can take many forms, from pretending choices are meaningless or random through convincing oneself that some form of determinism is true, to a sort of mimicry where one acts as "one should".

In existentialism, despair is generally defined as a loss of hope. More specifically, it is a loss of hope in reaction to a breakdown in one or more of the defining qualities of one's self or identity. If a person is invested in being a particular thing, such as a bus driver or an upstanding citizen, and then finds his being-thing compromised, he would normally be found in state of despair—a hopeless state. For example, a singer who loses the ability to sing may despair if she has nothing else to fall back on, nothing to rely on for her identity. She finds herself unable to be what defined her being.

What sets the existentialist notion of despair apart from the conventional definition is that existentialist despair is a state one is in even when one isn't overtly in despair. So long as a person's identity depends on qualities that can crumble, he is in perpetual despair—and because there is, in Sartrean terms, no human essence found in conventional reality on which to constitute the individual's sense of identity, despair is a universal human condition. As Kierkegaard defines it in *Either/Or*: "Let each one learn what he can; both of us can learn that a person's unhappiness never lies in his lack of control over external conditions, since this would only make him completely unhappy." In *Works of Love*, he said,

> When the God-forsaken worldliness of earthly life shuts itself in complacency, the confined air develops poison, the moment gets stuck and stands still, the prospect is lost, a need is felt for a refreshing, enlivening breeze to cleanse the air and dispel the poisonous vapors lest we suffocate in worldliness.... Lovingly to hope all things is the opposite of despairingly to hope nothing at all. Love hopes all things—yet is never put to shame. To relate oneself expectantly to the possibility of the good is to hope. To relate oneself expectantly to the possibility of evil is to fear. By the decision to choose hope one decides infinitely more than it seems, because it is an eternal decision. (p. 246–250)

Existentialists oppose definitions of human beings as primarily rational, and therefore they oppose positivism and rationalism.

Existentialism asserts that people actually make decisions based on subjective meaning rather than pure rationality. The rejection of reason as the source of meaning is a common theme of existentialist thought, as is the focus on the feelings of anxiety and dread that we feel in the face of our own radical freedom and our awareness of death. Kierkegaard advocated rationality as means to interact with the objective world (e.g., in the natural sciences), but when it comes to existential problems, reason is insufficient: "Human reason has boundaries."

Like Kierkegaard, Sartre saw problems with rationality, calling it a form of "bad faith", an attempt by the self to impose structure on a world of phenomena—"the Other"—that is fundamentally irrational and random. According to Sartre, rationality and other forms of bad faith hinder people from finding meaning in freedom. To try to suppress their feelings of anxiety and dread, people confine themselves to everyday experience, Sartre asserts, thereby relinquishing their freedom and acquiescing to being possessed in one form or another by "the Look" of "the Other" (i.e., possessed by another person—or at least one's idea of that other person).

Although nihilism and existentialism are distinct philosophies, they are often confused with one another. A primary cause of confusion is that Friedrich Nietzsche is an important philosopher in both fields but is also convinced of the existentialist insistence on the inherent meaninglessness of the world. Existentialist philosophers often stress the importance of angst as signifying the absolute lack of any objective ground for action—a move that is often reduced to a moral or an existential nihilism. A pervasive theme in the works of existentialist philosophy, however, is to persist through encounters with the absurd, as seen in Camus' *The Myth of Sisyphus* ("One must imagine Sisyphus happy"), and it is only very rarely that existentialist philosophers dismiss morality or one's self-created meaning: Kierkegaard regained a sort of morality in the religious (although he wouldn't himself agree that it was ethical; the religious suspends the ethical), and Sartre's final words in *Being and Nothingness* are, "All these questions, which refer us to a pure and not an accessory (or impure) reflection, can find their reply only on the ethical plane. We shall devote to them a future work."

Søren Kierkegaard and Friedrich Nietzsche were two of the first philosophers considered fundamental to the existentialist movement, though neither used the term *existentialism.* and it is unclear whether they would have supported the existentialism of the twentieth century. They focused on subjective human experience rather than the objective truths of mathematics and science, which they believed were too detached or observational to truly get at the human experience. Like Blaise Pascal, a follower of the Catholic theological movement of Jansenism that emphasised the original sin, human depravity, which compels divine grace, they were interested in people's quiet struggle with the apparent meaninglessness of life and the use of diversion to escape from boredom. Unlike Pascal, Kierkegaard and Nietzsche also considered the role of making free choices, particularly regarding fundamental values and beliefs, and how such choices change the nature and identity of the chooser. Kierkegaard's "knight of faith" and Nietzsche's bergens are representative of people who exhibit freedom, in that they define the nature of their own existence. Nietzsche's idealised individual invents his own values and creates the very terms they excel under. By contrast, Kierkegaard, opposed to the level of abstraction in Hegel, and not nearly as hostile (actually welcoming) to Christianity as Nietzsche, argues through a pseudonym that the objective certainty of religious truths (specifically Christian) is not only impossible but even founded on logical paradoxes. Yet he continues to imply that a leap of faith is a possible means for an individual to reach a higher stage of existence that transcends and contains both an aesthetic and ethical value of life. Kierkegaard and Nietzsche were also precursors to other intellectual movements, including postmodernism, and various strands of psychology. However, Kierkegaard believed that individuals should live in accordance with their thinking.

In Germany, the psychologist and philosopher Karl Jaspers—who later described existentialism as a "phantom" created by the public—was heavily influenced by Kierkegaard and Nietzsche and called his own thought *Existenzphilosophie.* For Jaspers, "*Existenz-*

philosophy is the way of thought by means of which man seeks to become himself … This way of thought does not cognize objects but elucidates and makes actual the being of the thinker". Jaspers was acquainted with Martin Heidegger but later became estranged over Heidegger's support of national socialism. They shared an admiration for Kierkegaard and Nietzsche. Nevertheless, the extent to which Heidegger should be considered an existentialist is debatable. In *Being and Time*, he presented a method of rooting philosophical explanations in human existence (Dasein) to be analysed in terms of existential categories (existential), and this has led many commentators to treat him as an important figure in the existentialist movement.

Most commentators associate Jaspers with the philosophy of existentialism, in part because he draws largely upon the existentialist roots of Nietzsche and Kierkegaard, and in part because the theme of individual freedom permeates his work. In *Philosophy*, Jaspers gave his view of the history of philosophy and introduced his major themes. Beginning with modern science and empiricism, Jaspers points out that as we question reality, we confront borders that an empirical (or scientific) method simply cannot transcend. At this point, the individual faces a choice: sink into despair and resignation, or take a leap of faith toward what Jaspers calls transcendence. In making this leap, individuals confront their own limitless freedom, which Jaspers calls *Existenz*, and can finally experience authentic existence. For Jaspers, transcendence (paired with the term "the encompassing" in later works) is that which exists beyond the world of time and space. Jaspers' formulation of transcendence as ultimate non-objectivity (or nothingness) has led many philosophers to argue that ultimately, Jaspers became a monist. (Monism is the view that attributes oneness or singleness (Greek: μόνος) to a concept such as existence). Jaspers himself continually stressed the necessity of recognising the validity of the concepts both of subjectivity and of objectivity. Although he rejected explicit religious doctrines, including the notion of a personal God, Jaspers influenced contemporary theology through his philosophy of transcendence and the limits of human experience.

Sartre had travelled to Germany in 1930 to study the phenomenology of Edmund Husserl and Martin Heidegger, and he included critical comments on their work in his major treatise *Being and Nothingness*.

Phenomenology is the philosophical study of the structures of experience and consciousness. It is not a doctrine or a philosophical school, but rather a style of thought, a method, an open and ever-renewed experience having different results. It has been criticised by different schools of philosophy, such as hermeneutics, existentialists, and others.

According to Heidegger, humanism is either grounded in metaphysics or is itself made to be the ground of one. Heidegger's thought had also become known in French philosophical circles through its use by Alexandre Kojève in explicating Hegel in a series of lectures given in Paris in the 1930s. The lectures were highly influential; members of the audience included not only Sartre and Merleau-Ponty but also Raymond Queneau, Georges Bataille, Louis Althusser, André Breton, and Jacques Lacan.[98] A selection from Heidegger's *Being and Time* was published in French in 1938, and his essays began to appear in French philosophy journals.

Heidegger read Sartre's work and was initially impressed, commenting, "Here for the first time I encountered an independent thinker who, from the foundations up, has experienced the area out of which I think. Your work shows such an immediate comprehension of my philosophy as I have never before encountered." Later, however, Heidegger distanced himself from Sartre's position and existentialism in general in his *Letter on Humanism*. Heidegger objected to Sartre's refusal to accept metaphysics, stating, "Existentialism says existence precedes essence." In this statement he is taking existentia and essentia according to their metaphysical meaning, which, from Plato's time on has said that essentia precedes existentia. Sartre reverses this statement. But the reversal statement of a metaphysical statement remains a metaphysical statement. With it, he stays with metaphysics, "in oblivion of the truth of being". The difficulty with theists is that they are unable to distance themselves of metaphysics. Heidegger's reputation continued to grow in France during the 1950s and 1960s. In the 1960s, Sartre attempted to reconcile existentialism and Marxism in his work *Critique of Dialectical Reason.* A major theme throughout his writings was freedom and responsibility.

French-Algerian philosopher, novelist, and playwright Albert Camus was a friend of Sartre until their falling-out over communism. Camus wrote several works with existential themes, including *The Rebel, Summer in Algiers, The Myth of Sisyphus,* and *The Stranger,* the latter being "considered—to what would have been Camus's irritation—the exemplary existentialist novel". Camus, like many others, rejected the existentialist label and considered his works concerned with facing the absurd. In the titular book, Camus uses the analogy of the Greek myth of Sisyphus to demonstrate the futility of existence. In the myth, Sisyphus is condemned for eternity to roll a rock up a hill, but when he reaches the summit, the rock will roll to the bottom again. Camus believes that this existence is pointless, but that Sisyphus ultimately finds meaning and purpose in his task, simply by continually applying himself to it. The first half of the book contains an extended rebuttal of what Camus took to be existentialist philosophy in the works of Kierkegaard, Shestov, Heidegger, and Jaspers.

Simone de Beauvoir, an important existentialist who spent much of her life as Sartre's partner, wrote about feminist and existentialist ethics in her works, including *The Second Sex* and *The Ethics of Ambiguity.* Although often overlooked due to her relationship with Sartre, de Beauvoir integrated existentialism with other forms of thinking such as feminism (unheard of at the time), resulting in alienation from fellow writers as Camus.

CHAPTER 15

Death

Death is the termination of all biological functions that sustain life. The natural cause of death is senescence or old age. The causes of premature death are manifold, such as predation, malnutrition, disease, suicide, homicide, starvation, dehydration, and accidents or trauma resulting in terminal injury. Bodies of living organisms begin to decompose shortly after death.[126]

Death is considered a sad occasion by the people who have a bond with the deceased, but it is greatly feared by the living themselves. This fear is also felt by the believers who though are convinced that death opens the gate to paradise. The Moslem self-destructing terrorists cry "Allah is great" while committing their murderous acts!

Extension of the lifespan has become the main objective of science.

The nature of death and humanity's awareness of its mortality has been the concern of philosophical enquiry for millennia and is unavoidably connected with religion. In the Abrahamic religions, death is followed by resurrection. In the Dharmic religions, there is a belief in reincarnation or rebirth. The atheists, not believing in the supernatural, are convinced that the end of permanent consciousness implies eternal oblivion.

Death anxiety is the morbid, abnormal, or persistent fear of one's own death or the process of one dying. Predatory death anxieties mobilise an individual's adaptive resources and lead to fight or flight, active efforts to combat the danger, or attempts to escape the threatening situation. Existing death anxiety is the basic knowledge and awareness that natural life must end. Awareness of human mortality arose though some 150,000 years ago. In that extremely short span of evolutionary time, humans have fashioned but a single basic mechanism to deal with death, and that is to try to deny it as final. The denial then leads to actions (violence against others, seeking of power or wealth) that are, in the short or long run, damaging to self and others. Denial is used when memories or feelings are too painful to accept and are rejected by the mind. Martin Heidegger, the illustrious and pious philosopher, shows death as something conclusively determined in the sense that it is inevitable for every human being, and on the other hand, it unmasks its indeterminate nature via the truth that one never knows when or how death is going to come. He argues that all human existence (*dasein)* is embedded in time—past, present, and future. When considering the future, we encounter the notion of death, which creates *angst.* In his religious conviction, he posits that *angst* clears the mind that death is a possible mode of existence. The thought of death causes a different degree of anxiety for different individuals, depending on many factors. Religiosity plays an important role. A 2013 study involving people from the United States, Turkey, and Malaysia found that religiosity is positively correlated with increased fear of death, meaning more religious individuals fear death more.[59] On the other hand, it has been shown through results of various studies that a strong sense of religion in a person's life can be related to a lower sense of anxiety towards the death. Although there has been no association discovered between religiosity and death anxiety, it has been shown that death anxiety tends to be lower in individuals who regularly attend religious meetings, gatherings, and mass. The Church indeed provides for a lifelong death attendance.

CHAPTER 16

Antiquity

Antiquity is generally referred to that period of history that begins with the emergence of culture in which writings were developed. All important cultures have an antiquity that for Western civilisation begins about 4,500 yrs before our era. The difference between culture and civilisation is hardly distinguished. Culture is the pattern of human behaviour that expresses the habits and customs of the people of a certain region. Cultural expressions include clothing, parties, food supply, eating habits, art, religion, and science. Civilisation is the establishment of a group of people in a certain region, where they develop a political structure under a central authority. Individually, civilisation can also indicate a sophisticated behaviour opposite uncivilised behaviour. Since the year AD 1500, civilisation has lost its specific meaning in history. Now, by levelling, only of empires is spoken. In Cicero's book *Tusculanae Disputationes* (forty-five years before our era) we find the modern meaning of culture. In the book comes a conversation for about the usefulness of the philosophy with a pupil who has doubts because he is of the opinion that philosophers have sometimes a debauched lifestyle. Cicero replied, "Nor that all fields that you cultivate bear fruit, nor bring all the souls you cultivate fruit. But the cultivation of the mind is the philosophy (*cultura animi, filosofia est).*"

Most cultures have an ancient time. The period of about 750 years before our era to 400 years of the current era are the civilisations of classical antiquity, especially Greece and Rome. That is in contrast with the ancient civilisations of Mesopotamia and Egypt, which are regarded as forerunners of the Western civilisation. Ancient China, Persia, and Meso-America also possessed important cultures. No one in the history of civilisation has shaped our understanding of science and natural philosophy more than the great Greek philosopher and scientist Aristotle, who exerted a profound and pervasive influence for more than two thousand years.[20]

The early civilisations are the large valley civilisations with fertile areas.

- The city-states of Sumer between the Euphrates and the Tigris
- Egypt along the Nile
- The Indus Valley civilisation
- China around the Yellow River and the Yangtze River

Classical antiquity is a broad term for a long period of cultural history centred on the Mediterranean Sea and the Middle East, comprising specially the interlocking civilisations of ancient Greece and ancient Rome. The modern world is immensely influenced by the language, politics, education systems, philosophy, science, art, and architecture of this period. The classical civilisations are:

- the Persian Empire
- Greece and the Hellenistic world
- the Roman Empire
- China of the Han dynasty
- India of the Chandragupta and Maurya
- the Olmec (Meso-American people)

The post-classical civilisations are:

- the Islamic world
- the Byzantine Empire
- the Tang and Song dynasties in China

- the Toltecs and Aztecs in Central America
- the Incas in the Andes

In the fertile area between the Tigris and the Euphrates rivers, agriculture started about 10,000 years ago. In this area, the Sumerian civilisation arose around 6,500 years ago. In 3,300 years before our era, writing was invented there. Sargon of Akkad was the first warlord to create a state around 4,300 years ago. The Persian ruler Cyrus the Great was the first king who managed to unite a whole region under his command. His successors tried in vain to conquer Greece for centuries.

The longest civilisation of ancient times was that of the old Egypt, which amounted to almost four millennia. There were thirty consecutive dynasties. The last dynasty, that of the Ptolemaic, ended in AD 30 when the Egyptian Empire was incorporated into the Roman Empire by Emperor Augustus I. Alexander the Great had conquered Egypt in 332 before the present era, but when he died, his general Ptolemy I Soter took power over the Nile area. During the existence of the Egyptian civilisation, it was often threatened and occupied by Assyrians, Persians, and Macedonian Greeks. Starting from five hundred years before the current era, the city-states of Greece came into being with a thriving society where science, philosophy, and art flourished. Philip II of Macedon overthrew all the Greek city-states, and his son Alexander the Great started a campaign which ended on the west bank of the Indus River in Pakistan. This great empire fell apart after the death of Alexander in 323 before the current calendar.

The tenth century before our era saw the first settlements on the hills of Rome established. Rome grew into the largest power of antiquity.

After the conquest of Greece, Rome was aware and open to the Greek culture, which they continued to preserve. In 117 of our era, the Roman Empire reached its greatest extent under Emperor Trajan, controlling much of Europe, North Africa, and the Middle East. Diocletian introduced an administrative division, and under Constantine the Great the capital was transferred to Byzantium. Rome itself fell in AD 476. The Eastern Roman Byzantine Empire section would still exist for nearly one thousand years. Constantinople was conquered by the Turks in 1453. Following the fall of Rome, intellectual darkness and economic regression came into being. Gradually, contacts with the Islamic world and the cognisance of Greek scientific and philosophical texts by Latin translations from the Arabic allowed an intellectual renaissance. It was not until the fourteenth century that the humanists started to collect Greek and Latin manuscripts and revived the antique heritage.

Although modern historians claim that the Renaissance is more a continuation of the culture of the Middle Ages than a rebirth of classical antiquity, there is a consensus that the Renaissance began in Florence in the fourteenth century. It is the era of new developments such as the demise of the feudal system, the discovery of new continents, the Copernican system of astronomy, the introduction of modern science by Galilei, Leonardo da Vinci's and Michelangelo's works of art, and the invention or introduction in Europe of the press, paper, compass, and gunpowder. An important contribution to the Renaissance was the migration of Greek scholars to Italy with their texts at the fall of Constantinople.

CHAPTER 17

Mythology

The word *myth* originally meant in Greek the spoken word, a story. In the time of Homer, the word had the meaning of a sacred story of people about its origin and religion. Myth is by no means fiction because that is something that has never happened and is a made-up story. In contrast to sagas, fairy tales, and fables, myths deal mainly about gods and demigods. The stories of gods, before writing was invented, relate how the world and man were created and how everything has an end. The stories about gods, apart from their extraordinary gifts, are a reflection of the daily life of man. The gods embody the lives of the people but show all the laws of humankind. At a later stage, the stories were put in writing, and they constitute the mythology. Today, myth is considered a story that may or may not be true.[99]

Mythology is not only defined as the collection of myths of people or group of people in the scientific, literary, mystical, and religious areas, but it is also the study of these myths and **a** particular people in a particular religious context (e.g., the Greek mythology, Norse mythology, Indian mythology).

Myths belong to the culture of people. Myths are stories and legends that were passed on orally from generation to generation. In all times, man has been at a loss to solve the deep recurring questions about himself and the world he inhabits. Myths are basic questions about themselves, nature, birth, death, and the rebirth or afterlife.

Although a myth is not necessarily false, the term is typically used in the ordinary language as a synonym for a lie.

Oral traditions have the disadvantage to be handed down with a lot of imagination.

There are several types of myths.

Creation myths are the stories about the universe, the Earth, and its inhabitants. In Norse mythology, there is a gaping abyss of Ginnungagap where Ymir is created and from whom worlds, gods, giants, and people are descended.

Theogony myths are the stories in which gods and demigods occur as creatures that represent real life. Greek mythology (described by Hesiod) is a typical example of this. From Chaos came the Earth (Gaia), and she brought forth the sea and sky (Uranus). Gaia and Uranus married and brought on Titan, the ancestor of all later Greek gods. A grandson, Prometheus, creates together with Pallas and Athens the human race. Prometheus steals fire from the gods and brings civilisation amongst the people. The occurrence of Prometheus is of a soteriological nature because he is a saviour (Soter) of humankind.

Eschatological myths are stories involving people punished by the gods for their misconduct. The flood story can be found in three hundred ancient cultures.

Finally, there are etiologic myths that provide an explanation of a particular use or event. Sometimes there is more than an explanatory myth, such as the founding of Rome by Romulus and Remus versus Aeneas.

In many religions, the ideas whereupon a particular faith is based first were first orally passed on but were later written down and collected. The collection of myths is called mythology.

CHAPTER 18

Deity

Humans are considered to have started attaining the status of Homo *sapiens* around 200,000 years ago and reaching the full status around 60,000 years ago, but their cultural development from a Western viewpoint only started in the first civilisation in Mesopotamia 6,500 years ago. Primitive man, in the context of culture, was an anxious and shy being overloaded with doubts about his person and the world in which he stood. To overcome his instability, he took to the existence of gods and goddesses to answer his many doubts. Human burials from between 50,000 and 30,000 BC provide evidence of belief in gods and afterlife, although it is not clear when human belief in deities took place.

To trace the origin and development of the God idea, one must go back to the time when civilisation was still in its infancy and science was still unknown. Primitive people, out of fear and admiration towards the natural phenomena, believed in different spirits and gods. They used their spirits and gods to form religions of their own. According to their respective circumstances and understanding capacity, different people founded different gods and different faiths.

At the beginning of the God idea, people worshipped many gods—gods of trees, streams, lightning, storm, winds, the sun, and all other terrestrial phenomena. These gods were related to each and every act of nature. Then man gradually began to transfer to these gods sex and form, as well as the physical and mental characteristics of human beings. Human attributes were given to the gods: love, hate, jealousy, fear, pride, envy, and other emotion found amongst human beings. From all these gods, there slowly grew a realisation that the phenomena of the universe were not many but were one. This understanding gave rise to the monotheistic God of recent ages.

In religious beliefs, a deity is a supernatural being with powers greater than those of ordinary humans, and which may be thought of as holy, divine, sacred, immortal, and responsible for various aspects of life and the world. Some religions have one supreme deity, whereas other religions have multiple deities of various ranks. Of course, many educated people simply deny the existence of deities.[100]

Gods are depicted in various forms, but for reasons of comprehension they are frequently expressed as having human form. Some faiths and traditions consider it blasphemous to imagine and depict the deity as having any concrete form.

Primitive man assumed that all that was above his comprehension and frightened him was due to "invisible intelligences". This was the case for all uncontrollable natural phenomena, such as lightning, earthquakes, and pests. All elements of nature such as the sun and the moon waked to wonder and then eventually worship. These invisible intelligences or supernatural entities were given in all cultures the name of gods. They were supposed to live on Earth but also in the sky and in the underworld. Gods were male, female, or hermaphrodite. In the Abrahamic religions, God is characterised as male, except for the female Eve in Genesis.

In the process of developing, the God idea went through a variety of changing social and intellectual climates. It was regarded by different men in different ways. Some idealised God as the king of heaven and earth, and they had a conception of God as a person. Others thought of God as an abstract principle. Some raised the ideal of supreme deity to the highest heaven, whereas others brought it down to the lowest depths of the earth. Some pictured God in a paradise, and others made an idol and worshipped it. Some went so far as to say that there is no salvation without God—no matter how much good you do, you will not receive the fruits of your actions unless you act out of faith in God. The theists said yes and went on to affirm that God really did exist. The atheists said no and went on to affirm that God did not exist at all. The sceptics or agnostics said, "We do not know, or we cannot know." The positivists said that the God idea is a meaningless problem because the idea of the term *God* is not clear. Thus, there grew a variety of ideas and beliefs and names for the God idea: pantheism, idolatry, belief in a formless God, belief in many gods and goddesses, and more.[115]

The Holy Trinity of the Roman Catholic Church is an expression of mythology without prejudice to monotheism but still recognising three distinct divine persons: God the father, God the son, and God the Holy Spirit. In Christianity, there is no mention of Eve except for granting the role of goddess to the holy Mary, who through the intervention of the Holy Spirit bore Christ and was accordingly honoured and revered. It's a lovely fable that is still believed by more than one billion people!

Some human rulers, such as the pharaohs of Ancient Egypt, the emperors of Japan, and some of Rome, were worshipped by their subjects.

The faith in gods was formerly widespread but is now waning. The belief in gods is strongly associated with various cultures that have endowed them with their own worship and institutionalisation. In addition to the monotheistic religions such as Judaism, Christianity, and Islamism, there are polytheistic religions such as Norse and Germanic mythology and Hinduism. The particularity of Hinduism rests in the existence of incarnation so that in fact a lot of God's worship can be combined with one universal, divine principle that manifests itself in all.

Metaphysics is the site of the philosophers and theologians who explore what, being (something rather than nothing), *dasein,* and God's existence is, and they wonder which and for which we exist. In short, they wonder whether life has meaning. Ancient and modern thinkers have made a distinction, corresponding to reality, coherent abstractions (thoughts of things that are imaginable but not real), and that which cannot even be rationally thought. By contrast, existence is often restricted solely to that which has physical existence or has a direct basis in it, in the way that thoughts do in the brain. Reality is often contrasted what is imaginary, delusional, only in the mind, dreams, what is false, fictional or abstract?

Contrary to science, metaphysics examines what immanently and transcendently is. Science denies the metaphysics and the supernatural, and accordingly it denies the existence of gods. The existence of gods cannot be scientifically established. Provided that one believes in the supernatural, science cannot rule out that gods, which are immaterial, exist. The supernatural means whatever transcends the powers of nature or human agency.

Theology is the systematic and rational study of concepts of god and the nature of the divine; whether there is a god (monotheism) or many gods (polytheism) or no gods (atheism), or whether it is unknown if gods exist (agnosticism), and whether a divine entity directly intervenes in the world (theism), or its sole function is to be the first cause of the universe (deism).[127]

Theology includes the study of the God's entity and is looking for the essential characteristics (transcendence and immanence) to unravel and systematise. Immanence (permanent pervading the universe) is the philosophical designation for that what belongs to the structure of something and does not exceed it. In the epistemology, immanence is the knowledge that does not exceed consciousness but remains inside the experience or awareness. The immanence philosophy limits the knowledge to that what is possible in the conscious experience. Not being but awareness gets the largest meaning to knowledge acquisition. In Western philosophy came immanence eventually undone of the scholastic view of John Duns Scotus and was later extensively treated by Wilhelm Dyke. Dyke claimed the concept of conscious immanence in an idea in which subject and object form a unit. It was the starting point of epistemology. Immanence can be found in the philosophy of Baruch Spinoza (pantheism) and also with Georg Wilhelm Hegel (*Phänomeologie des Geistes*). The concept of immanence is mainly present in religion. The immanence of God means that God is omnipresent, not only as an inner driving force that permeates all creation but also by its intervention in the daily events.

According to Christian theology, the transcendent God, who cannot be approached or seen in essence or being, becomes immanent primarily in the God-man Jesus the Christ, who is the incarnate second person of the Trinity. In Catholic theology, Christ and the Holy Spirit immanently reveal themselves, whereas God the father only reveals himself immanently vicariously through the son and the Holy Spirit. The divine nature, the godhead, is wholly transcendent and unable to be comprehended according to Paul in his letter to the Philippians.

Transcendence in philosophy is a concept that is defined as standing outside and exceeding the knowledge of humans. Kant used the concept in his knowledge theory. He called his epistemological investigation a "transcendental analysis" in which transcendental refers to the frontiers of knowledge and the meaning of "outside sensuous perception". Unlike Kant, the philosopher Edmund Husserl stood for the concept of transcendence from the phenomenological method, whereby the phenomena speak for themselves. Martin Heidegger then treats transcendence in his book *Sein und Zeit* (*Dasein*)showing a different meaning. It has to do with the being of man.

Martin Heidegger, widely acknowledged as one of the most original, seminal, and important philosophers of the twentieth century, is best known for his contributions to phenomenology and existentialism, the latter not acknowledged by Heidegger himself. In his first and best known book, *Being and Time,* Heidegger attempted to turn away from ontic questions about beings to ontological questions about being (dasein, or being-there) and recover what he claimed was the most primordial and philosophical question: the question of being, of what it means for something to be. This was in opposition to rational thinkers like René Descartes, who located the essence of man in his thinking abilities. Heidegger was a Christian, but he was a controversial figure due to his affiliation to Nazism.

In the fourth century BCE, Plato used the Greek *theologia* for the discourse on God. Augustine of Hippo defined the Latin equivalent as "reasoning or discussions concerning the deity". Theology includes the study of the God's entity and looking for the essential characteristics, which are transcendence and immanence, to unravel and systematise. One differentiates in the philosophy and theology.

In the philosophy and theology, the following distinctions are made.

- Agnosticism is the philosophical view that the truth of certain beliefs and claims—particularly metaphysical claims regarding theology, afterlife or the existence of gods—are not known or incoherent unknowable. The terms agnostic and agnosticism (belief in the unknowability of the existence of gods) were introduced by Thomas Henry Huxley in his book *Agnosticism,* in which he defended the rational honesty. Other famous agnostics were Robert G. Ingersoll (*Why I Am an Agnostic*) and Bertrand Russell (*Why I Am Not a Christian*); the latter was more atheist than agnostic.
- Animism is the belief that spirits exist that animals, plants, and resorts infuse, and even can be found in one way or another, in the major religions.
- Atheism is the explicit affirmation that gods do not exist because, as part of the supernatural, it is contrary to science.

Unproven religious propositions deserve as much belief as any other unproven theorem. Ninety per cent of scientists are theists.

- Bahá'i faith is a monotheistic religion that was founded by Bahá'u'llah in the nineteenth century in Persia. It emphasises the spiritual unity of mankind. Worldwide, there are an estimated six million believers spread in more than two hundred countries and territories. This religion, which is equally wanting conviction as any other religion, argues in an exalted way that the religious history is an unfolding of truth in which a series of divine messengers have occurred, each of which has installed a religion suited to the needs of their time and the capacity of their time. Bahá'u'llah mentions Abraham, Krishna, Buddha, Jesus,

Mohammed, and himself. This interpretation has the merit to provide a logical explanation about the time-phased flaws of the messengers. Humanity is supposed to stay in constant evolution so that in the future new messengers will occur.

- Buddhism is a non-theistic religion in which the existence of gods is not central to the religious experience. It recognises, however, the existence of gods and heavens but in a sphere of incarnation, and it does not recognise a supreme being. Gautama Siddartha Buddha stated that the god Maha Brahma was wrong when he declared that he had created the world. According to Buddha, the physical world exists from a very long term of cycles of genesis, growth, decline, downfall, and regeneration. Rebirth in a heaven is a favourable incarnation and is the result of karma, fate determined by the sum of good actions in previous successive existences.
- Deism is the belief that there exists a transcendent supreme being (an intelligence) as the creator of the physical universe but, in contrast to theism, without exerting a role in human life and the natural laws of the universe. Deists do not believe in a Trinitarian God, the divinity of Jesus Christ, supernatural happenings, prophecies and miracles, or the divine writings of Jews, Christians, and Muslims. According to deists, God has given man the gift to distinguish between good and evil.
- Dualism is the belief that, in addition to a god of goodness, an opposite deity of evil exists.
- Henotheism is the belief and worship of a single god while accepting the existence or possible existence of other deities.
- Hinduism is the belief in the absolute unity of a transcendent and immanent God, the infinite cosmic consciousness (Parama Purusha), who is the creator of the universe and with whom all beings are closely connected. The one god is Brahma, Shiva, or Vishnu, whereas other gods are incarnations or sequential phases.

- Monotheism is the belief in a single deity. In the Abrahamic religions (Judaism, Christianity, and Islamism), a single God is considered a supreme being who is the creator of the universe. This is similarly the case in the Persian Bahá'i faith, Hinduism, and Zoroastrian Brahmanism. In the Abrahamic religions, Abraham is regarded as the first prophet. Names for the deity in monotheism are YHWH, God, Gott, Allah, Jumala, Bog, and Brahma. He is regarded as all-powerful (omnipotent) omniscient, all-goodness (love and merciful), ubiquitous, and just. These properties of the monotheistic god make him an exceptional entity that managed to convince most people of his existence. Monotheism is the belief that God is both immanent and transcendent, infinite and exalted, and at the same time ubiquitous, which would mean that he interferes in worldly matters and which is hardly acceptable to the educated man. These properties of the monotheistic god make him an exceptional entity, and belief managed to convince most people of his existence.
- Non-theism holds that the universe can be explained without any reference to the supernatural. Some non-theists, refusing to accept the concept of God, accept it is significant to a large part of the world and that it is a symbol of human values and aspirations. Believers defend theology on the basis that the supernatural is non-empirical and thus the proper domain of theology.
- Philosophical logical positivism is the teaching that the term *God* has no meaning.
- Something is the view of people who do not wish to delve further into the subject and are satisfied that there is something that does not need to be a god but which is inexplicable. One would be surprised how often this statement is made.
- Panentheism is the faith that God contains the universe (immanence) but is not identical to that universe because God transcends the universe (transcendence). The Kabbalah, the Jewish mystical, provides a panentheistic view

of the essence of god. Christian (creation spirituality) and Islamic mysticisms also have panentheistic considerations.

- Pantheism is the belief that God is entirely immanent (inherently) and that the cosmos (the universe) is a god.
- Polytheism is the belief in the existence of many gods, and it preceded monotheism.
- Theism generally holds that God exists realistically, objectively, and independently of human thought; that God created and sustained everything; and that God is omnipotent, benevolent, omniscient, and eternal. God is considered personal and interacting with the universe. Theism holds that God is both transcendent and immanent. In theology, God is considered "the greatest conceivable existence".[30] Theists believe in a supreme being, but they cannot get rid of the thought that angels and demons also exist.

The Abrahamic belief in a single God is somewhat reflected in Zoroastrianism, as defined by Zarathustra in ancient Persia.

In all times and everywhere around the world, various notions of God turned up and gave rise to different religions. Many notable philosophers have developed arguments for the existence of God, but none ever succeeded in establishing a truth that could not be refuted. Even in modern times, philosophers continue to seek a way to convey God. Most theories, however, refute God.

The Abrahamic religions are equally based on the supernatural, and they dismiss the other religions as heresy—yet they themselves spread superstitions.

Notwithstanding their efforts, no religion has been able to produce a valid proof of God. Countless arguments have been proposed to attempt to prove the existence of God. One of the oldest is the ontological argument of Anselm, archbishop of Canterbury. In his *Prologion,* Anselm[21] defined his belief in the existence of God using the phrase "than that which nothing greater can be conceived" (in Latin: *Id quo malus nihil cogitari potest)*. He reasoned that if "that than which nothing greater can be conceived" existed only in the intellect, it would not be "that than which nothing greater can be conceived", because it can be thought to exist in realty, which is greater. It follows, according to Anselm, "that than which nothing greater can be conceived as God", and thus it establishes that God exists in reality. This *ratio Anselmi* was applied the term "ontological argument" by Immanuel Kant. Descartes reasoned similarly to Anselm, and the Jew Baruch Spinoza used it differently as a pantheistic view by considering the whole world as God. The philosopher and father of the Church, Thomas Aquinas, refuted the *ratio Anselmi* (ontological reasoning) and wrote his own argumentation to prove the existence of God, "The Five Ways of Aquinas", of which none survived modern times.[22] The Christian Gottfried Wilhem Leibniz, one of the greatest philosophers, mathematicians, and inventors of his time, was (along with René Descartes and Baruch Spinoza) one of the three great seventeenth-century advocates of rationalism. He concluded that our universe is, in a restricted way, the best possible one that God could have created. The idea was lampooned by others such as Voltaire. This conclusion is one of optimism but is rarely followed in modern times. Leibniz is also known for his justification of God. The works of Leibniz anticipated modern logic and analytic philosophy, but his philosophy also looks back to the scholastic tradition, in which conclusions are produced by applying reason of first principles or prior definitions rather than empirical evidence.

Spinoza argued that God existed but is abstract and impersonal. His writings were banned for two hundred years because of his criticism of the historical Bible. He denied the miracles of Jesus and suggested that the biblical prophets were ordinary people with exceptional imagination when they spoke on behalf of God.

The famous atheist Richard Dawkins wrote that God is a delusion[16] and that the existence of God is an empirical question, on the grounds that "a universe with a God would be a completely different kind of universe from one without it, and it would be a scientific difference".[23]

The gifted theoretical physicist Stephen Hawking and his co-author Leonard Mlodinow stated in their book *The Grand Design*[24] that it is reasonable to ask who or what created the universe, but if the answer is God, then the question has been merely deflected to that of who created God. They posit that science provides a better answer and needs no intervention of a divine being to create heaven and earth.

Believing in something is a hypothesis (cf. chapter XXIII, infra). A discussion of whether God exists is not possible as all believers depart from a starting point, which is the supernatural. However, the supernatural does not exist and makes further discussion impossible.[1] Furthermore, science and religion are completely incompatible, although some scientists are believers.[1]

We are in the twenty-first century, but no one can deny that poverty in the world is still very great. The yearly income of a European, American or Japanese citizen is around €30,000, but it is around €8,400 in Asia and only €2,400 in the countries of Africa below the Sahara.[25] The unhappy life of an impoverished human is centred on staying alive; though no dummy, he has no time to acquire knowledge. His beliefs are those of his forefathers. His gap of knowledge stunts his intellect. He fornicates without realising that he is not able to support his children. It is a tragedy that religions are unwilling to focus on this grave matter. Only knowledge can help man to remedy his beliefs and lust. Knowledge liberates man. But knowledge is dependent on economic welfare, out of which arises a vicious circle. Real intellect is dependent of having an open mind.

One of the most poignant and clear criticism of religion is the one stated by the monument of scientist Paul Dirac during a friendly conversation at the 1927 Solvay Centre Conference in Brussels with Wolfgang Pauli and Werner Heisenberg, discussing Einstein's and Planck's views on religion.

> I cannot understand why we idle discussing religion. If we are honest—and as scientist honesty is our precise duty—we cannot help but admit that any religion is a pack of false statements, deprived of any real foundation. The very idea of god is a product of human imagination. I do not recognise any religious myth, at least because they contradict one another.

The great scientist Steven Weinberg, in his talk *A Designer Universe*[128] given in April 1999 at the Conference on Cosmic Design of the American Association for the Advancement of Science in Washington D.C., remarked that today we do not think anymore that the world was designed by some sort of intelligence. Now, we understand that the world was created in terms of physical forces acting under impersonal laws—although we don't yet know the most fundamental laws, and we can't work out all the consequences of the laws we do know. The great monotheistic faiths are founded on miracle stories—the burning bush to allow Moses to find his way (Exodus, 3:1–4, 17), the Immaculate conception of the saviour of the world Sycophant in Zoroastrianism, the empty tomb of Jesus, Jesus transforming water into wine (New Testament), the archangel Gabriel dictating the Koran to Mohammed, the chronicle on golden plates presented to Joseph Smith by the angel Moroni in Mormonism, and the revelations made to L. R. Hubbard in Scientology. The evidence of these miracles is much weaker than the evidence of cold fusion. The universe is very large and perhaps infinite, so it should be no surprise that amongst the enormous number of planets that may support only unintelligent life and the still vaster number that cannot support life at all, there is some tiny fraction on which there are living beings who are capable of thinking about the universe as we are doing here. Thus, to judge whether our lives show evidence for a benevolent designer, we have to ask not only whether life is better than would be expected in any case from what we know about natural selection, but we also need to take into account the bias introduced by the fact that it is we who are thinking about the problem (not a supernatural entity). The prevalence of evil and misery (cancer, Alzheimer's, pogroms, crusades, and jihads) has always bothered those who believe in a benevolent and omnipotent God (for which they have no valid explanation). One of the great achievements of science has been, if not to make it impossible for intelligent people to be religious, then at least to make it possible for them not to be religious. We should not retreat from this accomplishment.

People who believe all this crap about miracles can certainly not be considered intelligent.

Therefore, it is completely irrational to believe in a deity. If God is an omnipotent entity who has created heaven and Earth, then it was a creature or intelligence that existed outside the universe. If faith in God has maintained 6,500 years, then that is for several reasons. The remarkable success of the concept of God is the myth that the almighty God is infinitely good and has been a guiding principle for mankind. Humanity cannot look back on a happy existence. It places the individual with his hard life open to happier perspectives, such as that God promises a paradise after death. The various religions have let no opportunity pass to assert themselves, even to practise genocide. The establishment of private schools was the easiest way to brainwash students.

Prophets in the Bible are treated as venerable persons. They were originally persons who performed at the courts of kings as fortune tellers, and they made predictions that were completely unfounded. In fact, they cannot be considered as anything other than quacks. Prophets are the foundation of faith. Their writings and traditions make out the holy books from which not the least truth can be distilled. In the Old Testament, one finds the books of different prophets. In the New Testament, the main writings are those of evangelists who have heard everything from hearsay. Paul (Saul of Tarsus), the author of the Apostolic letters, was not a prophet but underwent a vision of Christ. It is disconcerting that all this nonsense published about God continues to hold entrance. The man is prey for fantasy and perhaps has need of fantasy to overcome the stress and frustrations of life. However, such judgement is in fact humiliating for the human because he is portrayed as a weak, irrational creature who is mentally unable to live without placebos.

Imagination or fantasy is the ability of the mind to provide in situations in which to live or to think of events or entities that do not exist, which cannot exist, or whose existence is unproven.

Over the centuries, faith has been propagated by individuals who claim divine revelations. Revelations are simply imaginations or chimera that include fantasy and illusion. When someone attaches belief to his chimera, he deceives himself when he proclaims his chimera as truth to third parties, and then he deludes his fellow man. Prophets are figures from antiquity which in modern life have disappeared, apart from crooks who operate as sect leaders. Perhaps the most sensational cult leader was Joseph Smith, founder of the Church of Latter-day Saints (Mormons): every time he needed money or wanted a new wife, he had a revelation.

Some philosophers, pseudo-intellectuals, and even psychiatrists consider that faith is good for humans. God is an invention of man. This invention explains the immaturity of humans. The considerable influence that religion continues to exert is a sorry state of mankind.

The fear of death and the promise of eternal life have always dominated the life of rather unstable men, and religions have eagerly played on that. The Apostle Paul promised eternal life, but in the form of the soul. The soul is a metaphysical concept associated with the essence of the man. The soul does not die with the body, from which it is separated by death and with which it will be reunited in the final resurrection. The only thing we can determine about the soul is that it is immaterial. Paul is not able to explain the life of the soul or the reuniting by resurrection. What is immaterial includes no feelings. What does an incorporeal and eternal life mean in the hereafter? Is such an existence preferable to eternal oblivion, and is it not disappointing? Perhaps when people are really unhappy about their existence, it is fortunate that people do not think in depth and realise that eternal life is a sweet holder.

Notwithstanding the large scientific evidence of the creation of the universe, the majority of the world's population believes in God. The reasons are twofold. The first group of people, somewhat rational though not thinking in depth, cannot get rid of the thought that God is almighty goodness, the distinction between good and evil, and necessary for the order of the world. This is of course great nonsense because ethics does not need divine inspiration. Another group of people, which forms the majority of the world population, is fully seized by the urge to survive. Their sad existence finds a mainstay in the existence of God, a supernatural entity which sooner or later, possibly after death, will allow for a better life. The grace of God constitutes their comfort.

Religion is based on dogma and faith, whereas science is based on doubt and questioning. In religion is faith a virtue, but in science is faith a vice. The invention by man of God is a sop. Modern man needs to realise that the invention of God is both a delusion and illusion. A rational evolution demands an open mind.

The term *reality* seems a simple concept that needs no further text and explanation. Nevertheless, the concept in philosophy and in the philosophy of science is hotly contested on the matter. It has to do with the controversy of achieving reality when adoption by sensory perceptions. Einstein wrote, “The belief in an external world independent of the acting subject is the basis of all science. Because, however, sensory perception only provides indirect information from the external world, we can only conceive the latter with speculative (rational) means. As a result, our notion of physical reality can never be final.”[62]

CHAPTER 19

Theodicy

Theodicy is an aspect of God's existence. It is a justification of God's existence notwithstanding the dualism of good and evil. There is no problem in deism in which God does not interfere in the daily matters on earth; the occurrence of evil is of the freewill of humankind. In monotheism, a problem arises. How can a supernatural deity with extraordinary powers, benevolence, and omniscience allow the occurrence of evil (criminality and human suffering)? Theodicy attempts to resolve the evidential problem of evil by reconciling the traditional divine characteristics of omnibenevolence, omnipotence, and omniscience in either their absolute or relative form, with the occurrence of evil and suffering in the world.[101]

The term *theodicy* was coined in 1710 by the German philosopher Gottfried Leibniz in his work *Essais de Théodicée sur la Bonté de Dieu, la Liberté de l'Homme et l'Origine du Mal* (*Essays on the Goodness of God, the Freedom of Man and the Origin of Evil*). Leibniz's theodicy states that God of course created the best of all possible worlds, but that a created world is limited and so imperfect. He adds that even God cannot evade logic, in which case God's powers are very limited and constitute a mockery of theism. Leibniz's theodicy is actually not so much a justification of God but rather a writing that defends the widespread application of reason. He rejects the Pythagorean theorem that all possible worlds really exist. The term *multiverse* is apparent in quantum mechanics. It is a significant simplification for the faith reasoning if it is only necessary to demonstrate that it is better for each world to exist than to not exist— and no more to demonstrate that its existence is better than that of any other possible world. The existence of a multiverse is put forward in quantum mechanics to provide a solution in physics which otherwise is excluded.[1] The theory of multiverse stands against Leibniz's conviction that our known world is unique amongst other theoretical worlds but not existing worlds. The preceding is a significant paradigm of how the advance of science drives religion to the bay.

Because reason and faith must be entirely reconciled, Leibniz judges that any tenet of faith which could not be defended by reason must be rejected. He approached one of the central reasons of Christian theism: if God is all good, all wise, and all powerful, how did evil come into the world? Leibniz answers this delicate question that though God is indeed unlimited in wisdom and power, his human creations, as creations, are limited both in their wisdom and power (power to act). This predisposes humans to false beliefs, wrong decisions, and effective actions in the exercise of their free will. Further, although human actions flow from prior causes that ultimately arise in God and therefore are known as a metaphysical certainty to God, an individual's free will is therefore exercised within natural laws, where choices are merely contingently necessary, to be decided in the event by "a wonderful spontaneity" that provides individuals an escape from rigorous predestination. Leibniz, though burdened by the bias of belief, was a very intelligent man and could have added to his theodicy that if God had created humans in complete image and nature of himself, he would have created gods. He had many fervent admirers, and one of them was the genial mathematician Kurt Gödel, Einstein's closest friend.

There are many theodicies, and one is more ludicrous than the next. There's even one about original sin. God accepts the existence of evil in the world as a punishment for original sin because Adam and Eve ate from the tree of good and evil. If God's existence itself is at stake, it makes little sense in theology to advance justifications for detected subsidiary inconsistencies.

The French philosopher Voltaire, pseudonym of François Marie Arouet, disputed Leibniz's theodicy in his poem "Poème sur le Désastre de Lisbonne" ("Poem on the Lisbon Disaster"), in which he argued that the earthquake in the city of Lisbon in 1775 on a feast day that took the lives of so many people demonstrates that God has not created the best possible Earth at all. This criticism is also found in Voltaire's book *Candide*.

The natural disaster of Lisbon is not comparable to the Holocaust when it comes to human evil of the highest degree and which more than ever has cast doubt on the existence of God. Monotheistic theologians are still working in vain to seek a reconcilable theodicy for the genocide of the Jews.

The belief in God is expressed loudly and ludicrous in daily life. In the United States, it seems every speech is terminated with, "God bless America." The Muslims cry continuously, "Allah is great," even when murdering their fellow men.

CHAPTER 20

Religion

A. Generalities

As each religion came into existence and developed around the God idea,[135] each religion developed its own explanation of creation. Thus, as the God idea evolved within different religious systems, this idea became associated with various myths. People used the God idea as a vehicle for their explanations of the existence of man and the nature of the life. Today, intelligent men who have carefully reviewed all the available facts have concluded that, like the God idea, the creation myths must be regarded as an evolution of the human imagination which began by the misunderstanding of the phenomena of nature. These misunderstandings were rooted in the fear and ignorance of primitive man. Even today, man still retains his primitive interpretations of creation. In the light of recent scientific thinking, the theological definition of God is vague and hence has no place in the present civilisations.

If man is created by an external source, then he must belong to that source and not to himself. Buddhists believe that man does belong to himself and that he is responsible for everything he does. Thus, Buddhists have no reason to believe that man came into existence in the human form through any external sources. They believe that man is here today because of his own actions. He is neither punished nor rewarded by anyone but himself, according to his own good and bad actions. In the process of evolution, the human being came into existence. However, there are no Buddha words to support the belief that the world was created by anybody. The scientific discovery of gradual development of the world system conforms with the Buddha's teachings.

People who believe are, much to my regret, lacking intelligence or development, which is the case for 90 per cent of the world population.

Religion aims to explain the meaning of life, human origin, and the universe. Religion is a phenomenon of rules and values. It is also service and worship of an entity of the supernatural, represented by a deity (one God, many gods or goddesses). It is also the belief in a supernatural controlling power. The term *supernatural* means whatever transcends the nature of the universe.

Organised religion is a movement with an organised collection of beliefs, cultural systems, and world views that relate humanity to an order of existence. Most religions have narrative histories (mainly mythological) and symbols which aim to explain the meaning of life, the origin of life, and the universe. From these beliefs of the cosmos and human nature, religions derive different disciplines of morality, ethics, religious customs, laws, lifestyle, and life stand.[102] Anthropologists argue that religion and belief help mankind to deal with problems of human life that are significant, persistent, and intolerable. It comes down as a placebo necessary for people who are perhaps intelligent but undeveloped.

The origin of religion is uncertain. Probably the shamans and soothsayers of primitive tribes could convince their gullible fellow men that the phenomena of nature were manifestations of deities and that they must revere these gods. At the same time, the people were compelled to respect the authority of the intermediators. Later, paganism evolved to monotheism, in which so-called prophets claimed to have received divine inspirations. These prophets were able to gather followers, and organised religion was born. It is perhaps shocking to many people, but it must be said that all prophets are imposters. Some may have been of good faith, but nevertheless they acted out of ignorance, naivety, or sheer stupidity.

The only merit of religions consists of having introduced some good ethics, in so far that they prescribe the love of fellow man—and not as Islam, wherein the Muslims are dictated to exterminate the unbelievers (surah 8, verse 39 of the Koran).

There are 42 different religions in the world, which seems to demonstrate that humans need religion. A global poll of 2012 reports that 59 per cent of the world's population is religious, and 36 per cent is not religious, including 13 per cent atheists. However, there has been a 9 per cent decrease in religious belief from 2005. This is especially joyous for the rational human, who then can expect that religion is doomed to disappear. In the West, the decrease in religion will happen faster than elsewhere because in Africa, Asia, and many out-of-the-way corners of the world, people are still too attached to their customs and traditions, such as the marrying of young girls to older men—a fact never denounced by the Vatican. It will take some time before these people are ready to abandon their way of living. Generally, women are more religious than men, and that is why Muslim women are tolerating the autocratic manner of their husbands.

The five largest religious groups by world population, estimated in 2010 to account for 5.8 billion people and 84 per cent of the world population, are Christianity, Islam, Buddhism, Hinduism (with the relative numbers for Buddhism and Hinduism dependent on the extent of syncretism, merging of opposing tenets), and traditional folk religions.

Christianity:	2.2 billion, 32 per cent
Islam:	1.6 billion, 23 per cent
Hinduism:	1 billion, 15 per cent
Buddhism:	0.5 billion, 7 per cent
Folk religions:	0.4 billion, 6 per cent

Recent studies have shown that countries with a low IQ are overwhelmingly religious.[66]

The oldest religions were founded in the Indian subcontinent, with origins going back as far as prehistoric times. The general belief of Hinduism is that the spirit or soul (*atman*), which expresses the person's true self and which is the ultimate goal, is eternal. Hinduism is a synecdoche (partial description) of the similar philosophies of Vaishnavism, Shaivism, and related groups practised or founded in India and sharing the same concepts of karma, caste, reincarnation, mantras, yantras, and darsana. Hinduism is not a monolithic religion but a religious category containing dozens of separate philosophies amalgamated as Sanatama Dharma, which is the name by which Hinduism has been known throughout history by its followers. Most Hindus believe in the absolute unity of a transcendent and immanent deity, the infinite cosmic consciousness (Parama Purusha), who is the creator of the universe and where creatures are connected at the closest. Most Hindus revere but one god, such as Brahma, Shiva, and Vishnu. They believe that other gods are incarnations of that one god, as aspects or sequential phases.

Hinduism is based on a cycle in which the world created, destroyed, and recreated. It has many gods, and the people are (depending on the degree of dedication) quite busy keeping them satisfied. Hinduism still deals with temple prostitution and human sacrifices. In addition, concepts such as reincarnation and karma are taught. Karma is seen as a law of nature. It is a variant on the law of causality: action causes reaction, cause caused a result. By the principle of karma, people have a great responsibility. It further implies the acceptance of creation, the acceptance of a natural order, and the existence of natural laws established by the creator.

Abrahamic religions are the monotheistic religions which believe irrationally that they descend from Abraham and which science has proven false, just like all other religions.

Judaism is the oldest Abrahamic religion, and Christianity and Islam are derived from it. It originated in the people of ancient Israel and Judea. Judaism is based on the Torah (Old or Hebrew Testament), which Jews believe is handed down through the prophet Moses. The Jewish people were scattered (diaspora) after the destruction of the Temple in 70 CE. Today, there are about 13 million Jews, with about 40 per cent living in Israel and 40 per cent living in the United States.

Christianity is based on the fictive life and teachings of Jesus of Nazareth (first century BCE), as presented in the New Testament. The Christian faith is based on a manifestation of God in the person of Jesus, the supposed son of God. Christianity teaches the concept of the Trinity, the unity of God, son, and Holy Spirit as three figures in one Godhead. The trinity was highly criticised in the first three hundred years of Christianity and was only definitely settled at the first Council of Nicaea in 325 CE. The Nicene Creed declared the gospel of Mani, who declared himself to be the Paraclete (Holy Spirit), and the gospel of the prominent Arius to be apostasies and heresies. The noble Arius was later exonerated at the first Synod at Tyre in 335 CE, but after his death he was again pronounced a heretic at the first council of Constantinople in 381 CE. It was Roman Emperor Constantine I who, in order to ease the friction in his realm between the different factions of Jewish Christians, charged his high priest, Eusebius of Caesarea, to organise the Council at Nicaea. Constantine II and Valens were more inclined to Arianism, but it was Theodosius I who made Christianity the state religion in 392 CE, starting the persecution of non-Christians.

The concept of the Trinity does not appear in the Bible, but it was later advanced to prove the divinity of Jesus and the virginity of Mary. It is invented drivel. Judaism and Islam repudiate the Trinity. Judaism does not recognise Christ as the messiah, and Islam considers Jesus a prophet but not divine. Several verses of the Koran state that the Trinity doctrine is blasphemous.

Protestantism separated from the Catholic Church in the sixteenth-century Reformation and was split into many denominations.

Islam is a widespread religion based on the teachings of Prophet Muhammad, who in the seventh century, by divine revelations, was commanded to spread the name of the one and only God. That was the same God of Abraham and Jesus, but followers had lost their way and distorted the messages of their prophet.

Islam is a copy of Judaism, modified to appease the pagan convictions of the Arab tribes.

Sunni Islam is the largest denomination within Islam and follows the Koran, with the Hadiths reporting the Sunnah whilst placing emphasis on the Sahabah. The second largest denomination is the Shia Islam, the adherents, featuring the same holy writings but placing emphasis on Ali succeeding Muhammad and the importance of Muhammad's family. There is constant friction between the factions, to the extent of wars between them. Other and more extreme denominations are Ibadi, Sufism, and Wahhabism. Islam is a religion which inspires terrorism.

Iranian religions are ancient religions whose roots predate the Islamisation of Greater Iran and which are now practised by minorities. The most important of these religions is Zoroastrianism, founded by the philosopher and prophet Zoroaster in the sixth century BCE. The adherents worship the creator Ahura Mazda. In Zoroastrianism, good and evil have distinct sources, with evil trying to destroy the creation of Mazda, and with good trying to sustain it. It cannot be denied that the concepts of Zoroastrianism have greatly influenced the Abrahamic religions, although the followers of these religions will not admit it.

Buddhism was founded by Prince Siddhartha Gautama in the sixth century BCE. His teachings aimed to help sentient beings by alleviating their suffering (Dukkha) through understanding the true nature of phenomena, the cycle of suffering and rebirth (Samsära), which is achieving nirvana. Buddhism is not a religion but a philosophy because it lacks the conception of a deity. However, it does not deny the existence of gods and heavens. Buddha claimed that the god Maha Brahma wrongly claimed that he had created the cosmos because this was not possible for a god. The universe is a cycle of creation, growth, decline, and fall, which then follows a new creation. The original beginning is not perceptible according to Buddha. In Buddhist philosophy, there are twenty-nine different heavens with twenty-nine distinct types of godly entities' (devas) house. Rebirth in a heaven is an auspicious event and the result of karma, a previous well-made life. Creatures in a heaven reborn are devas which are not immortal but end up back in a cycle. Meditation is the recommended way of life in Buddhism regarding the good qualities of the devas.

East Asian religions consist of several religions based on the concept of the Tao (Do in Japan). Tao, or Dao, is a Chinese concept signifying path, which is the intuitive knowing of life that cannot be grasped full-heartedly but known nonetheless as the present living experience of one's every day being. The teachings began from the legendary figure of Laozi that gave rise to a religion in the sixth century BCE. The concept is also found in Buddhism and Confucianism. Taoist cosmogony emphasises the need for all sentient beings and all man to return to the primordial or to rejoin with the oneness of the universe by way of self-cultivation and self-realisation.

In the foundational text of Taoism, the *Tao Te Ching*, the Chinese Laozi explains that Tao is not a name for a thing but the underlying natural order of the universe whose ultimate essence is difficult to circumscribe and is likened to silence. The Tao is eternally nameless and can only be found in meditation. The Chinese philosopher Confucius, who subscribed to Taoism, espoused the well-known principle, "Do not do to others what you do want not done to yourself." This was an earlier version of the golden rule.

Chinese folk religions are the indigenous religions of the Han Chinese and include amongst others Confucianism and Taoism.

In Western civilisation, the Abrahamic religions have had the most impact, with Judaism as the oldest and the original, Christianity as the greatest denomination, and radical Islam as a threat to civilisation. Therefore, each of these religions shall be closely examined infra.

The roots of the irrational faith lurk in primitive man. Not in the sense of primitive man before the Homo *sapiens* era, but the little man evolved from ape at the stage of mental development, ten thousand years back and before the scientific and technological era. The primary experience that primitive man had in a world where so many things were happening shattered and stunned him, and he had no explanation for them. His primary experiences gave rise to imaginary solutions that hold projections of what is now present and resulted in modest knowledge identifying irrationality. A human is a being with needs and emotions, and he develops objectives which he carries out with trial and error. All that the mental faculties of humans were unable to understand was explained by the supernatural behaviour of mystic intelligences, gods, couched in an anthropomorphic world because otherwise it was not understandable. Unintelligence converted the unknown into known. The sun was a god who sails on a ship in the sky from east to west. Natural disasters were violences exhibited by disaffected gods and could be avoided by sacrifices to the supposed gods. But time gnaws at the ignorance and sets things right; gradually the ratio takes the upper hand. At first there were many gods, and then came a supreme god that drove out all other gods. Monotheism came about, but then again, man has a need for angels and demons to distinguish and sublimate evil and good.

The process of sublimation has taken 6,500 years since the first civilisation of the Sumerians in Mesopotamia, and it is far from complete. Civilisation takes a long time. There is still much evil. We witness that the Taliban and Islamic State exert an intense barbarity, and in particular that these barbarians assume a deep faith that encourages them to terror-suicide in order to reach paradise and to achieve the stupid promise of spending eternity with *houris.*

Already in the beginning of primitive man, he was afflicted with the twofold question from where we came, and which is our destiny. The anxieties of life show that there was already a primitive reasoning ability in human's present, and related is the arbitrariness of life due to illness, disabilities, setbacks, suffering, and failure, in conjunction with the finiteness. The human brain must camp with these factors and is looking for solutions and when they are not there; then frustration is created and leads to asking more questions. Salvation is sought in the supernatural to render answers to the asked questions even if those are not rational. Mythologies and religions provide the human pain killers and the solace systems to accommodate the people in their unanswered questions and to virtual reality. The faith is therefore nothing more than meeting the limited capabilities and weaknesses of man. The faith has no doubt helped a clumsy man in the past in so far that he is content with placebos, which are against reality. When the human becomes more intelligent and less clumsy, he will be able to undergo the arbitrariness of life and distance himself of the supernatural. However, one has to realise the unbearableness of life by fictional projections.

At the present, man can already boast of a lot of knowledge, and yet it is the question how it is possible that there is still belief in the supernatural. Science excludes all metaphysics from since long. God is an entity of the supernatural, and so if the supernatural does not exist, God cannot exist. Is this reasoning error? And if not, why are 90 per cent of the people unable to provide a rational response? It means that the roots of irrational belief are lurking deep in humans and are difficult to erase.

Priests are mediatory agents between humans and one or more deities. They have the authority (accorded or assumed) to administer religious rites, sacrifices to the deity, or propitiation to the deity. Priests and priestesses have existed since the earliest of times. Before the invention of writing, beliefs were transmitted orally from generation to generation, usually within the same family. When writing appeared, the priests had the task of collecting and preserving sacred texts. The first priests were sort of shamans or medicine men performing a variety of functions depending upon their respective cultures, such as placating the gods, healing, leading a sacrifice, preserving the traditions of storytelling or songs, and guiding souls. Shamans enjoyed great power and prestige in the community, and later, as priests they became more powerful than the secular leaders.

Priests exist in many religions today, such as in all or some branches of Judaism, Christianity, Shintoism, and Hinduism. They are generally regarded as having positive contact with the deity or deities of the religion to which they subscribe, often interpreting the meaning of events and performing the rituals of the religion. Their tasks include blessing worshippers with prayers of joy at marriages, births, and congregations, as well as easing grief at funerals and maintaining a spiritual connection to the afterlife in faiths where such a concept exists. The priesthood was at times the servant of cruelty to exercise authority; this was the case of priests in Mesoamerica and the Spanish Inquisition. The terms priests and priestesses are sufficiently generic that they may be used in an anthropological sense to describe the religious mediators of any religion. In Protestantism priests are coined: minister, pastor or presbyter. In Judaism the priesthood, rabbi is inherited in familial lines. Priests have always found it necessary to dress differently from other people in order to distinguish themselves. Now, the liturgical dress is only worn during services. The priesthood has always played a key role in society. Catholicism has dominated Europe for two thousand years and is only now declining; the pope was a political player as much as a spiritual leader, and he was one of the reasons for Protestant antagonism. Even in historic times, the priesthood played a significant role, competing with secular leaders and suppressing them. In a theocracy, society is governed by its priesthood (such as in modern Iran). Democracy is dependent on the separation of state and religion, which is refuted by Islam, and therefore such a religion is medieval and unacceptable.

In the United States, Mayo Clinic researchers have examined the association between religious involvement (and spirituality) and physical health, mental health, health-related quality of life, and other health outcomes. The researchers reported that most studies show that religious involvement and spirituality are associated with better health outcomes, including greater longevity, coping skills and health-related quality of life (even during terminal illness), and less anxiety, depression, and suicide.[26] Without showing prejudice, this research is really the concept of the application of a placebo that helps people in need of consolation. When people are sick, this is not the right time to point out their irrational beliefs; on the contrary, use all means to assist them. In particular, in the United States faith healing has quite a following.

The terms atheists (belief there are no gods) and agnostic (God is transcendent and unknowable), though specifically contrary to theistic teachings, do not by definition mean the opposite of religious. Indeed, religions such as Buddhism and Taoism classify some of their followers as atheistic, agnostic, or even non-theistic.

The true opposite of religion is irreligion, which describes an absence of religion. *Antireligious* describes an opposition or aversion towards religion in general.

As religion became a more personal matter in Western culture, starting with the Enlightenment discussions of society became more focused on political and scientific meaning, as religious attitudes dominantly in the Western culture were increasingly seen as irrelevant to the needs of the people. Ludwig Feuerbach recast Christian beliefs considering humanism, paving the way for Karl Marx's famous characterisation of religion as "the opium of the people". In the scientific world, in 1869 T. H. Huxley coined the term agnostic, and it further used by Robert Ingersoll and Bertrand Russell (*Why I Am Not a Christian*).

To parody the equal time argument employed by intelligent design creationism, some atheists constructed as a joke the church of the Flying Spaghetti Monster.[27]

Religions are barrels full of inconsistencies and contradictions. The founding fathers of the important religions date of an era in which scientific knowledge was minimal and technological know-how was missing. The big problem of sacred scriptures is that they rely on writers who have not experienced the events themselves. In the cases that they themselves are responsible for the event, it is merely a fictitious revelation, a communication from a message obtained by a vision without the least credibility.

Criticism of religion has always existed. The first criticism dates from the fifth century BCE. There were religious critics in ancient Greece, such as Diagoras, the atheist of Melos, in the fifth century BC, and in Rome, with Titus Lucretius Carus's *De Rerum Natura.* The Greek philosopher Celsus was the first to oppose Christianity in his book *The True Word.*

Even great thinkers who did not deny God felt obliged to write critical comments. In ancient times, Greek philosopher Epicurus, whose tenets and philosophy were spread by Lucretius, taught that people had to live happy and tranquil existence and that the gods could not reward or punish. He is the author of the famous paradox of evil, which is mentioned by Sextus Empiricus in his outlines of Pyrrhonism and by Lactatius, a Christian somewhat considered a heretical philosopher, in his book *De Ira Dei.* David Hume treated the paradox in his book *Dialogues Concerning Natural Religion*. He treated the problem of evil by a series of questions.

- Is God willing to prevent evil, but is unable? Then he is malevolent.
- Is he able, but not willing? Then he is malevolent.
- Is he both able and willing? Whence, then, cometh evil?
- Can he not or does he not want to? Then why do we call him god?[1]

The afore mentioned Lucretius ensured the peace of mind of the people by arguing that the fear of the gods and of death were without any foundation. In his work *De Rerum Natura* (On the Nature of Things), he stressed that no supreme being exists and that the universe is built up from small particles (atoms). After the preface in his work, he asks the reader to regard his teachings not as wickedly but to think about the cruelty of the religion.

Erasmus proved by his translation from Greek of the New Testament that the Vulgate of Jerome Bible was full of errors. He was accused of having laid the egg that gave rise to the Reformation ushered in by Luther, whom he admired but finally decried.

René Descartes is the father of modern philosophy. He rejected the philosophy of Aristotle and Scholasticism and built himself a philosophical system, the doctrine of rationalism. He suggested that knowledge alone on thinking may be based (cogito ergo sum). He made a distinction between the human soul and the body, which dualism collided with the Christian doctrine. Although seemingly convinced of God's existence, he had so many reservations about the faith, including transubstantiation, that he was reproached for being an atheist. His contemporary, the Catholic philosopher Blaise Pascal, wrote, "*Je ne puis pardonner à Descartes: il aurait bien voulu, pouvoir se passer de Dieu; mais il n'a pu s'empêcher de lui faire un chiquenaude pour mettre le monde en mouvement; après cela il n'a plus que faire de Dieu.*"[58] The Works of Descartes were banned by the pope in 1663.

Baruch Spinoza, a secular Jew called by Hegel and Wittgenstein called the prince of philosophers, was the first philosopher who denied the miracles of Christ on the basis to accept no other explanation than those based on reason. He suggested that the biblical prophets were ordinary people with exceptional imagination who did not speak on behalf of God. In his philosophy, the theology of any religion played no role. He suggested that God and nature are the same and are united in pantheism.

David Hume was an agnostic who believed in God as the creator of the universe, but God has no further role in the world. He did not believe in a perfect God or in paradise. For fear of his life, he was very careful in his statements because often he was accused of atheism. After him, the God problem (God's idea) was more openly debated, and there was even more doubt of the existence of Christ.[1]

The evolution theory of Darwin meant a first frontal assault on the credibility of the biblical Genesis, followed by the final blow when, in the twentieth century, the creation of the universe was scientifically and conclusively established. In the second half of the twentieth century, the churches in Europe started to run empty. At the end of the twentieth century, there were no longer enough Catholic priests to conduct mass. The failure of religion is accompanied by a violent response of the Islamic believers who find their salvation in more and more radicalisation at risk of world peace.

The theocratic government in Iran recently published a government policy which consists of promoting sexuality to enter as early as possible and to limit the contraceptives so that women are pushed to bear more children. The woman, whose role in Islam was always secondary, is now reduced to a baby factory. This function of the wife is already dealt with in a statement by the Turkish president Erdogan, who added that men and women are not equal. Also, it's not surprising that the Western world is starting to stir when the primary principles of democracy are trodden down; it has become necessary to more sharply watch the behaviour of the Muslims.

Religion has only one merit, and that is the ethic that is attributed to God. The ethical message is wrong by the lie of the divine origin and by the lie of the reward of paradise, but it has contributed to social peace, usually to the detriment of the common man. The authorities have always eagerly made use of religion to maintain law and order. The governments, and in particular kings, always could count on the support of the Church. The charisma of a figure like Christ has affected humans in the depths of their essence.

Our era is marked by the rise of the religious right not because of a "religious revival" but rather due to the rise of extreme-right political movements and states using religion for political supremacy. The Islamic State (IS; formerly ISIS), the Saudi regime, Hindutva (Rastrija Swayamsevak Sangh) in India, the Christian Right in the United States, Bodu Bala Sena in Sri Lanka, Haredim in Israel, AQMI and MUJAO in Mali, Boko Haram in Nigeria, the Taliban in Afghanistan and Pakistan, the Islamic Republic of Iran (a theocracy), and the Islamic Salvation Front in Algeria are examples of this.

The analysis of religion makes clear that amoral and immoral elements take shelter in the different religions. Religions show a false image of the world to the innocent and the credulous in order to bind the naive believers. Someone who has enjoyed an education but nevertheless remains religious is not innocent of gullibility. The doctrine of a blood sacrifice is an animal lust. The doctrine of the Atonement is an exercise of authority. The doctrine (delusion) of eternal reward or punishment is an inhuman perspective created to enslave the innocent and gullible believers. The same applies to the imposition of eating habits and sexual acts.

During the Middle Ages and continuing in the Renaissance, criticism of Christianity was not tolerated, and critics such as Giordano Bruno were burned at the stake.[28] Bruno was an Italian friar, philosopher, mathematician, and poet who was tried for heresy by the Roman Inquisition on charges of denial of several core Catholic doctrines, including the Trinity, the divinity of Christ, the virginity of Mary, and transubstantiation. He is considered a martyr of science, and his death was a landmark in the history of free thought. During the Middle Ages and even much later, Christianity persecuted and murdered many unbelievers.

A big step forward for civilisation was the Enlightenment at the end of the seventeenth century and the beginning of the eighteenth century. It was the era in which reason was advocated as the primary source of legitimacy and authority. The Enlightenment was more a set of values than a set of ideas, including the right to question the authority of king and the Church, and traditional institutions, customs, and morality. Thinkers such as the Scot David Hume, the French François Dupuis, and Constantin François Chasseboeuf were the forerunners of the Jesus myth theory.[1] Also, the French writer Voltaire criticised religion.

In the nineteenth century, Charles Darwin and Albert Wallace, with their theory of evolution proving Genesis wrong, led to increased scepticism about religion. Thinkers such as Thomas Huxley, Jeremy Bentham, Marx, Charles Bradlaugh, Robert Ingersoll, and the writer Mark Twain were noted nineteenth-century and early twentieth-century critics. In the twentieth century, Bertrand Russell, Sigmund Freud, and many others continued criticism.[1] In the late twentieth century and early twenty-first century Sam Harris, Daniel Dennett, Richard Dawkins, Victor J. Stenger, and the late Christopher Hitchens were active critics. Modern science shows why God does not exist. Lack of knowledge is the primordial reason that people believe.

Scientific method, contrary to belief, acquires knowledge by testing hypotheses to develop theories through elucidation of the facts or evaluation by experiments to find answers to cosmological questions about the universe, which can be observed and measured. All scientific knowledge is subject to new evaluation, refinement, and even outright rejection in the light of additional or new evidence. Theories such as general relativity theory and evolution were proven by gathering additional evidence. In 1940, Albert Einstein stated that science could only determine what is, but not what should be, and outside of its judgement, domain of all kinds continue to be necessary. Religion, on the other hand, covers only evaluations of human thought. It is not able to speak correctly about facts and relationships between facts.[116]

After the French philosophers Charles François Dupuis and Constantin-François Volney, the main proponents of the Christian myth were the German Theologian David Strauss, the German historian Bruno Baur, the German philosopher Arthur Drews, the English philosopher George Albert Wells, the Swedish linguist Alvar

Ellegard, the English philosopher Bertrand Russell, the American theologian Thomas L Compton, and the ethologist and evolutionary biologist Richard Dawkins.[1]

Critics consider religion medieval, outdated, harmful to the individual (e.g., brainwashing of children, faith healing, female genital mutilation, circumcision), and harmful to society (e.g., holy wars, terrorism, wasteful distribution of resources). It impedes the progress of science, exerts social control, and encourages immoral acts (e.g., blood sacrifice, discrimination against homosexuals and women). Religious beliefs lack scientific or rational foundations, and it is a mystery that educated people hold beliefs that are irrational, unscientific, and unreasonable. The Iranian Peace Laureate Shirin Ebadi has spoken out against undemocratic Islamic countries justifying oppressive acts in the name of the Islam.[1]

The origin of religion is vague. Many anthropologists pose that religion is the vision of a charismatic thinker or prophet who fired the imagination of the people in need of a better life. People have always been in need of better lives, and thus everywhere in the world, there were visionaries who gathered supporters. When there was a large group of followers, the religion became institutionalised. The development of religion has taken different forms in diverse cultures. The merit of some religions lies in the fact that they have been associated with the care of people such as education (albeit one-sided), hospitals, family, government, and political hierarchies. It does seem that religions and belief help the weak and uneducated people to deal with problems of human life that are significant, persistent, and intolerable. For those people, the abolition of religion creates a problem as long they are not fully educated.

In nineteenth-century Japan, Buddhism was radically transformed from a pre-modern philosophy of natural law into a religion, which it is not, by the Japanese political leaders in order to address domestic and international political concerns. However, Japan remains a secular nation.

George Lindbeck is an American Lutheran liberal theologian who propagates that religion does not refer to a belief in God or a transcendent absolute, but rather to "a kind of cultural and/or linguistic framework or medium that shapes the entirety of life and thought".[29] That is certainly reasonable, but on the other hand, it does not imply a necessity or usefulness. Lindbeck is an active ecumenicist striving to bring all religions together, which is impossible to realise with Islam.

Theology is the systematic and rational study of the concepts of deity and of nature of religious truths. Augustine of Hippo, renowned for his writing on free will and original sin, defined theology as "reasoning or discussion concerning the deity (supreme being)".[31]

Aristotle divided theoretical philosophy into mathematics, physics, and theology, the latter being metaphysics, which included the nature of the divine (God as the first unmoved mover).[32]

Already in antiquity, there was scepticism about theology. In modern times, beginning with the Enlightenment, as knowledge increased, the irrationality of theology gained more ground. It is indeed impossible to have a reasoned discussion about the divine which belongs to the realm of the supernatural.

In the fifth century BCE, Protagoras, who is reputed to have been exiled from Athens because of his agnosticism about the existence of the gods, said, "Concerning the gods I cannot know that they exist or that they do not exist, or what form they have, for there is much to prevent one's knowing: the subject and the shortness of man's life."[33]

Thomas Paine, English and American political activist, philosopher, deist, revolutionary, and author of (amongst other works) *Common Sense* and *The Rights of Man*, wrote in his book *The Age Reason* that "the study of theology, as it stands in the Christian churches is the study of nothing; it is founded on nothing; it rests on no principle; it proceeds on no authority, it has no data; it can demonstrate nothing; and it admits of no conclusion. Not anything can be studied as a science, without our being in possession of the principles upon which it is founded; and as this is the case with Christian theology, it is therefore the study of nothing".[34]

Ludwig Feuerbach, German atheist, philosopher, and anthropologist, sought to dissolve theology in his work *Principles of the Philosophy of the Future*: "The task of the modern era was the realisation and humanisation of god—the transformation and dissolution of theology into anthropology."[35] This mirrored his earlier work, *The Essence of Christianity,* in which he said that God did not create man, but man created God to anthropomorphic form. This cost him his teaching career.[36]

Robert G. Ingersoll was one of the great intellectuals of his time. He was a lawyer and agnostic who advocated free-thought and humanism. In English literature, he is often quoted. One great tribute is by James Joyce in his novel *Ulysses,* where the figure of an American Evangelist proclaims, "You can rub shoulders with a Jesus, a Gautama, an Ingersoll."[37] Ingersoll stated that when theologians had power, most of the people lived in hovels while a few privileged had palaces and cathedrals. Not religion but science improved people's lives. Trained theologians reason no better than a person who assumes the devil must exist because pictures resemble the fictive devil so exactly.[38]

Charles Bradlaugh was a political activist and famous atheist who believed that theology prevented human beings achieving liberty.[39] He noted that theologians of his time stated that scientific research contradicted sacred scriptures, and therefore the scriptures cannot be anything else but wrong.[40]

The particle physicist Victor Stenger, author of the bestseller of *God: The Failed Hypothesis: How Science Knows That God Does Not Exist,* was a strong advocate for removing the influence of religion from scientific research. He was a prominent critic of intelligence design and the aggressive use of the anthropic principle in quantum mechanics, applied by some to support the paranormal, mysticism, or supernatural phenomena, which he debunked as pseudoscience.

The very intelligent Richard Dawkins, ethologist, evolutionary biologist, and writer, finds that theology is not a subject to be taught at the university because it is not scientific.[41] He states that although science has enabled spectacular achievements ranging from space exploration to development vaccines and other life-saving treatments for infections, religion has achieved nothing.[41]

Jerry Allen Coyne is a professor of biology at the University of Chicago specialising in the theory of evolution. He considers himself a secular Jew. He is a great critic of creationism, theistic evolution, and intelligent design,[1] which he calls "the latest pseudoscientific incarnation of religious creationism, cleverly crafted by a new group of enthusiasts to circumvent recent legal restrictions".[42] He considers theology to be "beliefs that have no basis in fact" and suggests that theologians are deliberately obscure and baffling. He queries how theologians know that reality corresponds to what they say and how they know that they personally are closer to reality than others.[43]

Mark Twain, penname of Samuel Langhorne Clemens, author of the great American novel *Huckleberry Finn*, was a Presbyterian but was critical of organised religion and renowned for poking fun at religion. He stated that several mutual incompatible religions claimed to be the true religion and that people cut the throats of others for following a different religion.[44]

The former Catholic nun Karen Armstrong,[1] an authoritative author in religious circles, seeks in her new book *Fields of Blood. In the Name of God, Religion and Violence* to refute that religion especially leads to bloodshed. It's a disappointing book. She does not agree with the separation of church and state because she finds that the secular state is too anti-religious, which of course is nonsense. To palliate religious violence, she puts the blame on the shoulders of politics and the governments, which is hardly acceptable for any rational human. It recalls to mind that this noble figure of yesteryear has gone somewhat out of her mind, or she is trying to book her place in the afterlife paradise. In contrast to Ludwig Feuerbach, Karl Marx, Friedrich Nietzsche, and Arthur Schopenhauer, she sees the human as a religious being who enjoys the guidance and solace provided by religion in a chaotic world. The religious charity for which she stands, and which is present in all her books, is not enough to be able to follow her train of thought in her latest book.[45]

Coincidence is a remarkable concurrence of events or circumstances which have no apparent causal connection with each other. Plutarch stated, "It is no great wonder if in the long process of time, while fortune takes her course hither and thither, numerous coincidences, should spontaneous occur" (*Parallel Lives,* vol. II, "Sertorius"). On the contrary, synchronicity states that remarkable coincidences occur because there is a causal connecting principle. The Jung-Pauli theory of synchronicity conceived by a psychiatrist and a physicist, both eminent in their fields, represented perhaps the most radical departure from the world view of mechanistic science. It was only possible to conceive by spiritually minded scientists hackneying quantum mechanics principles to form mumbo-jumbo theories.

Inevitably, over the century's religion has affected the culture of groups of people. A religious life stand cannot help but influence everyday life.

What religion is typically referred to and what spirituality is typically referred to often lie close to each other. In a strict sense, consciousness is meant with it, showing the human soul or the inner self. Its origin is to be found in a divine or transcendent state or another state in relation to a higher reality. The spirituality is a special, but not necessarily understood, denominational confessional life, holding a religious life stand whereby one concentrates on the transcendence and immanence of God and the transcendent truth of highest reality finds. After World War II, the points of spirituality and religion were conceptually disconnected from each other. There was a new discourse in which humanistic psychology (group psychology) prevailed. The "true self" can be achieved by self-disclosure, free expression, and meditation. Spirituality became more than mysticism or someone's experience; it was more open to new ideas and influences, less dogmatic, and pluralistic in respect of established religions. Absolute truths were questioned, and intolerance was banned.

Secularisation is the transformation of society from close identification with religious values and institutions (as in the United States) towards non-religious values and secular institutions, such as in Norway, Sweden, and Denmark.

Religion has a significant impact on the political system in many countries. Notably, most Muslim-majority countries adopt various aspects of the Sharia, the ridiculous Islamic law. Much more serious, and a danger to peace in the world, is the application of the notorious Hadith scriptures. Islam refutes democracy. As long as Muslims abide in the Western world according to their religion, there will be friction which can develop into revolution and war. Some countries even define themselves in religious terms, such as the Islamic Republic of Iran. The Sharia thus affects up to 23 per cent of the global population, or 1.57 billion people who are Muslims. However, religion also affects political decisions in many Western countries. For instance, in the United States, 51 per cent of voters would be less likely to vote for a presidential candidate who did not believe in God, and only 6 per cent were more likely. Christians make up 92 per cent of members of the US Congress, compared to 71 per cent of the general public (as of 2014). At the same time, although 23 per cent of US adults are religiously unaffiliated, only one member of Congress (Kyrsten Sinema, D-Arizona), or 0.2 per cent of that body, claims no religious affiliation. In most European countries, religion has a much smaller influence on politics, although it used to be much more important. For instance, same-sex marriage and abortion were illegal in many European countries until recently, following Christian (usually Catholic) doctrine. Several European leaders are atheists (e.g., France's ex-President Francois Hollande or Greece's Prime Minister Alexis Tsipras). In Asia, the role of religion differs widely between countries. For instance, India is still one of the most religious countries, and religion still has a strong impact on politics, given that Hindu nationalists have been targeting minorities like Muslims and Christians, who historically belonged to the lower castes. By contrast, countries such as China or Japan are largely secular, and thus religion has a much smaller impact on politics.[102]

B. Abrahamic Religions

Abrahamic religions are a joint designation of three great monotheistic religions (Judaism, Christianity, and Islam) and a number of related religions such as Druzism and the Bahá 'Í faith, the latter dating from the nineteenth century. They form a quite distinct collective from the other two groups of world religions also somewhat of supernatural yet more of philosophical nature—namely, the Indian tradition, including Hinduism, Jainism, Buddhism and Sikhism, and the East Asian tradition, including Taoism, Confucianism, and Shinto. All these religions and traditions include the vast majority of believers scattered throughout the world.

Historically, the Abrahamic tradition has its origin in the Bronze Age of the Levant around the fourteenth century BC. At that time, there lived in the Levant primarily polytheistic Semitic tribes, including the Israelites. During the polytheistic faith was Yahweh, one of the many gods who were worshipped by the tribes in Canaan. The faith was not codified or monotheistic and became gradually completed around at the time of the Babylonian exile in the sixth century BC. Christianity (first century BC) and Islam (seventh century AD) are each in their own way split off, though predominantly retaining the Abrahamic thought. In addition to a mythological reflection, each of the Abrahamic religions has a theological framework in which it explains its origin and position.

In the Abrahamic religions is the belief that God is personal, appears as an individual, and is considered an entity that exists beyond this world. He has created the cosmos and can intervene in human conditions. He is omnipotent, omniscient, and omnipresent, and he has the features of infallible justice and all-encompassing love. He is traditionally identified as male, such as the Lord. Abrahamic monotheism is characterised by the assumption that the individual contacts the deity through prayer or through dreams. Within the Abrahamic religions consists the human body from a physical element and a spiritual soul. The soul has the will, the intellect, and the emotions that science rejects. Notwithstanding the human being created in the image of God, it is forbidden to depict God as a man because of the danger that his portrayal would be worshipped as an idol. The man has only one life in the material world, which is linear and not cyclical (reincarnation) as in Asian religions. Human behaviour in the physical world determines his existence in the afterlife.

God is in all god's traditions elusive for the mind of man, which means that a man as an unwise being should abstain to reflect or to question the existence of God. This is the dialectic of the religions to counter all arguments about their untruths.

The mythological descent from Abraham is already more than enough to write the Abrahamic religions off as myths, which makes it incomprehensible that so many people attach faith to religion. Myths as traditions may contain some truth but seldom do.

Judaism is the basic religion of all Abrahamic religions. If Judaism is untrue, then Christianity and Islam also fail.

Recent archaeological excavations have been a death blow to Abrahamic religions (cf. B, infra).

Religion is a life stand based on a lie.

C. Judaism

Judaism's most important feature is the worship of a single, incomprehensible, transcendent, indivisible, absolute being who created and governs the universe. Closeness with the God of Israel is through study of his Torah and adherence to its Mitzvot (divine laws). In traditional Judaism, God established a special covenant with his people, the people of Israel, at Mount Sinai, giving the Jewish commandments. The Torah comprises the written Pentateuch and the transcribed oral tradition, further developed through the generations. The Jewish people are intended as "a kingdom of priests and a holy nation"[88] and a "light to the Nations", influencing the other peoples to keep their own religio-ethical Seven Laws of Noah. The messianic era is seen as the perfection of this dual path to God.

Jewish observances involve ethical and ritual, as well as affirmative and prohibitive, injunctions. Modern Jewish denominations differ over the nature, relevance, and emphasis of Mitzvot. Jewish philosophy emphasises that God is not affected or benefited, but individuals and society are benefitted by drawing closer to God. The rationalist rabbi Maimonides sees the ethical and ritual divine commandments as a necessary but insufficient preparation for the philosophical understanding of God, with its love and awe.[89] Amongst fundamental values in the Torah are the pursuit of justice, compassion, peace, kindness, hard work, prosperity, humility, and education. The world to come, prepared in the present, elevates man to an everlasting connection with God. Simeon the Righteous says, "The world stands on three things: on Torah, on worship, and on acts of loving kindness." The prayer book relates, "Blessed is our God who created us for his honour … and planted within us everlasting life." Of this context, the Talmud states, "Everything that God does is for the good," including suffering.

The Jewish mystical Kabbalah (esoteric teaching of Judaism) gives complimentary esoteric meanings of life. As well as Judaism providing an immanent relationship with God (personal theism), in Kabbalah the spiritual and physical creation is a paradoxical manifestation of the immanent aspects of God's being (panentheism), related to the Shekhinah (divine feminine). Jewish observance unites the *sephirot* (divine attributes) on high, restoring harmony to creation. In Lurianic Kabbalah, the meaning of life is the messianic rectification of the shattered sparks of God's persona, exiled in physical existence (the *Kelipot* shells) through the actions of Jewish observance. Through this, in Hasidic Judaism the ultimate essential "desire" of God is the revelation of the omnipresent, divine essence through materiality, achieved by man from within his limited physical realm when the body will give life to the soul.

The Torah, given by God to Moses and whose existence is a myth doubted,[1] comprises the first five books of the Tanakh (the Hebrew Bible), which forms the basis of the Jewish faith and hence the main holy book of Judaism.[103]

The Torah is a written narrative which describes how the world and humankind were created, as well as the further course of the Israelites, who are the forerunners of the Jews and which denomination is now used by the State of Israel for its people. The Torah offers a way of life for the Jews. Before the written Torah, there was an oral version. The oral Torah consists of interpretations and amplifications, and according to rabbinic traditions, they have been handed down from generation to generation and are now embodied in the Talmud and Midrash.[46] Starting from the second century BCE, there are Jewish communities which describe the biblical books as holy scriptures.

The five books of the Torah, also known as the books of Moses or the Pentateuch, are as follows.

- Genesis ("In the beginning") tells the primeval history of Judaism according to rabbinic tradition. It is a story relating the beginning of the world and the descent of Abraham. It includes a narrative about the three patriarchs (Abraham, Isaac, and Jacob), Joseph and the four matriarchs (Sarah, Rebekah, Leah, and Rachel), the promise by God for the land of Canaan, and the departure for Egypt to find grain.

Genesis is a collage of some oral traditions because the book expires repeated times in repetition but in a different way.

* Creation: Genesis 1:1–2:3; Genesis 2:4–25
* The wife of a patriarch goes through for his sister: Genesis 12:13; Genesis 20:2; Genesis 27
* Jacob steals Esau's birthright: Genesis 25:29–34; Genesis 27
* Jakob is named Israel: Genesis 32:28–29; Genesis 35:10
* Jacob changes the place name Luz in Bethel: Genesis 28:19; Genesis 35:15

Another flagrant incongruity is the age of almost a thousand years of patriarchs (Methuselah and the like).- Exodus (departure) tells the story of God's revelation to his people through Moses, who leads them out of Egypt to Mount Sinai. There, the people accept a covenant with God. Moses receives the Torah, to which the people of Israel must abide. The first violation of the law occurs when the golden calf is constructed. Exodus ends when the tabernacle is built.

- Leviticus (related to the Levites) contains the instructions to use the Tabernacle, further teachings of what is chaste and unchaste, the correct way of slaughtering animals, the Day of Atonement, and multiple laws of morality, punishment, and ritual.

- Numeri (numbers) relates the consolidation of the community of the Israelites, the search for the Promised Land and the condemnation, due to doubt, to forty years wandering in the desert before finding the Promised Land.
- Deuteronomy (second law) is a repeat and elaboration of laws previously given in Exodus, Leviticus, and Numeri.

The Pentateuch is a cruel story in which the heirs of Abraham acted without any humanism. Everything indicates that the story was written by multiple authors all showing narrow aspects of their side.

Since God is one, Judaism regards the idea of a duality or a trinity of God a heresy and akin to polytheism. Judaism, in contrast with Christianity, is still waiting for the arrival of a Messiah. Judaism believes that the soul is pure at birth. People are born with the tendency to do good as well with the tendency to do bad, so that the people are free to choose their own paths. In consequence, there is no original sin.

Although Judaism has some solid principles of faith, there is no binding catechism, and neither is there a constraint to conscript followers, for the Jews are indeed God's chosen people. After all, there is no central authority agreed; that would dictate an exact religious dogma. Because of this, many different variations on the basic beliefs are considered by the rabbi, but all are well within the scope of Judaism based on the Tanakh, Talmud, and Midrash. Judaism also recognises the biblical Covenant between God and the patriarch Abraham, as well as the additional aspects of the Covenant revealed to Moses, who is considered Judaism's greatest prophet. In the Midrash, a core text of rabbinic Judaism, acceptance of the divine origins of this covenant is considered an essential aspect of Judaism, and those who reject the Covenant forfeit their share in the world to come.

The Midrash is the body of exegesis of Torah texts along with homiletic stories as taught by Chazal (Rabbinical Jewish sages of the post-Temple era) that provide an intrinsic analysis to passages in the Tanakh.

Midrash is a method of interpreting biblical stories that goes beyond simple distillation of religious, legal, or moral teachings.

It fills in gaps left in the biblical narrative regarding events and personalities that are only hinted at.[2]

The purpose of Midrash was to resolve problems in the interpretation of difficult passages of the text of the Hebrew Bible, using Rabbinic principles of hermeneutics and philology to align them with the religious and ethical values of religious teachers.

The Torah declares two attributes that are decisive for Judaism. On the one hand, because it dares to posit that God made a Covenant with the patriarchs of the Jews, that makes them God's chosen people. On the other hand, because God has issued his law through Moses in the Sinai desert, including the Ten Commandments, these are not justified and must be considered mere inventions.

The creation of Earth, the creation of Adam, the creation of Eve with a rib of Adam, the fall (allusion to sex) caused by Eve (for which woman is responsible and eternally inferior compared to the man), banishment from paradise, Abraham and his son Isaac and grandson Jacob as the patriarchs of the tribe of Israelites, the exodus from Egypt under the leadership of Moses, and the Promised Land Canaan are all facets of a ridiculous story. Today the creation of the universe and Earth are scientifically proven by the Big Bang, modern man is the product of the evolution of life.

Throughout the centuries, rabbis have tried in vain to figure out the symbolism that lurks behind the childish narration of the Torah. It seems that it is intended for people who are little developed, as an introduction to religion. The scanty development of the humans 2,500 years ago is perfectly normal. However, what is not normal at all is that this creed is still widely accepted in modern times.

According to Jewish tradition, there are indications in the Torah and the Deuteronomic history that the final form of the Torah dates to the seventh century before our era, after several editorial operations. These edits show differences between the Masoretic text, the Septuagint, and the Samaritan Pentateuch (being a Greek translation to which seventy translators are considered to have worked). The original text according to the current biblical textual criticism, without any historic proof, was composed of probably four different texts between the tenth and fourth century BCE before being put in writing and combined into a single text.

There should be borne in mind that concrete evidence to substantiate all these assumptions is absent. Famous rabbis over the centuries have written detailed commentaries on the Torah without managing to succeed to provide real proof and meaning to the composition of the Torah.

The five books of the Torah are part of the twenty-four books of the Hebrew Bible (the Tanakh).

Today, most academic scholars agree that the Torah has multiple authors and that its composition took place over many centuries. The consensus of scholarship is that the stories are taken from four different written sources and that these were brought together over the course of time to form the first five books of the Bible as a composite work. This view contradicts heavily with the fairy tales of the orthodox rabbinic tradition, which posits that the Torah was dictated to Moses by God in the year 1280 or 1312 BCE.

The academic sources of the Torah are J, the Jahwist source, from the German transliteration of the Hebrew YHWH; E, the Elohistic source; P, the Priestly source; and D, the Deuteronomist source. Thus, the Torah comprises material taken from six centuries of human history to paint a picture of the beginning of the world and of humanity to give a basis to religion.[47]

The holy books of Judaism are the Tanakh (Hebrew Bible), the Talmud, the Midrash, and the Kabbalah. The Tanakh, mainly written in Hebrew except the books of Daniel, Ezra, and a few others (which are written in Aramaic), contains twenty-four books divided into three parts: the five books of the Tora (the Pentateuch), the prophets, and the writings. The oldest manuscripts of the Tanakh in Hebrew and in Aramaic date from the tenth century CE.

The second part of the Tanakh deals with the prophets of the faith. There are two subgroups: the early prophets (which contain the stories of Joshua, Judges, Samuel, and Kings) and the later prophets (which contain the stories of Isaiah, Jeremiah, Ezekiel, and the twelve minor prophets).

Isaiah was not the earliest prophet but was the most important. He would have historical existence but by no means was in accordance with the Jewish tradition. According to the Tanakh, he lived around 725 BC and was a prophet to the court of the kingdom of Judah at the time that the kingdom of Israel was conquered by the Assyrians. The Jews were then polytheistic, and Isaiah would, according to Judaism, have been already monotheistic. There is absolutely no historicity in the book of Isaiah. He is recognised as a prophet both by Christianity and Islam. The oldest manuscripts of the book of Isaiah are two rolls of the scrolls of the Dead Sea, which date to approximately 150–100 BC. The book of Isaiah identifies itself as the words of the eighth century before our era, but this is wrong because studies have shown that the book was started over a hundred years later and compiled over hundreds of years. Part would be written by the Jewish exiles in Babylon, and a part after the return from Babylon. The prophecies of Isaiah can be situated with regards to successive kings of the kingdom of Judah, while Israel was occupied by the Assyrians, but even this is not historically correct. Isaiah made predictions about Judah, Israel, and Jerusalem, as well as about Persian King Cyrus, whom he never knew. For the Christians honouring from the prophecies of Isaiah, the coming of Jesus requires a great deal of imagination; it is rather the coming of a Jewish Messiah. Isaiah prophesied (Isaiah 7:14; Isaiah 8:8; Matthew 1:23) that Immanuel (Hebrew for "God with us") would be the deliverer of Judah. The Christians interpreted Immanuel as Christ. The texts of Isaiah are not prophecies but the sources of a "level-headed thinking" in which various mythologies were merged. Isaiah would have made a prediction in connection with the Persian Prince Cyrus, but certainly not related to a Messiah. The book of Isaiah is linked to three different eras and cannot be assumed to concern the same author; neither is there any truth to be distilled out. Nevertheless, the Gospels refer to the prophecies of Isaiah (Matthew 3:3; Luke 3:4–6; Luke 4:16–41; John 12:38; Acts 8:28; Romans 10:16–21).

The third part of the Tanakh includes the three poetic books: Psalms, Proverbs, and Job. Then there are the five scrolls: Song of

Solomon, Ruth, Lamentations, Ecclesiastes, and Esther. Finally, there are the other books: Daniel, Ezra, and the Chronicles.

Though the Torah dates as possibly from the fifth century BC, it was regarded as canonical with the prophets from the second century BC. This was for the last part of the Tanakh only, starting from the second century of our era. The Jews only recognise the Hebrew Tanakh as canon, whereas the Christians go out of the Greek translation, the Septuagint. According to classical rabbinic texts, this parallel set of material was originally transmitted to Moses at Sinai, and then from Moses to Israel. At that time, it was forbidden to write and publish the oral law because any writing would be incomplete and subject to misinterpretation and abuse. However, after exile, dispersion, and persecution, this tradition was lifted when it became apparent that in writing was the only way to ensure that the oral law could be preserved. After many years of effort by a great number of rabbis,[147] the oral tradition was written down around 200 CE by Rabbi Judah haNasi, who took up the compilation of a nominally written version of the oral law, the Mishnah (Hebrew: משנה). Other oral traditions from the same time period not entered into the Mishnah were recorded as "Baraitot" (external teaching) and the "Tosefta". Other traditions were written down as "Midrashim". After continued persecution, more of the oral law was committed to writing. A great many more lessons, lectures, and traditions only alluded to in the few hundred pages of Mishnah became the thousands of pages now called the Gemara, which is written in Aramaic, having been compiled in Babylon. Orthodox and conservative branches of Judaism accept these texts as the basis for all subsequent *halakha* and codes of Jewish law, which are held to be normative. Reform and Reconstructionist Judaism deny that these texts, or the Torah itself for that matter, may be used for determining normative law (laws accepted as binding), but accepts them as the authentic and only Jewish version for understanding the Torah and its development throughout history. Humanistic Judaism holds that the Torah is a historical, political, and sociological text, but it does not believe that every word of the Torah is true or even morally correct. Humanistic Judaism is willing to question the Torah and disagree with it, believing that the entire

Jewish experience, not just the Torah, should be the source for Jewish behaviour and ethics.

While Christianity includes the five books of Moses (the Pentateuch) amongst their sacred texts in its Old Testament, Islam states that only the original Torah was sent by God. In neither religion does the Torah retain the religious legal significance that it does in Orthodox Judaism.

Amongst early centres of Christianity, the Septuagint was used by Greek speakers, whereas Aramaic Targums were used by Aramaic speakers such as the Syriac Orthodox Church. It was regarded as the standard form of the Old Testament in the early Greek Christian Church, and it is still considered canonical in the Eastern Orthodox Church. Though different Christian denominations have slightly different versions of the Old Testament in their Bibles, the Torah as the "Five Books of Moses" (or "the Mosaic Law") is common amongst them all.

The Koran refers heavily to Moses to outline the truth of his existence and the religious guidelines that God had revealed to the Children of Israel.[148] According to the Koran, Allah says, "It is He Who has sent down the Book (the Koran) to you with truth, confirming what came before it. And He sent down the *Taurat* (Torah) and the *Injeel* (Gospel)." Muslims consider the Taurat as the word of God given to Moses. However, Muslims also believe that this original revelation was corrupted (*tahrif*, or altered by the passage of time and human fallibility) over time by Jewish scribes and hence does not revere the present "Jewish version". The Torah in the Koran is always mentioned with respect to Islam. The Muslims' belief in the Torah, as well as the prophethood of Moses, is one of the fundamental tenets of Islam.

The Torah, held to be the most ancient of histories, without historicity exists today in three separate versions.

- The Hebrew, considered authentic by the Jews and the Protestant clergy
- The Greek Septuagint, which was used as authoritative in the Greek and other eastern churches

- The Samaritan Torah, the standard authority for that people

These three versions differ greatly from another, even with regards to the lifetimes of the most celebrated figures. In the Hebrew Torah, it is recorded that from Noah's flood until the birth of Abraham, there was an interval of 292 years. In the Greek, that time span is given as 1,072 years, whereas the Samaritan, the recorded span is 942 years. Moreover, according to the text of the Hebrew Torah, from the creation of Adam until Noah's flood, the elapsed time is recorded as 1,656 years, whereas in the Greek Torah the interval is given as 2,262 years, and in the Samaritan text the same period is said to have lasted 1,307 years. The Jews and Protestants belittle the Greek Torah, to the Greeks the Hebrew version is spurious, and the Samaritans deny both the Hebrew and the Greek versions. 'Abdu'l Bahá's elucidations in 1906 are found in his letter to Ethel Jenner Rosenberg.[143]

Although fundamentalists claim that the Bible is as a whole revealed, the Torah is possible from the fifth century BC regarded as canonical. For the prophets from the second century BC, this was for the last part of the Tanakh, only starting from the second century of our era. The composition started in the fifth century BC, when the exiled Jews came back from Babylon with the knowledge of the supreme god Marduk,[1] and it is supposed to have ended in the third century BC by the entire translation from the Hebrew and Aramaic into Greek (the Septuagint). It was, according to the fundamentalists, a lengthy process of oral traditions to capture in writing.

Scholars have tried in vain to track down the history of oral traditions. Consequently, the Tanakh has little historicity.

The Masoretes between the seventh and tenth century CE were a group of Jews who kept themselves busy with the composition, processing, and dissemination of the Hebrew text of the Tanakh. This configuration is still authoritative for believers. The oldest known surviving Masoretic manuscripts date back to the ninth century (Code Aleppo; Damascus Keter). A seventh-century fragment of the Tanakh, including the song of the Sea (Exodus 13:19–6: 1), is one of the few remaining texts of the Hebrew Bible between the Dead Sea scrolls and the codex Aleppo. With the discovery of the Dead Sea scrolls, manuscripts became available dating more than one thousand years older. These writings show that the Masoretic composition and translation is a reliable tradition. However, it is also evident from the Dead Sea scrolls that another text type is related with the Septuagint and that does not match with the Masoretic text, bestowing the Septuagint more archaic value.

The Talmud is the most important book after the Tanakh in Judaism. A part of it forms even for the Christians a part of the Old Testament. It includes the comments of important rabbis and other scholars on the Tanakh, often in the form of discussions between supporters and opponents of one or different point of view. The Talmud consists of two parts, the Mishnah and the Gemara. The Mishnah contains written commentaries on the Tanakh recorded from around two hundred years of our era, while the Gemara are commentaries on the Mishnah. The Mishnah is the first major written redaction of the Jewish oral traditions known as the Oral Torah. It is also the first major work of Rabbinic literature at which approximately 120 rabbis contributed. The period during which the Mishnah was assembled spanned about 130 years, or five generations, in the first and second centuries CE. Yehudah haNasi is credited with the final redaction and publication. There is a distinction between the Babylonian Talmud and the Jerusalem Talmud, although both have the same Gemaras as the core. The Babylonian Talmud is most used and is recorded between the years 500 and 1000 BC in Mesopotamia, where in that period thriving Jewish communities were established. The Jerusalem Talmud, so called because it originated in Jerusalem and was standardised, dates from 350 CE. The work is less important because it mainly addresses Mosaic laws that apply to the agricultural land use and cleaning laws in the temple service.

The Midrash embodies the exegesis of biblical texts. The discussions contained therein are metaphorically and can hardly be taken literally, which is the case for the liberal Jews. The purpose of Midrash was to solve the interpretation of difficult passages in the Tanakh by the use of the hermeneutics and philology of the rabbis, in line with the religious and ethical values of the religious teachers.

When fiction is written, there is always the chance that grave incongruities occur. Examples of this are the two versions of the creation of man in Genesis, each with a distinct perspective. In the first story are a man and woman in God's form created, who are commanded to multiply and to act as administrators of all that God has created. In the second more colourful story, God creates Adam from the dust of Earth and places him in the Garden of Eden, where he is banned from eating of the tree of knowledge and good and evil. Because the man was lonely, God created Eve from a rib of Adam. Eve was tempted by a serpent to eat fruit from the tree of knowledge, and she enticed Adam to do the same (an allusion to sex). Adam and Eve were banished from the Garden of Eden.

Another flagrant incongruity is the age of almost a thousand years of patriarchs (Methuselah and the like). The first temple referred to in the writings of Judaism, to make the distinction with the temple destroyed by the Romans, may have never existed and is rather a reference to the Tabernacle on God's command founded by the fictional Moses in Shiloh. What a death blow for all Abrahamic religions are the archaeological excavations in the biblical world. In the last hundred years, many excavations were done in the Middle East to figure out the civilisations of ancient times. The last three decades in particular, the Bible was archaeologically examined. Ze'ev Herzog, an Israeli archaeologist and a professor at the University of Tel Aviv, published in 1999 a report by a group of archaeologists that, under his leadership from 1997 to 1999, had carried out a series of thorough excavations to scientifically establish the origin of the Bible. It was discovered that the Jews had never been in Egypt and that the glorious kingdoms of David and Solomon have never existed because David and Solomon were really only the heads of small tribes. More disconcerting was the finding that Jehovah had a spouse. The findings of Ze'ev Herzog, who was only known by scientists in 2001, were confirmed by archaeologists I. Finkelstein and N. A. Silberman in their book *The Bible as Myth* (title badly translated from *The Bible Unearthed: Archaeology's New Vision of Ancient Israel and the Origin of its Sacred Texts*).[49]

In dialectic reasoning, there is an enormous difference between the expression "There are no findings found for the occurrence of the exodus" and the express reasoning "There is evidence that the exodus did not take place". It is indeed an enigma that billions of people, after the express scientific data provided by science on the creation of the universe and the recent archaeological finds, continue to stick to the supernatural faith. The Bible is a severe and captivating story, often severely cruel but totally fabricated, covering all aspects of life and in which are intertwined hate, love, revenge, atrocities, murder, enslavement, incest, and prostitution. God is a shepherd of a flock of people he is unable to curb.

The Kabbalah (Revelation) is a discipline that belongs to Jewish mysticism. It is a Jewish philosophical system that claims to provide insight into the divine nature. The Kabbalah refers to esoteric doctrines about God and the universe, only accessible to some chosen ones. The first book on the Kabbalah is the *Sefer Jetzira* (Book of Creation) written in the tenth century, and it is still often quoted. It was followed by the *Bahir* (Enlightenment) in 1176, also known as the Midrash of Rabbi Nechoenja ben haKana. But the most famous work is the *Zohar* (Glittering) according to orthodox Jewish traditions, written in the second century by Rabbi Shimon Bar Yochai. The books are incomprehensible to people who lack the extensive background of the Tanakh, Talmud, and Midrash. The ultra-Orthodox Jews of Jerusalem devote their whole lives, in rather marginal conditions, to the study of the Kabbala.

In Judaism, as in all God's traditions, is God elusive to humans, which means that a human as an unintelligent being has to abstain from doubting God. It is the dialectic of religions to couch untruths.

Judaism, in contrast to Christianity, is still waiting for the arrival of the messiah, a policy of the never never.

Judaism argues that the soul of the human is pure at birth. Humans are born with an equal tendency to do good or bad and are free to choose their own way. There is no question of original sin.

The claim of mythological descendance from Abraham should be significant to confirm that Judaism is myth, like all Abrahamic religions.

It is impossible for the rabbi to objectively judge. People who assume that they are the chosen people of God can only be judged as partisan, making them mentally taxed. Tzipi Hotovely, a thirty-six-year-old Orthodox Jewish woman and current deputy minister for the Foreign Affairs of Israel, bewildered the Israelite diplomats during a speech when she stated that the ground truth of the Bible granted the Jews the full right to return to their country, for which the Jews have the full right to place settlements in their homeland.[104] How can people with a certain development not waive their mythological traditions? What is even worse is that Hotovely and the like, in God's name, are the cause of inhumanity and prevent a peaceful solution in the Middle East. The majority in Israel are orthodox Jews who cart aside democracy and humanism; their government can only be condemned as bad as the jihadists.

C. Christianity

Christianity is a departure from Judaism that came up when a small flock of Jews in the first century BCE were discontented that there was no sign of the promised Messiah. The development began in the second half of the first century by a Jewish second temple sect of our era to become a full-fledged religion after three centuries around the world.[1] Christianity is a religion based on the Gospel and the life of the fictional prophet Jesus,[1] but it depends on belief in the Hebrew Bible. The Gospel maintains that through this belief, the barrier that sin has created between man and God is destroyed, and that allows God to change people and instil in them a new heart after his own will and the ability to do it. This is what the terms *reborn* or *saved* almost always refer to.

The faith in Jesus is narrated in the New Testament and is based on the Hebrew Bible. Because Judaism has no credibility, Christianity has no credibility—these religions are fabricated. The success of Christianity as a world religion is due to the charisma of the symbolic figure Jesus. In contrast to Christianity, the Hebrew

Bible (Old Testament) deals with a cruel deity, though doggedly defended by the Jews.[105]

Christianity has its roots in Judaism and shares much of the latter faith's ontology. Its central beliefs derive from the teachings of Jesus Christ, as presented in the New Testament. Life's purpose in Christianity is to seek divine salvation through the grace of God and intercession of Christ (cf. John 11:26). The New Testament speaks of God wanting to have a relationship with humans both in this life and in the life to come, which can happen only if one's sins are forgiven (John 3:16–21; 2 Peter 3:9).

In the Christian view, humankind was made in the image of God and perfect, but the fall of man caused the progeny of the first parents to inherit original sin. The sacrifice of Christ's passion, death, and resurrection provide the means for transcending that impure state (Romans 6:23). The means for doing so varies between diverse groups of Christians, but all rely on belief in Jesus, his work on the cross, and his resurrection as the fundamental starting point for a relationship with God. Faith in God is found in Ephesians 2:8–9—"For by grace you have been saved through faith; and that not of yourselves, it is the gift of God; not as a result of works, that no one should boast" (New American Standard Bible). A recent alternative Christian theological discourse interprets Jesus as revealing that the purpose of life is to elevate our compassionate response to human suffering. Nonetheless, the conventional Christian position is that people are justified by belief in the propitiatory sacrifice of Jesus's death on the cross.

In the *Westminster Shorter Catechism*, the first question is, "What is the chief end of man?" That is, "What is man's main purpose?" The answer is, "Man's chief end is to glorify God and enjoy him forever." God requires one to obey the revealed moral law, saying, "Love the Lord your God with all your heart, with all your soul, with all your strength, and with all your mind; and your neighbour as yourself." The *Baltimore Catechism* answers the question "Why did God make you?" by saying, "God made me know Him, to love Him, and to serve Him in this world, and to be happy with Him forever in heaven."[149]

The Apostle Paul also answers this question in his speech on the Areopagus in Athens.

> And He has made from one blood every nation of men to dwell on all the face of the earth, and has determined their pre-appointed times and the boundaries of their dwellings, so that they should seek the Lord, in the hope that they might grope for Him and find Him, though He is not far from each one of us.

Catholicism's way of thinking is better expressed through the principle and foundation of St Ignatius of Loyola.

> The human person is created to praise, reverence, and serve God Our Lord, and by doing so, to save his or her soul. All other things on the face of the earth are created for human beings to help them pursue the end for which they are created. It follows from this that one must use other created things, in so far as they help towards one's end, and free oneself from them, in so far as they are obstacles to one's end. To do this, we need to make ourselves indifferent to all created things, provided the matter is subject to our free choice and there is no other prohibition. Thus, as far as we are concerned, we should not want health more than illness, wealth more than poverty, fame more than disgrace, a long life more than a short one, and similarly for all the rest, but we should desire and choose only what helps us more towards the end for which we are created.

Original sin, also called ancestral sin, is the Christian doctrine of humanity's state of sin resulting from the fall of man by Adam, stemming from the latter's disobedience (desire) in Eden. Even the intelligent Augustine lowered himself to exert such rubbish. Only baptism can grant remission of original sin. This provoked the difficulty that dead born children are in limbo. The Church later relented in this matter, but only concerning unbaptised children. The state of limbo was maintained for unbaptised adults. The question of original sin and baptism are the principles which enable the Church to exert on a child a way to indoctrinate its belief.

A competitor of Christianity was Manichaeism, founded by Mani in ancient Persia. The religion initially had a large following but is now extinct. Mani taught that laozi, Buddha, Zoroaster, Hermes Trismegistus, Plato, and Jesus were messengers of God, and Mani himself the promised Messiah. It is a syncretic religion by elements of various religions. It is a dualism in which good (light) and evil (darkness) fight each other. Eschatology consists of a coming last judgement, where light and darkness are differentiated from each other forever. The concept of reincarnation is also available. After protection by the King Sjapoer I of Persia, Mani, on instigations of the priest caste of Persian magicians, was captured by his successor Bahram I and died from torture in 276 CE. The beliefs of Mani were based on local Mesopotamian Gnostic movements. Augustine of Hippo was for nine years a fervent supporter of Mani but became a fanatic adversary of Manichaeism.

Christianity has 2.1 billion adherents and has had Western civilisation in its grasp for two thousand years.

Christianity has its roots in Judaism and shares much of the latter faith's ontology. Its central beliefs derive from the teachings of Jesus Christ, as presented in the New Testament. Life's purpose in Christianity is to seek divine salvation through the grace of God and intercession of Christ (cf. John 11:26). The New Testament speaks of God wanting to have a relationship with humans both in this life and the life to come, which can happen only if one's sins are forgiven (John 3:16–21; 2 Peter 3:9).

D. Islam

Islam (submission) is a version of the Abrahamic religion from an Arabic perspective. The religion was introduced by Muhammad, who is regarded by Muslims as a prophet and the last messenger of God. Various verses of the Koran stress that a new religion is not founded by Muhammad. His task imposed by God only existed from the calls of creation and humanity, to return to the original religion that was distorted. Also, the judgement day was provided. Before the introduction of Islam, the Arab tribes that inhabited the Arabian Peninsula practised polytheism and worshipped spirits. Their idol was the Ka'aba, the black stone in the mosque of Mecca, where 360 gods were worshipped.[106, 107, 108]

Although one adopts (usually in contrast with Moses and Jesus) that Muhammad has existed historically, the lack of reliable first-hand sources prevents real historicity. The earliest known biography of Mohammad was 120 years written after his death by Ibn Ishaak. This biography, *The Life of God's Messenger,* is not surrendered and is kept in an edited version by a later author named Ibn Hisham, which dates back to the ninth century.

According to the Muslim tradition, Muhammad was a merchant, statesman, social reformer, philosopher, orator, teacher, general, and philanthropist. According to tradition, Mohammad would have withdrawn in 610 in the Hira cave to meditate, where he obtained visions of God through the Archangel Gabriel. He was designated as a prophet and ordered to spread the name of the one and only God, who was the same as that of Abraham and Jesus, but whose followers had lost their way and had distorted the messages of their prophet.[1] As a merchant, Muhammad had contact with Jewish and Christian tribes and gained knowledge about their life habits and religion.

The Koran, the holy book of Islam, is not written by Muhammad because he was illiterate and could not read or write, but according to tradition, it was entrusted to him by God verbatim. The Koran contains the creed, the admonitions, and the instructions that must be complied with by the Muslims, as well as the stories about other peoples and their fate and their messengers (Moses and Jesus).

The Koran is divided into 114 surahs (chapters) and 6226 ayah (verses), and it includes four religious doctrines.

- Monotheism, referring to the unity of God with the rejection of polytheism, as well as the other peoples associated with God (amongst others Surah the Cow, 22, 255, Imran 2, Maryam/Mary and Isa/Jesus, Surah Surah, the Inflated, and the Award 2, 23)
- Prophet confirmation of Muhammad, and the fact that the Koran is the word of God (amongst other things, the Surah Imran Award 1, 31-31, Surah the Bees 64, Surah Narration 85–87, Surah Ya Sin 2–3)
- Eschatology, referring to the resurrection and judgement day (amongst others, Surah Surah Ta Ha, the Tilt 187, Gemma Sin 51, Surah QAF Consultation 9, 42–43)
- Reward and punishment, usually represented by a contrast, where the faithful will be rewarded with paradise and infidels will be punished with hell in the hereafter (amongst other things, the Surah the Cow 81–82, the Byzantines 15–16, Surah 88–94, the Insurmountable Events Cheats 9–10). According to Islamic tradition, Muhammad entrusted the revelations to his followers, which they memorised by recitation and also partly wrote on parchment, bones, and wood. The first caliph, Abu Bakr, started gathering the loose fragments after the death of Mohammed, and the third caliph, Uthman ibn Affan, started the process of official codification. The oldest known full Koran likely dates from the late eighth to early ninth century.

In 1972, old Koran remnants were discovered in the great mosque of Sana'a, Yemen, coined as the Sana'a palimpsest, which the Yemen authorities subjected to a German research institute. A palimpsest is a manuscript page, either from a scroll or a book, from which the text has been scraped or washed off so that the page can be reused for another document. Parchment and other materials for writing or engraving upon were expensive to produce, and in the interest of economy, they were reused whenever possible. The manuscript is written on parchment and comprises two layers of text. The upper text conforms to the standard Uthmanic Koran, whereas the lower text contains many variations to the standard text. An edition of the lower text was published in 2012. A radiocarbon analysis has dated the parchment containing the lower text to before AD 671 with a 99 per cent accuracy, a 95.5 per cent probability of being older than AD 661, and a 75 per cent probability from before AD 646. The restoration project was under the leadership of German palaeontologist Gerd Rüdiger Puin. His research revealed examples of an unusual arrangement of the verses, minor text variations, rare styles of orthography, and artistic embellishments compared to the authorised version. This refutes the claim that the Koran was never changed once was it written down. The scriptures were written in the early Hijazi Arabic writings, a rare and (as far as is known) the oldest form of Arabic script, matching the pieces of the earliest known Koran fragments. The Islamic world did not appreciate at all the discovered differences. In 1987, Parvez Manzoor angrily wrote in the *Muslim World Book Review* that the researchers were out to undermine the faith of Muslims in the Koran. More than 15,000 Yemen sheets of the Koran were examined, cleaned, sorted, handled, and photographed via 35,000 photos of the manuscripts.

In a 1999 article in *Atlantic Monthly*, Gerd Puin is quoted as saying,

> My idea is that the Koran is a kind of cocktail of texts that were not all understood even at the time of Muhammad. Many of them may even be a hundred years older than Islam itself. Even within the Islamic traditions there is a huge body of contradictory information, including a significant Christian substrate; one can derive a whole Islamic anti-history from them if one wants.
>
> The Koran claims for itself that it is "mubeen", or "clear", but if you look at it, you will notice that every fifth sentence or so simply doesn't make

> sense. Many Muslims—and Orientalists—will tell you otherwise, of course, but the fact is that a fifth of the Koranic text is just incomprehensible. This is what has caused the traditional anxiety regarding translation. If the Koran is not comprehensible—if it can't even be understood in Arabic—then it's not translatable. People fear that. And since the Koran claims repeatedly to be clear but obviously is not—as even speakers of Arabic will tell you—there is a contradiction. Something else must be going on. (Observations on early Koran manuscripts in Sana'a)[50, 51]

The wife of Puin, Dr Elisabeth Debris, published in 2008 and 2009 detailed results of the analysis of the Sana'a manuscript DAM (dar almakthutat) 01.27-1, which proved that the manuscript was a twice-written palimpsest and shows that between the first and the second text, the language was still in movement (fluxion).[52]

The Koran is punctuated by themes and stories relating to Judaism (the Torah, Abraham, and Moses), and to a lesser extent Christianity (the Psalms, the Gospel, Jesus, and Mary), in such a way that the scientific consensus identifies the Koran as inspired from previous texts without taking everything literally. Amongst other things, Jesus is not accepted as the son of God, and neither is it believed that he was crucified. In addition to Judeo-Christian elements, Islam contains pagan traditions that preceded the teachings of Mohammed, such as the worship and ritual of the Ka'aba.

The surahs and verses of the Koran are very vague and lead to different interpretations.

What is not arguable is that the Koran focuses on the primitive Arab tribes of that time and not on the world's population. After all, the instructions apply to the tribes regarding the habits that they should resign and the new life habits which they should respect in future. The Islam accounts for many barbaric atrocities, such as the penalties provided for in the adopted Shariah, the legal system of the Koran, on theft (amputation of the limbs) and adultery (death by stoning). What is most distasteful is the treatment of the woman. Although the woman is supposed to be equivalent to the man, a set of restrictions is imposed on her that made it clear that she lives a second-class role. In Surah 34, the man is recorded as the agent or intermediary of the woman. The husband may admonish and punish the woman with a slight branch without hurting her. The legal status of the woman is brought down: she is forbidden to marry an unbeliever; the woman has fewer rights than the man; in court the testimony of the woman is worth half of the man. In the Cow Surah, verse 281, it is stated that two women in the place of one man must testify in case "one of the two women would be mistaken"—in other words, a woman is less believable. Finally, man can have up to four wives, female slaves not counted. Throughout the centuries, the Islamic potentates kept harems.

The worst practitioners of the Islam faith are the Afghans who have contempt for womanhood. They consider education of women utterly waste and forbid the education of girls above the age of twelve.

Wearing a headscarf by Muslim women is a controversial issue in the West. To date, no Muslim is in doubt that the woman should wear a headscarf, whereas fifty years ago this was not explicitly so.

Fundamentalism in Islam is now rampant, which results in radicalisation motivated by the increasing hatred of Islam for the West, in particular the United States. There are several different interpretations of whether the headscarf is an obligation for the Muslimah. In Surah the Party Hosts 59 it is mentioned, "O Prophet! Say to your wives and your daughters and the women of the believers that they portion her shawl over her head to hang. This is better, so that they may be distinguished and not molested. And god is forgiving, merciful". Surah the Light 31 and several Ahadith talk of the requirement to wear head scarves and veils for faithful women. In several European countries, there is a headscarf ban in public functions, for violation of neutrality in a secular state. The Catholics tend to contest the ban to promote their own religion. Socialists throw all their ideology (democracy, separation of church and state, equality of women) overboard in order to be able to recruit Muslims based on plurality.

In addition to the Koran, sacred writings are the Sunnah (later included in the Hadith) and the Shariah. The Sunnah includes the writings that describe the life of Muhammad and his behaviours and actions that were recorded by his companions in order to serve as a guide in life. It comes to oral traditions which were patchily recorded more than a hundred years after the death of Mohammed. The danger of oral traditions is that something is lost with each tradition, and something is added that originally did not exist. Nevertheless, the Muslims believe that the Sunnah are rules in so far as they are not contradicted by the Koran. In the Shariah, based on the Koran and the Hadith, Islamic religious law is enacted. The Shariah contains all the aspects of daily life, including politics treated as the subject of religiosity, economics, banking, business, contracts, family, sexuality, hygiene, and social issues. It is a barbaric law, including amputation of the limbs in the event of theft, death by stoning in the case of adultery, and hanging in case of murder when the murderer is unable able to pay compensation to the relatives of the victim. The introduction or reintroduction of the Shariah is the leitmotif of most Muslims, which to the Western civilisation is repulsive.[1] Islam is the least valuable religion of Abrahamic religions. The religion is paradoxical and lacking charisma. Muslims are a fundamentalist and fanatical set, and so it is difficult to agree with them. Religions have always been a plague that thwart democracy and threaten world peace, and Islam is the worst of all.

The Koran includes, in addition to grove incongruities, beneficial use of urine of camels, prohibition to wearing gold (silver is allowed) and breastfeeding by women to strange men, and all sorts of alarming instructions. The concept of Taqiyya (Koran 2:195; 4:29; 40:28) reveals the ambiguity of Islam on truth and lie in order to allow the Muslims to defend themselves and manifest themselves in front of infidels. The Koran is the word of God, but is God then a cheat?

Islam states sign international agreements, but at the same time they close agreement to treaties that go against the signed international conventions and in which all applications of the Koran in all its aspects are confirmed.[1] Much worse is Surah 8:39, relating to the holy jihad: the war against the infidels continues until "all the chaos ends and all religion belongs to Allah". According to Surah 60:4, enmity and hatred will always exist between Muslims and non-Muslims "until you believe in Allah".

Fortunately, the influence of religions wanes in most countries, but far too slowly because education fails in many parts of the world or is inhibited in the Middle East.

When Islamic history is consulted, it is striking to find that in the Islamic golden age, which lasted from about 750 to 1257 CE, the authorities were particularly indulgent in their treatment of unbelievers. This happened because the Islamic philosophers and scientists delivered progressive work. The golden age is characterised by using glass, metal, textiles, and ceramics. Significant contributions to the field of science by Islamic scholars were the development of trigonometry, optics, mathematics, astronomy, anatomy, ophthalmology, pharmacology, physiology, and surgery. During

the Islamic golden age came many eminent scholars (Al-Kindy, Al-Farabi, Avicenna, and Averroës) who studied Greek philosophy and Neoplatonism and who affected the non-religious aspects of both the Islamic and Christian world. They exacted the teachings of Socrates, Plato and Aristotle, as well as Neoplatonism, to combine with other ideas of the Islam. The translations of the Arabic philosophy in Latin contributed to the European philosophy, such as that of Thomas of Aquino. The cosmological argument in theology and philosophy is cited to demonstrate the existence of God (God's proof). The dialectic is that there must have been a first cause of all that exists. The causality principle (the first cause) is, according to Aristotle, "an immovable mover" without understanding God's existence. In his work *Physics* (VIII, 2), Aristotle posits, "there has never been a time there was no movement and there will never be a time that there is no movement." This postulate is reminiscent of the theoretical physicist Lawrence Krauss with his physicist field in which the Higgs particle manifests and creates energy and matter as the origin of the universe.[53]

Many medieval Muslim thinkers pursued humanistic, rational, and scientific discourses in their search for knowledge, meaning, and values. A wide range of Islamic writings on love, poetry, history, and philosophical theology show that medieval Islamic thought was open to the humanistic ideas of individualism, occasional secularism, scepticism, and liberalism.[73]

According to Imad-ad-Dean Ahmad, Palestinian American scholar, another reason the Islamic world flourished during the Middle Ages was an early emphasis on freedom of speech, as summarised by Al-Hashimi (a cousin of Caliph al-Ma'mun) in the following letter to one of the religious opponents he was attempting to convert through reason.[74]

> Bring forward all the arguments you wish and say whatever you please and speak your mind freely. Now that you are safe and free to say whatever you please appoint some arbitrator who will impartially judge between us and lean only towards the truth and be free from the empery of passion, and that arbitrator shall be Reason, whereby God makes us responsible for our own rewards and punishments. Herein I have dealt justly with you and have given you full security and am ready to accept whatever decision Reason may give for me or against me. For "There is no compulsion in religion" (Koran 2:256) and I have only invited you to accept our faith willingly and of your own accord and have pointed out the hideousness of your present belief. Peace be with you and the blessings of God!

What a great pity that Islamic humanism lasted only a short golden period and disappeared due to the lack later of erudite philosophers. The teachings returned to the original conservative form and peak today to radical fundamentalism.

E. Considerations

The essence of religion is hard to define. The basic structure of theism is essentially a distinction between a transcendent deity and all else, between the creator and his creation, and between God and man.

The philosopher Simplicius of Cilicia was the last pagan philosopher and connoisseur of Aristotle. He explained Aristotle in disambiguation pages in a non-Christian way without openly attacking the Christian doctrines. He was in 524 banned by Christian Emperor Justinian, along with the conclusion of the Athenian philosophical school. The Kalam argument is the version of the cosmological argument formulated by the Islamic thinkers during the golden age of Islam. It was ushered in by Al-Kindy and refined by Al-Farabi, Avicenna, and Averrous. The Kalam argument is built on the following three premises.

- Everything that begins has to exist for its existence
- The universe began to exist
- Therefore, the universe has cause for its existence

There may be, according to the Kalam argument, two causes of the existence of the universe: an object (a thing) or a subject (consciousness). But because an object is abstract and causally inert, it can cause nothing. Should the universe be originally caused by an intangible consciousness that God is? William Lane Craig is a Protestant analytical philosopher who defends the Kalam argument. However, he drowns in metaphysical considerations which lack any scientific basis. Can one have respect for somebody who, proclaiming himself a divine command theorist, believes that God had the moral right to command the slaughter of the Canaanites if they refused to leave their land, as depicted in the book of Deuteronomy? Craig was put to point severely through his apparent catechism by the scientist Lawrence Krauss and by acclaimed journalist and author Christopher Hitchens, who in all his books and countless articles campaigned for antitheism. Hitchens was an important friend of the scientists

Dawkins and Krauss, who from New York to Melbourne campaigned for atheism. Hitchens is referred to by believers (amongst whom are the conservative Theodore Dalrymple) and taunted as a hedonist. He died after oesophageal cancer from by violent smoking and excessive alcohol consumption.

For Western culture, Arab philosopher Averrous was certainly the most important figure. He was not only the pre-eminent Aristotle commentator but was also the founding father of secular thought in Western Europe. He was a Homo *universale*, a master of Islamic philosophy, theology, Maliki law, Islamic jurisprudence, logic, psychology, politics, medicine, astronomy, geography, mathematics, physics, and celestial mechanics. In his most important philosophical work, *Gibberish of the Entangled,* he refuted the work of Al-Ghazali's *Gibberish of the Philosophers* and was in trouble with the spiritual government.[54] In another work, *The Final Treatise*, he explicitly covered what in Al-Ghazali's eyes was a contradiction between the revelations of Muhammad and conclusions of the philosophers. According to Averrous, there is no difference between religion and philosophy, both lead to the truth. He rejected the merger of Plato and Aristotle's ideas, which were mistakenly due to the Neoplatonic philosophers Plotinus and Proclus. He was exiled to Morocco because of his philosophy, which was considered not in accordance with the Islam. Many of his works are permanently lost due to the censorship exercised by radical Muslims.

The decline of the Islamic culture found a start with the Crusades of the eleventh and twelfth centuries, but it knew the greatest threat from the Mongolian Empire, first led by Hulagu Khan and later under the leadership of Dzengis Khan, who destroyed Baghdad in 1258. In the Iberian Peninsula, in 1482 the Catholic monarchs retook the Emirate of Granada, and so the Golden Islamic era knew a full expiration. Al-Ghazali, Persian philosopher and soeffist (mystical and fundamentalist movement in Islam), has with his work *The Philosophers* initiated the confusion of the stagnation and decline in Islam.[54] The conservative Al-Ghazali disputed causality because everything is done by hand and will of God. He found it waste and sin of intellect to approach God through philosophy, exerting a brake on scientific progress. In Islam itself, he enjoys high regard and is considered the most important teacher of Islam after Muhammad. Al-Ghazali condemned Socrates and Plato as corrupted sinners. All intellect needed to be harnessed to the divine laws, the Sharia, extracted from the Koran, the Sunnah, and the Hadith. The influence of Al-Ghazali as an anti-rationalist is still valid in fundamental and radical circles. Kemal Atatürk, the first Turkish president who led his country out of the middle ages, deemed it necessary to ban his work. The present president, Erdogan, is leading his country back to conservatism. Once an example for European culture, after the fall of Baghdad and Granada, Islam culture began to stagnate. There was a flare with the Ottoman Empire and a low point with the colonisation by European countries of North Africa and the Middle East. When colonisation ended in the middle twentieth century, there were prospects for a rebirth of Islamic culture. Unfortunately, this was not realised because of the phenomenon of Zionism and the creation of an Israeli State with the approval of the West. The small but powerful state of Israel managed to defend itself against the Allied Arab States. The humiliation of the Arabs led to frustration and bitterness. Salvation was searched for in the dark passages of the Koran in order to find a form of resistance. Fundamentalism prevailed and resulted in radicalisation and terrorism. All this was also facilitated by the failure of the Arab immigration in Europe that took place from on 1950. The Islamists could not integrate and gathered in ghettos, where they involved in practising their own habits, morals, and religion. The natives of Europe have taken vast pains to assimilate the immigrants without looking down upon them, yet they have some scepticism on this strange race. The children and grandchildren of the Muslims do poorly in school. They leave school without qualifications and find no work. They hang around and form a breeding ground for radicalisation. Willy-nilly, there is a serious problem that will culminate in a world conflict if Islam remains unchecked. Black people do not have the same problem to integration. US President Obama states, "Religion is not the enemy, but those who exploit the religion." If there were no religions, there would be no rancour or radicalisation. The United States consists mainly of believers. All religions are a plague, and Islam is the bubonic plague. No politician has the honesty to proclaim the truth, fearful of being elected. The faith is still encapsulated in man and certainly in the United States. The truth is different because the history tells a different story: the Crusades, the reconquest of Granada by Spaniards on the Islamists, the genocide of the Albigenses (Cathars) by the Catholic Church, the Thirty Years' War between Christians and Protestants in Germany, the eternal battles between Sunni and Shia, the religious war between Christians and Protestants in Northern Ireland, and the failure of Pope John Paul II to intervene when the Catholic Hutus murdered a million Tutsis in Rwanda.

People are in general not mentally gifted. Even developed people enthuse about life stands that baffle them. Centuries of indoctrination prevent them from objective reasoning. One says that the Bible is the most widely read book, but I have yet to encounter a person on the European continent, priests excepted, who reads the Bible. The same goes for Shakespeare, although he wrote the most ingenious literature ever written, like "To be or not to be" and "Man is a poor player that struts and frets his hour upon the stage and then is heard no more". One can hardly regard humans as wise when they need a supernatural deity to get through life. However, there is hope!

We can accept that it is difficult for uneducated people to surrender the indoctrinated deity. Consciousness must be able to undergo the thought process, while the life environment and the social situation make it difficult. Otherwise there lies the condition of the bourgeoisie or the establishment for whom no excuse exists. This layer of the population has a reasonable development, is usually proud of her Christian beliefs, but is vain. These people are too lazy for a thought process that leads them further than the Christ figure to reach the concept of the Big Bang and its consequences. They are so smug that they will look at you as though it thunders in Cologne. Their civilisation is a thin veneer for seeing the outside world, but their introspective is minimal. They look no further than the length of their noses. The messenger, whether fictitious, of their fictional deity (Moses, Zoroaster, Christ, Mohammad, Bahi i, Joseph Smith, and L. R. Hubbard) is sufficient to believe, but for the cause of the

Big Bang, outside a divine spark and the composition of the space, they find it unnecessary to investigate. They are only too glad to limit themselves to ostrich politics, by which their dilettantism and hypocrisy are expressed. Many groups of people in the world are the protagonists of narrow-mindedness, which is the why it is so difficult for people to agree with each other.

Typical reasons for adherence to religion include the following.

- Belief in God is seen by some to be necessary for moral behaviour.
- Many people consider religious practises to be serene, beautiful, and conducive to religious experiences, which in turn support religious beliefs.
- Organised religions promote a sense of community amongst their followers, and the moral and cultural common ground of these communities makes them attractive to people with the same values. Indeed, while religious beliefs and practises are usually connected, some individuals with substantially secular beliefs still participate in religious practises for cultural reasons.
- Each religion asserts that it is a means by which its adherents may come into closer contact with God, truth, and spiritual power. They all promise to free adherents from spiritual bondage and bring them into spiritual freedom. It naturally follows that religion, which frees its adherents from deception, sin, and spiritual death, will have significant mental health benefits.

Typical reasons for rejection of religion include the following.

- The fundamental doctrines of religions are considered to be illogical, contrary to experience, or unsupported by sufficient evidence, and they are rejected for those reasons. Even some believers may have difficulty accepting particular religious assertions or doctrines. Some people believe the body of evidence available to humans to be insufficient to justify certain religious beliefs. They may thus disagree with religious interpretations of ethics and human purpose, or various creation myths. This reason has perhaps been aggravated by the protestations of some fundamentalist Christians.

- Some religions include beliefs that certain groups of people are inferior or sinful and deserve contempt, persecution, or even death, and that non-believers will be punished for their unbelief in an afterlife.
- The values that a specific religion promotes (e.g., Islamic attitudes towards women) are unacceptable. This includes the proposition that those who do not believe will go to hell or be damned.
- The maintenance of life and the achievement of self-esteem require a person the fullest exercise of reason—but morality, which people are taught, rests on and requires faith.
- Deities are concepts invented by ignorant humans to explain all they do not understand. From that grew the institutions of religions, who enslaved the people.

CHAPTER 21

Hereafter

The hereafter (afterlife) is a representation of a life after death. It is peculiar to all religions and a placebo for people in their fear of death. In addition to a religious understanding, it also holds a spiritual and metaphysical understanding involving that the current, not physical human life does not end at death but continues in a different form after dying. There is usually suggested in religion the idea that something exists as the soul in the body of a human and is immortal. It's all very vague and confusing, and all the more ludicrous from one religion to the next.

The lifespan of man is, in the perspective of the universe, extremely minimal. Although the reproduction of human beings seems to expand life to an infinite continuation, the very short duration of the human being on Earth is regarded by the religious believers purely as a run-up to eternal life, in which case it is incomprehensible that death is feared. Consequently, these people believe that life on Earth has little meaning and constitutes a test to determine whether one is eligible for eternal life. However, religions remain vague on the matter of death, whether death results in a possible resurrection or reincarnation, or in a continuation of life in the form of a soul without any form. According to the most widely used meaning in religions, philosophy, and mythology, the soul is the non-material, spiritual component of a living being. In another sense (rather an esoteric concept), the soul is the carrier, the expression or the vehicle of the ego or eternal spirit. Already in antiquity, the soul was defined. According to Plato, the soul is the moral and intellectual itself; this is in contrast to the passions and lust, including fun and all kinds of sensory aspects of human life. Aristotle added to the understanding of Plato a divine or supernatural aspect, the *intellectus agens*. The concept of soul is found in Egyptian mythology. Buddhism denies the existence of a permanent soul. In Hinduism, the soul is a synonym of "the universal" now, with the soul the immaterial part of man, what the rational is for the individual act and life of human. It constitutes the "true self" of the individual. It also defines the soul as the set of all non-material components of the human: consciousness, self-awareness, character, thinking, intuition, experience, will, life, and desire. The soul as an immaterial entity cannot be scientifically demonstrated.

The philosophy of life (life stand) is a vision of life regarding the meaning of life, its value, and how it should be lived. The philosophy of life is an essential part of the life of the believers, who would be distraught without the fate of the possible existence of an afterlife. Theists of any denomination also believe in some sort of afterlife when they die.

The sciences focus on phenomena that are falsifiable or verifiable and which can be derived on rational grounds. The soul concept can of course be approached scientifically in terms of concept, but it's rather descriptive or from a linguistic perspective. However, by the progress of the sciences and mainly in psychology, genetics, and neurology, the idea of the soul is yesteryear and rendered out of date, and yet it's very logical in view of the many different opinions and often mystical packaging. Modern neurologists associate the soul of man with his temperament and personality, and they situate the phenomenon of the soul in the functioning of the frontal lobe. There, it is assumed that the constant interaction between the frontal brain lobe, which allows for thinking, and the limbic system, which controls our emotions and instincts, are responsible for the choice of trading between good and evil. The intended choice inevitably differs from person to person and depends on many factors such as heredity, education, and environment. The great difficulty is how to inform people properly, pointing out the bamboozlement which in the past has occurred and which the established religions are certainly not prepared to do.

The term *soul* is interpreted differently by the various religions. All religions, usually in varied form, promise that their God ensures eternal life. However, they don't agree whether the afterlife holds a spiritual or material life. In any case, it would be for most believers a heavy disappointment if the promise of an afterlife is not realised, ensuring a life of much better quality than the one enjoyed on Earth. Another question mark is whether there is a resurrection that happens from the worn body, whether there is granted a new young body, or whether it is the soul that survives (as in Christianity).

The believers of the Abrahamic religions believe in a further existence of the soul, whereas Hindus and Buddhists believe in reincarnation. Both types of believers hold that the status of an afterlife is dependent on the assessment of one's life on Earth.

There was quite an evolution in the religious idea of a life hereafter. Jewish eschatology is concerned with events that will happen at the end of days (end of times), according to the Hebrew Bible (Tanakh) and Jewish tradition. The eschatology covers the ingathering of the exiled diaspora, the coming of the Jewish Messiah, afterlife, and the revival of the death (Isaiah 26:19). The tenets of the Jewish eschatology are found in the books of Isaiah, Jeremiah, and Ezekiel of the Tanakh and in the Talmud.

In writings of Judaism (later included in the Tanakh), the place of the dead is Sheol. In Ecclesiae (Ecclesiastes 3:19–21 NKJV), one finds the funeral ritual "all living things are from dust and to dust shall perish". It is the Talmud that holds the train of thought of the hereafter. After death, the soul is judged. The previous life is examined as to whether the soul is entitled to the upcoming world (the world to come). A doctrine as the eternal curse is not to be found in Judaism. The afterlife of Judaism is vague but less ludicrous than those of Christianity and of Islam. The essence of Judaism is waiting for the Messiah who will usher in a new world. There is disagreement whether there is reincarnation because clear texts on this subject are missing in Judaism. The Zohar, the work of Jewish mysticism, mentions reincarnation several times without being specific. The non-Kabbalists suggest reincarnation. Reincarnation is incompatible with the new world of the expected Messiah. The hereafter is the perspective in which all religions are biting.

In the Judaic world view, the meaning of life is to elevate the physical world (Olam HaZeh) and prepare it for the world to come (Olam HaBa), the messianic era. This is called Tikkun Olam ("Fixing the World"). Olam HaBa can also mean the spiritual afterlife, and there is debate concerning the eschatological order. However, Judaism is not focused on personal salvation but on communal (between man and man) and individual (between man and God) spiritualised actions in this world.

The end of the world is a belief held by the Jews and by the early Christians. After the end of the world, a new world is predicted, which will be inaugurated by the Messiah—not a godhead but of the line of King David (world of tribes), who shall restore the former glory of Israel. All nations will recognise that the God of Israel is the only true God, who will resurrect the dead and create a new heaven and a new earth. All these fables could not stand the wear and tear of time, and new insights and interpretations came about to give some rationality to the beliefs. The advent of a Messiah remains the main tenet and is not disputed by believers. Neither is an afterlife, but the world beyond is difficult for human understanding. The resurrection of the dead is heavily divided: some reject it, and others speak of supernatural events culminating in a bodily resurrection of the dead. Essenes believed in the immortality of the soul. The day of judgement is disputed. Some rabbis hold that there will be such a day following the resurrection of the dead. Others hold that there is no need for that because of the yearly atonement, or it only applies to the Gentile nations.

Surely one cannot believe the nonsense contained in the Talmud, the Midrash, and the Kabbalistic work the Zohar, when they state that the deadline by which the Messiah must appear is six thousand years from the creation of the earth. Orthodox and Hasidic Jews believe that the Hebrew calendar dates back from the time of creation. The year 2009–2010 (the Hebrew New Year begins during

September or the beginning of October) of the Gregorian calendar corresponds to the Hebrew year 5770. This is all a clear example of the fiction of religion and of the absurdity to which it leads.

The Rabbi Maimonides, the best known and most highly regarded theologian of post-Talmud Judaism, had a solution for the absurdity of tangible or intangible resurrection. He argued that resurrection was physical but temporarily, until a new world came about by the coming of the Messiah. This divination stresses the extent to which Maimonides was willing to tell bullshit to defend his theodicy. Maimonides was far from being a humanist. In his book (translated into English) *The Guide to the Perplexed,* concerning unbelievers he condemned Turkish and black nomadic people as having a nature of mute animals.

In Christianity, the soul is considered the indivisible and immortal part of man, his essence. In metaphysics, essence is the meaning of the soul and is used as a synonym. According to Soren Kierkegaard, the emphasis of essence is on nature, but there is no human orientation that determines his character. Jean-Paul Sartre, the more materialistic existentialist, promoted the teaching of Kierkegaard by flatly refuting any metaphysical essence and soul while only recognising the mere existence, with attributes of the essence.

In Christianity, man is spirit, soul, and body, and the body constitutes the packaging. That part of man, which in the secular psychology is referred to as the “unaware” or “subconscious”, is in Christianity classified as spirit. The spirit knows features as intuition, conscience, and God consciousness, while the soul recognises functions as feeling, thought, and will. In short, the soul is the personality of the man and makes all the difference with animals and plants. Because spirit, soul, and body belong together and form one, the Christians consider death as unnatural, imposed by God as punishment for the original sin for violation of God’s command. According to Ecclesiastes 12:7 of the Old Testament (Tanakh), returns the spirit, man at death, back to God who has given it, while the soul descends into Hades.

In his second letter to the Corinthians, the apostle Paul declared that the body is transient but not the spirit. The hereafter will consist of disembodied spirits that have no feelings. His presentation of the hereafter is as unappealing as the one of physical resurrection touted by the other Abrahamic religions because no one can be enchanted by an existence without feelings. What signifies a life without feelings? Surely not much.

In the creed of the first Council of Nicea of the Christian Church in 325, it is stated that "we look forward to the resurrection of the dead and to the life of the world to come". What sort of life!

The Christian eschatology deals with death, the intermediate status, heaven, hell, the second coming of Christ, the resurrection of the dead, and the last judgement. The latter examines life on Earth by the deceased whether he has lived in accordance with Christian ethics. Eternal curse is the fate of the sinner. It is conspicuous that the holy writings sometimes make mention of the resurrection of the dead, and on the other hand that it has taken vast pains regarding the evaluation of the soul of the deceased. Apparently, one does not know very well how the life hereafter should be dressed. In any case, the soul is immaterial, and the afterlife is something entirely different from this on Earth. When Jesus was questioned by the Sadducees about the spouses who were married more than once, he answered that the question was irrelevant because the soul is immaterial and knows no sex urge.[56] The notion of purgatory is associated particularly with the Catholic Church. In the Catholic Church, all those who die in God's grace, but still imperfectly purified, are indeed assured of their eternal salvation, but after death they must undergo a certain form of purification to achieve the joy of heaven. Certain texts of scripture speak of "cleansing fire", which is preferred to purgatory because other religions reject the notion of purgatory. The notion of purgatory, Limbo, which was elaborated upon by theologians beginning in the Middle Ages, was never recognised as a dogma of the Roman Catholic Church, though it was much debated within the church. Limbo is a theory, introduced by Pope Gregory the Great in 593, that unbaptised but innocent souls, such as those of infants, virtuous people who lived before Jesus Christ was born, or those that die before baptism was inaugurated exist in neither heaven nor hell. Therefore, these innocent souls did not merit the beatific vision, but neither did they merit punishment. They bear the original sin, and so they are generally seen as existing in a state of natural, but not supernatural, happiness until the end of time. It means that the millions of people of preceding civilisations exist, bodily or not, in a place which is not heaven or hell but in complete happiness. It really is astounding fiction which the Church could hardly condone in modern times. On 21 April 2007, Pope Benedict XVII declared the theory of Limbo to be void, but only in case of unbaptised dead children. Augustine, confronted with the question, esteemed (notwithstanding his intellect) that only baptism can erase original sin. He answered affirmative but added that the babies would get a mild punishment. Is anyone still in doubt that the hereafter is complete nonsense?

Islam is a mixture of Jewish and Christian eschatology. In the Koran is the description of the lush Garden of Eden. regarded purely as ornate. Paradise (*Jannah*) has seven levels and is the reward to have lived in accordance with the commandments of Allah as proclaimed by the Prophet. Hell (*Jahannam*) likewise has seven levels, depending on the severity of the sinful life. The purpose of life is worship of the creator of heaven and Earth. The world is destined to perish, whereupon the day of reckoning for the risen comes. The last day of the world is at the same time the day of resurrection.

The Koran shows a garden with plenty of water (important for desert peoples) and the disposal of houris (perpetual virgins with black eyes) for the sexual needs of the faithful. The houris are the lure used by radical Muslims terrorists to recruit suicide bombers. An afterlife is a fictitious place invented by man to sublimate the death anxiety.

It is odd that the Koran, by contrast with the Gospel where Christ argued that there is no place in heaven for sex desires, expressly states that the Muslim men will be fully sexually satisfied.

The afterlife is a stupid invention for stupid people who need a placebo to survive the hardship of life.

CHAPTER 22

Truth and Belief

Truth is the fact or reality which is not disputed. Secondary, it can be fidelity to an original or to a standard or ideal.[109]

Various theories and views of truth continue to be debated amongst scholars, philosophers, and theologians.

The analytical philosopher Richard Kirkham wrote a much-cited *Theories of Truth* in 1992, describing the largely overlooked fact that the various theories of truth proposed through the centuries are not really all competitors of each other because they are often intended to answer distinct questions about truth.[154] Language and words are means by which humans convey information to one another, and the method used to determine what is a "truth" is termed a criterion of truth. There are differing claims on such questions as what constitutes truth: what things are truth bearers capable of being true or false; how to define and identify truth; the roles that faith-based and empirically based knowledge play; and whether truth is subjective or objective, relative, or absolute. It is the opposite of truth falsehood or lie which gives more meaning to truth.

According to Kirkham, truths can have a limited validity depending on the frame of reference: the statement "one and one is two" is valid for numbers in the decimal number system, but not for binary numbers. Similarly, a truth can depend on the person: the statement "Fish is delicious" applies to the one, though for the other it does not. The verdict "person A likes fish" takes these into account.

Opposite relativism or contextualise state that truth depends on the context; there are also universalist beliefs which, for example, hold that there is always an "overarching truth" that applies in all circumstances, and that apparently contradictory truths (or axioms) can reconcile with each other at a higher level.

The classical definition of knowledge, described but not ultimately endorsed by Plato, specifies that a statement must meet three criteria in order to be considered knowledge: it must be justified, true, and believed.

Epistemologists argue over whether belief is the proper truth-bearer.

In common speech, a statement of belief is typically an expression of faith and/or trust in a person, power, or another entity. Although it includes such traditional views, epistemology is also concerned with what we believe. This includes the truth and everything else we accept as true for ourselves from a cognitive point of view.

Whether someone's belief is true is not a prerequisite for the belief itself.

There is the belief that a saying or reasoning is true. The conviction can be weaklier expressed if one speaks of sights, consider, think, assume, believe, trust, postulate, and delusions. The claim of rejection does not necessarily mean that the inverse theorem is adopted. If someone does not accept the claim "God does not exist: as true, it doesn't necessary follow that those claiming "God does not exist" is true. According to the philosopher Martin Heidegger, the term *believe* "has no place in thinking" (*Der Glauben hat keinen Platz im Thinking*).[57] On the other hand, why does Heidegger believe in God, or does he consider that God is beyond discussion?

Reality is the conjectured state of things as they actually exist, rather than as they appear or might be imagined. Metaphysics is the philosophical doctrine that does not examine the reality as coming from data from sensory perceptions (physics), but goes in search of the essence of that reality—a reality that goes out over the matter. In philosophy, essence is the attribute or set of attributes that make an entity or substance what it fundamentally holds, and which it has by necessity, and without which it loses its identity. In contrast to accident, essence is a property that provides the entity or substance contingency.

Friedrich Nietzsche famously and beautifully suggested that an ancient, metaphysical belief in the divinity of truth lies at the heart of and has served as the foundation for the entire subsequent Western intellectual tradition.

> But you will have gathered what I am getting at, namely, that it is still a metaphysical faith on which our faith in science rests--that even we knowers of today, we godless anti-metaphysicians still take our fire too, from the flame lit by the thousand-year old faith, the Christian faith which was also Plato's faith, that God is Truth; that truth is 'Divine'.[150]

An analytic truth is a statement whose truth value is dependent on the meaning of the statement itself. An example is, "All bachelors are unmarried." This theorem is true because of the meaning of the word bachelor. Bachelor means unmarried man. In a language where bachelor would stand for something other than an unmarried man, it would not (always) be true.[156]

There are synthetic truths, as in the sentence "All bachelors are happy". A synthetic truth is the truth value not determined by the ruling itself and its meaning, but by something outside of the ruling. Often it is the reality that determines whether the pronunciation may or may not be true. "All bachelors are happy" is true if all actual bachelors in the world are effective happy.

Necessary truths are called those statements that are true in all possible cases. Also, one can say that they are the statements where the denial (negation) would lead to a logical contradiction—for example, "All circles are round." (If the object were not round, it would be no circle).

There are also contingent truths, which are not in all possible cases true but only in some cases. It is thus about statements whose denial not necessarily leads to a logical contradiction. An example: "The number of planets is equal to eight."

The question of what truth is, is a classic question in philosophy. In Western philosophy, the first attempts of analysis of the concept of truth were already found within ancient philosophy. According to Plato, truth concerns ideas. Truth for Plato, could have nothing to do with the actual world which man sees because this is increasingly variable and transient. But on the other hand, truth must rather be something stable and eternal. Central is the opposition between truth and appearance.

Aristotle proposed a classical definition of truth: "Truth of something is saying that it is so, and something that it is not the case, saying that it's not." This is a first formulation of the correspondence theory, which remained very dominant throughout the history of philosophy. For example, in the medieval philosophy truth was defined as an agreement between sense (knowledge) and facts (reality).

Correspondence theories emphasise that true beliefs and true statements correspond to the actual sitation. This type of theory stresses a relationship between thoughts or statements on one hand and things or objects on the other. It is a traditional model tracing its origins to ancient Greek philosophers. This class of theories holds that the truth or the falsity of representation is determined in principle entirely by how it relates to things, as well as by whether it accurately describes those things. An example of correspondence theory is the statement by the thirteenth-century philosopher and theologian Thomas Aquinas: *Veritas est adaequatio rei et intellectus* (Truth is the equation of things and intellect). Correspondence theory centres heavily around the assumption that truth is a matter of accurately copying what is known as objective reality and then representing it in thoughts, words, and other symbols. Many modern theorists have stated that this ideal cannot be achieved without analysing additional factors. For example, language plays a role in that all languages have words to represent concepts that are virtually undefined in other languages. The German word *zeitgeist* is one such example: one who speaks or understands the language may "know" what it means, but any translation of the word apparently fails to accurately capture its full meaning. (This is a problem with many abstract words, especially those derived in agglutinative languages.)

Within the modern and contemporary philosophy, this theory started being questioned. Immanuel Kant brings the concept of truth, for example, related to his understanding of *a priori* (in advance) and means concepts of which the meaning is immediately obvious. These concepts are completely independent of personal experience because the things of experience are not accessible, like the things of the mind, directly by reason: they have, after all, the need of the mediation of the experience (cf. his distinction between the *intellectus ectypus* versus the *intellectus archetypus*). Kant notes what exists is no general criterion for "truth" outside the predicate statements of truth or falsity. If one still tries to formulate such a general criterion for truth anyway (which would say something about truth outside the predicate statements), then one would have to say something about knowledge while abstracting it of its concrete objects. But if one abstracts of all objects, then there is no more knowledge because knowledge is knowledge about objects. That knowledge exists in the form of predicate statements. (*Kritik der reinen Vernunft*, B, 83).

A nominal definition explains the meaning of a linguistic expression. A real or actual definition describes the essence of certain objects and allows us to determine whether a part falls within the definition. Kant considers that the definition of truth is only nominal and therefore cannot be used to determine whether certain statements really add up. According to Kant, the ancient sceptics were critical of the logicians who, by means of only a nominal definition of truth, judged which statements were right. They tried something that is "impossible without qualification and for every man".

Immanuel Kant endorses a definition of truth along the lines of the correspondence theory of truth. Kant writes in the *Critique of Pure Reason*, "The nominal definition of truth, namely that it is the agreement of cognition with its object, is here granted and presupposed." However, Kant denies that this correspondence definition of truth provides us with a test or criterion to establish which judgements are true. Kant states in his logic lectures,

> Truth, it is said, consists in the agreement of cognition with its object. In consequence of this mere nominal definition, my cognition, to count as true, is supposed to agree with its object. Now I can compare the object with my cognition, however, only by cognizing it. Hence my cognition is supposed to confirm itself, which is far short of being sufficient for truth. For since the object is outside me, the cognition in me, all I can ever pass judgement on is whether my cognition of the object agrees with my cognition of the object. The ancients called such a circle in explanation dialectic. And actually the logicians were always reproached with this mistake by the sceptics, who observed that with this definition of truth it is just as when someone makes a statement before a court and in doing so appeals to a witness with whom no one is acquainted, but who wants to establish his credibility by maintaining that the one who called him as witness is an honest man. The accusation was grounded too. Only the solution of the indicated problem is impossible without qualification and for every man.

This passage makes use of his distinction between nominal and real definitions. A nominal definition explains the meaning of a linguistic expression. A real definition describes the essence of certain objects and enables us to determine whether any given item falls within the definition.

The political philosopher Giambattista Vico was amongst the first to claim that history and culture were man-made. Vico's epistemological orientation gathers the most diverse rays and unfolds in one axiom: *verum ipsum factum* (truth itself is constructed).

Hegel and Marx were amongst other early proponents of the premise that the truth is or can be socially constructed. Marx, like many critical theorists who followed him, did not reject the existence of objective truth but previously made a distinction between true knowledge and knowledge by power or ideology. According to Marx, scientific and true knowledge is in accordance with the dialectical understanding of history and ideological knowledge is an epiphenomenal expression of the relation of material forces in each economic arrangement.

A logical truth (also called an analytic truth or a necessary truth) is a statement which is true in all possible worlds or under all possible interpretations, as contrasted to a fact (also called a synthetic claim or contingency) which is only true in this world as it has historically unfolded.

Logic deals with patterns in reason that can help us if a proposition is true or not. Logic, however, covers no truth in absolute terms, as for instance a metaphysician does. Logicians use formal language to express truths that they are working on, such that there is only one truth under some interpretation or truth within some logical system. Georg Wilhelm Friedrich Hegel is the philosopher who brought the dialectic method to a new high point of development. According to Hegel in his science of logic, the dialectic method consists of three steps. First, a proposition which can consist of any proposition in logic; second, the antithesis of the theorem; and finally, a synthesis in which both the theorem and the antithesis figure. Hegel believed that there is no guarantee at all that the thesis can be taken as the whole truth. Only the whole can be true, and the dialectic synthesis is how the whole can be examined with respect to a specific proposition. Truth consists of the entire process. Looking at thesis, antithesis and synthesis separately results in one way of other to an untruth. According to Hegel, the concept of not arises from the outset. The whole is by Hegel called absolute and should be regarded as spiritual.

There are two main approaches to truth in mathematics. They are the model theory of truth and the proof theory of truth.

Historically, with the nineteenth-century development of Boolean algebra, mathematical models of logic began to treat "truth", also represented as T or 1, as an arbitrary constant. Falsity is also an arbitrary constant, which can be represented as F or 0. In propositional logic, these symbols can be manipulated according to a set of axioms and rules of inference, often given in the form of truth tables.

The works of logician and mathematician Kurt Gödel, mathematical biologist Alan Turing, and others shook this assumption with the development of statements that are true but cannot be proven within the system. Two examples of the latter can be found in the mathematician David Hilbert's problems. Work on Hilbert's tenth problem in the late twentieth century led to the construction of specific Diophantine equations for which it is undecidable whether they have a solution—or even if they do, whether they have a finite or an infinite number of solutions. (The Diophantine equation is a polynomial equation, usually in two or more unknowns.) The word *Diophantine* refers to the Hellenistic mathematician of the third century Diophantus of Alexandria, who made a study of such equations and was one of the first mathematicians to introduce symbolism into algebra. More fundamentally, Hilbert's first problem was on the continuum hypothesis. Gödel and mathematician Paul Cohen showed that this hypothesis could not be proved or disproved using the standard axioms of set theory. In the view of some, then, it is equally reasonable to take either the continuum hypothesis or its negation as a new axiom.

Psychologist and philosopher Erich Fromm finds that trying to discuss truth as "absolute truth" is sterile and that emphasis ought to be placed on "optimal truth". He considers truth as stemming from the survival imperative of grasping one's environment physically and intellectually, whereby young children instinctively seek truth to orient themselves in "a strange and powerful world". The accuracy of their perceived approximation of the truth will therefore have direct consequences on their ability to deal with their environment. Fromm can be understood to define truth as a functional approximation of reality. His vision of optimal truth is described partly in *Man from Himself: An Inquiry into the Psychology of Ethics*, from which excerpts are included below.

> The dichotomy between "absolute = perfect" and "relative = imperfect" has been superseded in all fields of scientific thought, where "it is generally recognised that there is no absolute truth but nevertheless that there are objectively valid laws and principles".

In that respect, "a scientifically or rationally valid statement means that the power of reason is applied to all the available data of observation without any of them being suppressed or falsified for the sake of the desired result". The history of science is "a history of inadequate and incomplete statements, and every new insight makes possible the recognition of the inadequacies of previous propositions and offers a springboard for creating an adequate formulation."

As a result, the history of thought is the history of an ever-increasing approximation to the truth. Scientific knowledge is not absolute but optimal; it contains the optimum of truth attainable in each historical period." Fromm furthermore notes that "distinct cultures have emphasised various aspects of the truth" and that "increasing interaction between cultures allows for these aspects to reconcile and integrate, increasing further the approximation to the truth".

Truth, says the philosopher Michel Foucault, is problematic when any attempt is made to see truth as an "objective" quality. He prefers not to use the term truth itself but "regimes of truth". In his historical investigations, he found truth to be something that was itself a part of, or embedded within, a given power structure. Thus, Foucault's view shares much in common with the concepts of Nietzsche. Truth for Foucault is also something that shifts through various phases of epistemology throughout history.

Hilary Putnam has suggested that the reconciliation of anti-scepticism and fallibility is the central goal of American pragmatism. Although all human knowledge is partial, with no ability to take a God's-eye view, this does not necessitate a globalised sceptical attitude, a radical philosophical scepticism (as distinguished from that which is called scientific scepticism). The analytical philosopher

Charles Sanders Peirce insisted that first in reasoning there is the presupposition, and at least the hope, that truth and the real are discoverable and would be discovered, sooner or later but still inevitably by investigation taken far enough. Second, contrary to Descartes' famous and influential methodology in the *Meditations on First Philosophy*, doubt cannot be feigned or created by verbal *fiat* to motivate fruitful inquiry, and much less can philosophy begin in universal doubt. Doubt, like belief, requires justification. Genuine doubt irritates and inhibits, in the sense that belief is that upon which one is prepared to act. It arises from confrontation with some specific recalcitrant matter of fact (which Dewey called a situation) which unsettles our belief in some specific proposition. Inquiry is then the rationally self-controlled process of attempting to return to a settled state of belief about the matter. Note that anti-scepticism is a reaction to modern academic scepticism in the wake of Descartes. The pragmatist insistence that all knowledge is tentative is quite congenial to the older sceptical tradition.

Pragmatism was not the first to apply evolution to theories of knowledge: Schopenhauer advocated a biological idealism as to what's useful to an organism to believe might differ wildly from what is true. Here, knowledge and action are portrayed as two separate spheres with an absolute or transcendental truth above, and they are beyond any sort of inquiry organisms used to cope with life. Pragmatism challenges this idealism by providing an "ecological" account of knowledge: inquiry is how organisms can get a grip on their environment. *Real* and *true* are functional labels in inquiry and cannot be understood outside of this context. It is not realist in a traditionally robust sense of realism (what Hilary Putnam would later call metaphysical realism), but it is realist in how it acknowledges an external world which must be dealt with.

Other modern philosophers such as Spinoza and Hegel ran (opposite the correspondence theory) a coherence theory: something is true if it is consistent with a series or system of other pronunciations (Hegel's *Phänomenologie des geistes*). In addition, one can also speak of an "evidence" theory of truth with René Descartes. A sentence is true when it bears a clear judgement. This theory is also reflected with Franz Brentano and Edmund Husserl. One can see the truth in contemporary philosophy theories even further splintering. In this way, the beginning of the twentieth century saw the pragmatic theory of truth authors such as Charles Sanders Peirce, William James, and John Dewey. According to the pragmatism, truth is that which is useful and usable, that which works. Although Peirce is seen as the founder of pragmatism, he kept to himself another truth theory: true is what the community of scientists eventually will agree on. Still, it would later be above all the pragmatic theory of James that would be most influential—for example, in the works of the analytical philosopher Richard Rorty.

However, the correspondence theory continues to have its supporters, including the young Ludwig Wittgenstein and Bertrand Russell. In his *Tractatus Logico-Philosophicus,* Wittgenstein sets a statement that truth is what portrays the reality correctly. According to Wittgenstein, words obtained their meaning because they represent certain states of affairs in the world (picture theory of meaning). Later, Wittgenstein renounced his former position in *Philosophische Untersuchungen.* He is inspired by the concept of truth as expressed in logic by authors such as Gottlob Frege and Alfred Tarski. Truth is seen here on a minimalist or deflationary mode: "true" is a concept that cannot be analysed. The statement "The grass is green" is true if the grass is green indeed (and the truth value of the ruling is 1, not 0). Frank Plumpton Ramsey formulates a specific variant, the redundancy theory: the term "true" is unnecessary. On the other hand, the late Wittgenstein is also linked to another truth theory—namely, the constructivist theory of truth. Truth is something that is not independent of man and his culture, but dependent on it. This relates to the new concept of language in the later works of Wittgenstein. The meaning is no longer determined by reflection of a reality but through the use of the words within so-called language plays and life forms (meaning is used). In this truth theory, this principle applied to the concept of truth: what is described as true or false depends on the language game in which one moves. Truth outside language games search is, in that sense, pointless because words have no meaning, and so truth does not either outside of language games.

According to the philosopher Martin Heidegger, truth is the "public nature of being". In doing so, he refers to the Greek term for truth, *aletheia*, which means unhidden. From a phenomenological perspective, Heidegger posits that things as such can only entry on the foreground in an ontological background of being (*das sein*). Further, there is also the consensus theory of truth of sociologist Jürgen Habermas and language philosopher Karl-Otto Apel, who state that a statement is true when an unlimited number of people who have all the desirable means of communication would endorse this ruling. Finally, one can also speak of a performance theory by the analytical philosopher Peter Frederick Strawson. According to him, the term "true" in a sentence underlines the predicate.

Although in fact a sociologist, Niklas Luhmann also has his own vision of truth. Within his system theory is truth taken as a symbolically generalised communication medium. At the basis, there is a distinction between knowing and truth, and what as true will apply shall, in second instance, be determined. This eventually leads to the paradox that truth is true and untrue.

In religion, truth primarily has a transcendent meaning. Because religion is based on revelations by not purely empirical or rational demonstrable personalities or actors (God, gods, spirits, angels, and so on), it is also closely related to understanding such supernatural revelations. Truth can then be understood as a supernatural (metaphysical) provision on the upper world in itself, or about the connection of the upper world with the natural world. Mostly it goes also about statements about validity and authenticity. The insights about that walk very widely between and within the various religions. Insight into the truth or truths could be obtained through meditation, prayer, study of sacred writings, obedience to use, being forbidden, rituals, and community practise.

Because in science (mathematics excepted) one is always pushing to the limits of the possible perception and absolute truth is found difficult, there are indications of what is true (or provisional) can be adopted as truth; the concept of paradigm refers to it. A possible indication is simplicity: the simplest explanation is adopted as the right one. For example, the movements in our solar system can be explained mathematically with the assumption that Earth is in the middle of the solar system. However, this is a much more complicated formula than with the assumption that the sun is in the middle, where upon the second explanation is adopted. This can also be seen as a manifestation of beauty. A nice solution is seen as an indication of accuracy (it is too good to not be true). This problem exists: the phases of Venus are in violation of Earth in the centre, but not with the sun.

In mathematics, absolute truth is achieved by proving axioms. The number system 1 + 2 = 3, for example, delivers absolute truths, known from sensory perceptions. (Incidentally, the claim "absolute truth does not exist" is in a fight with itself.)

One could also argue that science does not pursue truths but approaches them. Science posits (abstract) models, which describe and predict, as well as possible local behaviours without explaining them. An operating device, construction, and so on can be seen as an absolute truth. A mobile phone functions thanks to Maxwell's equations and the condensed matter physics—a practical proof of "truth".

Using lie detectors nowadays, one can examine whether someone is lying. One considers that a lie causes someone so much stress that the heart rate quickens and the perspiration increases. A fool proof evidence is it not, because there may be other reasons for excitement at interrogation, and on the other hand causes lying to many people no measurable stress.

Behavioural psychology has numerous characteristics because of which one can discover whether a partner is lying. Signals that indicate lie are dilated pupils; hand movements in the direction of the face, especially the mouth; and general nervousness. In addition, when lying the voice changes. The vocal cords make more effort; the voice is higher and under higher pressure. Also, this can be discovered with appropriate measuring equipment. But again, someone can be nervous, or someone may be a seasoned liar so that there is nothing to measure. Apparently, people urgently need to be able to distinguish truth from lie, and the solution to the problem is not yet found. Most societies therefore punish the lie. Children are generally harshly treated if they do not speak the truth. It is the fear of punishment that is the basis for the functioning of lie detectors, which indeed does only measure stress.

Views of experts or of a majority could already be regarded as authoritative truth according to Aristotle, provided the key of philosophical criticism was met, although the latter requirement was not always strictly observed. Such "authority" in history meant that new ideas were suffocated. Where the authority, by counterargument, was undermined, it was not always possible to dispose simply over the truth. Authority was then precisely divisive, whereby views about the truth of something splintered. The fight over truth that so ignited was often fought with power resources and happened not rarely at the expense of the authority of scientific expertise. When Copernicus, with his work on the revolutions of the celestial spheres in 1543, brought the then Western world into turmoil, he showed that it was impossible that Earth was the God-defined centre of the universe (the Copernican revolution). His work was placed on the index by the Inquisition. In 1633, Galileo Galilei was forced to renounce his scientific findings when they appeared to be contrary with the authoritative worldview.

Known too is the fight against the evolution theory of Charles Darwin, who immediately gave rise to a fierce public debate between Thomas Huxley and Richard Owen, and on which scientific truth to this day is heavily challenged by conservative creationist groups, with a large following on the basis of religious authority.

A truth that other apparently contradictory truths reconcile with each other at a higher level is an overarching truth. Theorems can be proven as true and yet hold contradictory axioms, which can only (with the greatest difficulty in an overarching understanding) be brought into line with each other. So went the special theory of relativity by Einstein of the apparent contradiction between a constant speed of light and the equal validity of laws of nature for any observer.

However, such an overarching truth is not always appropriate, partly because there are still apparent inconsistencies existing that cannot be solved by any science (such as those between quantum mechanics and gravity). In part this is because such an overarching truth on an everyday level is not always experienced as equally relevant. Within science, one often speaks of a "theory of everything", which means all fundamental theories of physics would unite with each other.

In a religious context, especially the Abrahamic religions (Christianity, Islam, and Judaism), perfect knowledge of all truth over all things (omniscience) is considered a characteristic of a divine being. In the Abrahamic view[160] on the divine judgement on the dead, God judges because of perfect knowledge of their lives.

Belief (faith) is the state of mind in which a person thinks something to be the case, with or without there being empirical evidence to prove that something is the case with factual certainty. In other words, belief is when someone thinks something is a reality and is true when he has no absolute verified foundation for his certainty of the truth or the realness of something. Another way of defining belief is as a mental representation of an attitude positively orientated towards the likelihood of something being true. In the context of Ancient Greek thought, two related concepts were identified with regards to the concept of belief: *pistis* and doxa. Simplified, we may say that *pistis* refers to trust and confidence, whereas doxa refers to opinion and acceptance. The English word *doctrine* is derived from doxa. Belief's purpose is to guide action and not to indicate truth.[110] In epistemology, philosophers use the term *belief* to refer to personal attitudes associated with true or false ideas and concepts. However, belief does not require active introspection and circumspection. For example, we never ponder whether the sun will rise. We simply assume the sun will rise. Because belief is an important aspect of mundane life, according to the *Stanford Encyclopaedia of Philosophy*, the question that must be answered is how a physical organism can have beliefs.[144]

Epistemology deals with delineating the boundary between justified belief and opinion, and it is in general concerned with a theoretical philosophical study of knowledge. The primary problem in epistemology is to understand exactly what it takes to acquire knowledge. Plato condemned the sophists who defined knowledge as "justified true belief".

In epistemology, philosophers use the term *faith* to refer to personal attitude, view, and way of thinking with regards to true or false ideas and concepts.

Mainstream psychology and related disciplines have traditionally treated belief as if it were the simplest form of mental representation and therefore one of the building blocks of conscious thought. Philosophers have tended to be more abstract in their analysis, and much of their work consists in examining the viability of the belief concept using philosophical analysis.

The concept of belief presumes a subject (the believer) and an object of belief (the proposition). Like other propositional attitudes, belief implies the existence of mental states and intentionality, both of which are hotly debated topics in the philosophy of mind and whose foundations and relation to brain states are still controversial.

Beliefs are sometimes divided into core beliefs (that are actively thought about) and dispositional beliefs (that may be ascribed to someone who has not thought about the issue). For example, if asked "Do you believe tigers wear pink pyjamas?" people might answer that they do not, despite the fact they may never have thought about this situation before.

This has important implications for understanding the neuropsychology and neuroscience of belief. If the concept of belief is incoherent, then any attempt to find the underlying neural processes that support it will fail.

Historically, *belief-in* belonged in the realm of religious thought, and *belief-that* instead belonged to epistemological considerations.

When people are asked to estimate the likelihood that a statement is true, they search their memory for information that has implications for the validity of this statement. Once this information has been identified, they estimate (a) the likelihood that the statement would be true if the information were true, and (b) the likelihood that the statement would be true if the information were false. If their estimates for these two probabilities differ, people average them, weighting each by the likelihood that the information is true or false. Thus, information bears directly on beliefs of another related statement.

Religious belief (faith) refers to attitudes towards mythological, supernatural, or spiritual aspects of religion. Religious belief is distinct from religious practise or religious behaviours, with some believers not practicing religion and some practitioners not believing religion. Religious beliefs, being derived from ideas that are exclusive to religion, often relate to the existence, characteristics, and worship of a deity or deities; divine intervention in the universe and human life; or the deontological explanations for the values and practises centred on the teachings of a spiritual leader or group. In contrast to other belief systems, religious beliefs are usually codified.

Although it is popularly conceived that religions each have identifiable and exclusive sets of beliefs or creeds, surveys of religious belief have often found that the official doctrine and descriptions of the beliefs offered by religious authorities do not always agree with the privately held beliefs of those who are identified as members of a particular religion.

First used in the context of early Christianity, orthodoxy is a religious belief that closely follows the edicts, apologies, and hermeneutics of a prevailing religious authority. In the case of early Christianity, this authority was the communion of bishops, and it is often referred to by the term *magisterium*. The term *orthodox* was applied almost as an epithet to a group of Jewish believers who held to a pre-Enlightenment understanding of Judaism, now known as Orthodox Judaism. The Eastern Orthodox Church of Christianity, as well as the Roman Catholic Church, consider themselves to be the true heirs to the early Christian belief and practise. The antonym of orthodox is heterodox, and those adhering to orthodoxy often accuse the heterodox of apostasy, schism, or heresy.

The Renaissance and the Enlightenment in Europe were associated with varying degrees of religious tolerance and intolerance towards new religious ideas. The *Philosophes* took exception to most of the fantastical claims of religions and directly challenged religious authority and the prevailing beliefs associated with the established churches. In response to the liberalising political and social movements, some religious groups attempted to integrate Enlightenment ideals of rationality, equality, and individual liberty into their belief systems, especially into the nineteenth and twentieth centuries (Reform Judaism and Liberal Christianity).

First self-applied as a term to the conservative doctrine outlined by anti-modernist Protestants in the United States of America, fundamentalism as a religious belief is associated with a strict adherence to an interpretation of scriptures that are generally associated with theologically conservative positions or traditional understandings of the text and that are distrustful of innovative readings, new revelation, or alternate interpretations. Religious fundamentalism has been identified in the media as being associated with fanatical or zealous political movements around the world that have used a strict adherence to a particular religious doctrine as a means to establish political identity and enforce societal norms. In the United States, the Republicans use religion as a political platform.

A term signifying derogation that is used by the religious and non-religious alike is superstition, the deprecated belief in supernatural causation. Those who deny the existence of the supernatural generally attribute all beliefs associated with it to be superstitious. A typical religious critique of superstition holds that it either encompasses beliefs in non-existent supernatural activity or that the supernatural activity is inappropriately feared or held in improper regard (idolatry). Occultism, animism, paganism, and other folk religions were strongly condemned by the Christian Church as mean forms of superstition, though such condemnation did not necessarily eliminate the beliefs amongst the common people; many such religious beliefs persist today.

In Buddhism, practise and progress along the spiritual path happen when one follows the system of Buddhist practise. Any religion which follows (parts of) the fundamentals of this system has, according to the teachings of Buddha, good aspects to the extent it accords with this system. Any religion which goes against (parts of) the fundamentals of this system includes bad aspects too. For any religion which does not teach certain parts of this system, it is not because this is a "bad" religion; it simply lacks those teachings and is to that extent incomplete.

As a religious tradition, Hinduism has experienced many attempts at systemisation.

Beliefs about the supernatural or metaphysical may not presuppose a difference between any such thing as nature and non-nature, or between science and what the most educated people believe.

People with exclusivist beliefs typically explain other religions as either in error or as corruptions or counterfeits of the true faith. This approach is a fairly consistent feature of smaller new religious movements that often rely on the doctrine that claims a unique revelation by the founder or leaders, and that considers it a matter of faith that the religion has a monopoly on truth. All three major Abrahamic monotheistic religions have passages in their holy scriptures that attest to the primacy of the scriptural testimony. Indeed, monotheism itself is often couched as an innovation characterised specifically by its explicit rejection of earlier polytheistic faiths.

Some exclusivist faiths incorporate a specific element of proselytization. This is a strongly held belief in the Christian tradition which follows the doctrine of the Great Commission, and it is less emphasised by the Islamic faith where the Koranic edict "There shall be no compulsion in religion" (2:256) is often quoted as a justification for toleration of alternative beliefs, though it is a very isolated passage having no impact at all on the many other passages condemning other religions. The Jewish tradition is one that does not actively seek out converts.

Exclusivism correlates with conservative, fundamentalist, and orthodox approaches of many religions. Pluralistic and syncretistic approaches either explicitly downplay or reject the exclusivist tendencies of the religion.

People with inclusivist beliefs recognise some truth in all faith systems, highlighting agreements and minimising differences. The attitude is sometimes associated with interfaith dialogue or the Christian Ecumenical movement, though in principle such attempts at pluralism are not necessarily inclusivist, and many actors in such interactions (for example, the Roman Catholic Church) still hold to exclusivist dogma while participating in inter-religious organisations. People with pluralist beliefs make no distinction between faith systems, viewing each one as valid within a particular culture. Examples include extracts from the Sri Guru Granth Sahib Ji (Sikh Holy Scriptures): "There is only the One Supreme Lord God; there is no other at all" (Pannaa 45). "By His Power the Vedas and the Puranas exist, and the Holy Scriptures of the Jewish, Christian and Islamic religions. By His Power all deliberations exist" (Pannaa 464). "Some call Him, 'Ram, Ram', and some call Him, 'Khudaa-i'. Some serve Him as 'Gusain', others as 'Allaah'. He is the Cause of causes, the Generous Lord. He showers His Grace and Mercy upon us and amen" (Pannaa 885).

People with syncretistic (combination of different often contradictory) views blend the views of a variety of different religions or traditional beliefs into a unique fusion which suits their particular experience and context. Unitarian Universalism is an example of a syncretistic faith.

The role of belief in representing reality is widely debated in pragmatism. Is a belief valid when it represents reality? Copying is one (and only one) genuine mode of knowing.[114] Are beliefs dispositions which qualify as true or false depending on how helpful they prove in inquiry and in action? Is it only in the struggle of intelligent organisms with the surrounding environment that beliefs acquire meaning? Does a belief only become true when it succeeds in this struggle? In pragmatism, nothing practical or useful is held to be necessarily true, and neither is anything which helps to survive merely in the short term. For example, to believe my cheating spouse is faithful may help me feel better now, but it is certainly not useful from a more long-term perspective because it doesn't accord with the facts (and is therefore not true).

Accepting what is not true is not something educated people do. It is claimed that intelligence has nothing to do with education because people can have potential which has not been able to emerge.

But the lack of knowledge will disarray the truth. Stupidity is the cause of hatred and envy in the world.

Many members of the establishment practise religion to please their fellow men but do not really believe in religion. This hypocrisy is common with politicians.

The nuances of the definition of the concept of truth seem to indicate that it is difficult to find out the truth. This is by no means the case. Although sophists often exploit nuances to doubt the truth and to launch false theories, the truth can be clearly distinct. The truth is, today, all that by nothing can be denied. It forms the essential and necessary component to meaningful information, discussion and reasoning. Without truth, logic and dialectic are empty boxes. The opposite of truth is falsehood, but it is the contrast of belief that in its description defines truth.

There is nothing that makes it possible to prove that a deity exists. When believers thereupon riposte that nothing proves that God does not exist, they forget also that there is also nothing which admits proving the non-existence of the flying spaghetti monster. A proof of something that does not exist cannot be approached or proved.

Civilisation has a variety of meanings related to human development. Typically, it is used to describe the development of people groups (races) or to describe a society with a certain degree of complexity. Since the sixteenth century, one talks about empire or realm rather than civilisation.[157] Culture is synonymous with civilisation and indicates all achievements of man. It includes language, social behaviour, technology, arts, and sciences.[158]

The current stage of human development is limited and has yet to grow tremendously. This is perfectly normal, considering that the universe exists since about 13.8 billion years ago and that man as a rational animal can only look back on a few million years of development. Recently it was discovered that Homo *sapiens* developed 300,000 years ago. Civilisations date back only 10,000 years ago. Great thinkers, including Friedrich Nietzsche and Arthur Schopenhauer, judge that the human is actually stupid. It's hard to disbelieve them. Nietzsche, who inspired existentialists to conclude that life is absurd, divided the humanity in two categories: a small fraction that dominated the people, and a herd-dominated theory on which the Nazis built their *herren class* and *übermenschen*.

Human intelligence is a mental property and the intellectual ability of humans, which is characterised by a high level of cognition, motivation, and self-awareness. Intelligence enables people to remember descriptions of things and to use them (memory) in future behaviour. It is a cognitive process. It provides people the cognitive skills to learn, form concepts, understand, and reason, including the ability to recognise patterns, understand ideas, plan, solve problems, and use language to communicate. Intelligence enables people to experience and think. Note that many of the above definitions apply too, though in a limited extent, for the intelligence of animals.[159]

Innate cleverness or intelligence is also referred to as ability and talent. It is a characteristic of personality. Some are more intelligent than others, or certain facets of intelligence are more developed. For example, some learn a language more easily, whereas others are more proficient in sums. However, social background, education, and culture play important roles. The potential of intelligence in humans is present, but the expression can vary greatly so that degrees of intelligence are inevitable.

People with a lot of knowledge are not necessarily more intelligent, although they have a big lead on the ignorant.

Scientists are researchers who pursue the truth, although it is sometimes hard to find or only approachable. Only the physicists are capable, by the means of their extensive knowledge of the laws of nature, of making true predictions. Most intellectuals who are not scientists are not researchers. Notwithstanding their extensive knowledge, they are influenced by all kinds of factors that affect their thinking and reasoning. The big problem of many intellectuals is their belief in a supernatural, almighty entity for which no evidence exists. They may go out of a priori permeated principles based on nothing or on fictitious grounds such as religious values, including the values of the Christian faith, so that they are unable to make the necessary distinction between fiction and reality. They forget that religious ethics do not outweigh humanism. They find it outrageous that the hereafter would not exist and that life would have no purpose or meaning. Gullibility is a weakness of man and a placebo.

Today, religious faith is still the cause of many wars in which millions of people die. Sex without birth control is the direct cause of great poverty in the world. In many continents, the inhabitants practise sex without worrying about the possible birth of children for whom they do not have the economic means to provide an upbringing. In Asia, children are conceived as future providers of income and as insurance against the old age of the parents. A sizeable percentage (about 77 per cent) of the world's population is faithful. It is therefore very sad that so many people in the world still believe, notwithstanding the existing extensive scientific knowledge, that heaven and Earth were created by a supernatural, almighty entity. That low-educated people continue to believe such a thing still is somewhat acceptable due to their ignorance. What cannot be accepted is that so many highly educated people are believers. There must be something wrong with those people, or else what lies behind their belief? Missing intelligence? This is undoubtedly the case with those who brandish the concept of life stand. But what of the highly intelligent people who are religious? Are they sincere? Is it a show to the people that they must respect divine ethics so that law and order may be maintained? It is then deceit to obtain a pragmatic result. The obtained result is, however, very moderate because the world is still in turmoil because war and massacres reign supreme.

Man drowns in huge, preposterous things.

The Jews are by no means a chosen people. Moses is an invented symbol. Jewish scientists, including many prominent ones, have long renounced their faith.

The Christians were originally radicalised Jews who abandoned their faith because there was no sign of the promised Messiah. They adopted the writings of the Jewish Bible (Old Testament). There is no evidence that Christ has ever existed. Christianity is by no means an exclusive religion. The schisms in the churches prove the fragile contents of the teachings. Christians are hypocrites who cheat their faith every day.

Islam is a barbaric copy of the old and the New Testament. It is a religion invented by Muhammad, who was by no means a divine envoy. He had political ambitions and used his invented religion to unite the pagan tribes of the Arabian Peninsula while respecting their morals and customs. Muslims, as their former tribes, despise women as only needed for their maintenance and catering to their sex urges.

The United States is the most powerful country in the world, but more than half of the inhabitants are low-educated, resulting in the election of a clown as president. The first plenary cabinet meeting held by President Trump was one à la Saddam Hussein: each minister expressed his affection for Trump and paid honour to him.

The stupidity of the people is the cause that evil reigns in the world. The people are unable to follow the golden rule "do not do to others what you do not want to be served to you". There have been many civilisations in the world, usually as a result of the intervention of leaders who were not concerned about the fate of their nationals. Actually, there are several different civilisations in the world in which most people do not really feel happy and simply endure life. In Iran and Turkey, there is a sort of ill-used democracy in which the numerous minorities are suppressed.

CHAPTER 23

Happiness

What all people (theists or atheists) seek without exception is happiness, which is a mental or emotional state of well-being.[111] Happiness is rather a vague concept and can mean different things to many people. The adaptation to living conditions (Darwinism) differs from man to man. What is important is not the momentary emotion of intense joy such as an orgasm, but the permanent state of well-being. Happiness derives from many things. Contentment of the life one leads varies in its definition according to the biological, psychological, religious, and philosophical approach of the matter by the individual. Life is not without hardships, which are present in every level of the community. Take for example the case of rich movie stars who take drugs to overcome the strains and stress of their lives. A positive approach to happiness is the adoption of the presence of pleasant or desirable situations, though these situations may be few. The consciousness of the painful aspects of life helps human to overcome them. What everyone is doing, without distinction between the intelligentsia and the large mass of the world's population, is the pursuit of happiness. The happiness can be defined as the satisfaction of its living conditions. This can include several positive emotions such as joy, pleasure, peace, tranquillity, and happiness. The living conditions of most of the world's population are far from ideal. There is, after all, a constant fight against poverty so that life is a struggle for existence and lacks the necessary positive emotions. In science, the feeling of happiness is caused by morphine-like substances called endorphins. Biogenic amines (dopamine) cause pleasure. From the biological point of view, there is a difference between pleasure and happiness. Other substances in our brains produce serotine, which influences romantic love and pleasure.

Happiness is purely personal and needs different needs per person. The quality of life depends therefore on the extent to which one manages to meet the required needs. Most of the world's population is not eager to learn beyond meeting primary needs.

Scientific inquiry may be able to reveal which aspects of life are of essential value and, if realised, grant peace of mind and satisfaction. A full engagement of activities in a career (job, sport, charity) will certainly further happiness. Materialist philosophies such as dialectical materialism challenge the very idea of an absolute value of meaning of life. As stated before, neuroscience describes reward, pleasure, and motivation in terms of neurotransmitter activity, especially in the limbic system of the ventral tegmental area in the brain.

Within science, there is an important hedonistic flow, the psychological hedonism, which propagates that every motivation is driven by a minimisation of pain and a maximisation of pleasure. The assumptions of the psychological hedonism are on the same line as that of the micro-economy, which is based on maximising the utility of goods and services.

Happiness is of fundamental importance. In the United States' Declaration of Independence, "life, liberty and the pursuit of happiness" were deemed unalienable rights. The United Nations, to recognise the relevance of happiness and well-being, declared 20 March the International Day of Happiness.

Nirvana is a state of everlasting peace in Buddhism and forms a central theme in the Buddhists' teachings of happiness. For Aristotle and Epicure, the happy life is a good life—that is, a life in which a person fulfils human nature in an excellent way (cf. chapter X, "Morality and Ethics"). Augustine and Thomas Aquinas agree that man's last end is happiness, but according to Aquinas, who agreed with Aristotle, happiness cannot be reached solely through reasoning about consequences of acts of happiness; it also requires a pursuit of worthy cause for acts, such as habits according to virtue. Aquinas posits that these habits and acts, which lead to happiness, are caused by natural and divine laws, which are caused by a first cause, God. Perfect happiness is then contemplation of God's ways, which will hardly satisfy common man.

The placebo effect of religions has been the cause that paraphrasing truth led to various faulty conceptions. Results of surveys seem to illustrate that religion has a beneficiary effect on people, but it is merely the effect of the placebo consisting of prayers, parochial community, and especially the fable of life hereafter. Much of the world's -population is theistic and cannot but give an erroneous view on the matter of happiness. It has been proved that people with sufficient means live longer than poor people because their means are greater to pay more attention to their health, which is a crucial factor in life.

Living in harmony with your fellow man is essential for a happy existence. It means to observe certain rules, called morality or ethics. The observance of the golden rule or ethic of reciprocity, a moral maxim or principle of altruism, is a universal rule of society: one should treat others as one would like others to treat oneself (cf. chapter XIV, "Existence and Existentialism").

Rationalism, opposed to empiricism of Descartes (Cogito ergo sum) and the existentialism of Heidegger (the observer exists; Dasein), aims to prove the existence of man. It remains questionable whether these philosophies have really contributed something or mean something for man, and whether they are purely rhetorical. The bearing has to do with metaphysical nonsense which theistic philosophers and a few rare scientists propagate. The existence of man seems not susceptible to be pulled in doubt.

CHAPTER 24

Purpose and Meaning of Life

A. Generalities

In the previous chapters, the data provided on religious, philosophic, and scientific issues should allow to judge whether life has any purpose or meaning. A thorough distinction should be made according to whether one assumes a theistic or atheistic point of view. In the end, only a position emanating from a scientific background is acceptable.

There is no such thing as sanctity of life. For many theists, because humans are made in God's image, the sanctity of life (inviolability) refers to the idea that human life is sacred, holy, and precious. In the fable of Genesis 9:3–6, God has authorised humanity to kill other forms of life, but he has expressly forbidden the murdering of other human beings, with the penalty being death. In contrast, in many schools of Eastern philosophy state that all animal life is sacred.

According to theists, humanity was created in God's image, but sin has corrupted that image. They assume that there is nothing inherently sacred in fallen man. The sanctity of human life is not because we are such wonderful and good beings. The only reason the sanctity of life applies to humanity is the fact that God created humans in his image and sets them apart from all other forms of life. Although that image has indeed been marred by sin, his image is still present in humanity. We are like God, and that likeness means human life is always to be treated with dignity and respect.

The sanctity of life means that humanity is more sacred than the rest of creation. Human life is not holy in the same sense that God is holy. Only God is holy in and of himself. Human life is only holy in the sense of being "set apart" from all other life created by God. Many apply the sanctity of life to issues like abortion and euthanasia, and though it applies to those issues, it applies to much more. The sanctity of life should motivate humans to combat all forms of evil and injustice that are perpetuated against human life. Violence, abuse, oppression, human trafficking, and many other evils are also violations of the sanctity of life. In Matthew 22:37–39, Jesus says, "You shall love the Lord your God with all your heart, and with all your soul, and with all your mind." This is the great and foremost commandment. The second is, "You shall love your neighbour as yourself." In these commandments, it is seen that the actions of humans are to be motivated by love for God and love for others. If humans love God, they will value their own lives as part of God's plan to do his will until it comes about that his will is better served by our deaths. And humans will love and care for his people (John 21:15–17). We will see to the needs of the elderly and sick. We will protect others from harm, whether from abortion, euthanasia, human trafficking, or other abuses. The sanctity of life can be the foundation, but love must be the motivation.[141] These ethics cannot be criticised were they not the basis of fanaticism that leads to fighting abortion, contraception, euthanasia, and embryonic stem cells.

Ethics form a very important part of religion and philosophy. They do not really contradict each other but differ on grounds, starting point, and scope. They differ when religion does not allow the least deviation. There are huge hypocrisy and insincerity on the account of the theists in the developed countries on the part of their sex lives. They mate continuously while avoiding pregnancy, trespassing God's commandment. However, anticonception is a necessity to avoid overpopulation and poverty, cf chapterXIII.

"To be or not to be" is not the question. The question is whether *to be* has any purpose or meaning. The meaning of life pertains to the significance of living or existence in general, out of which many questions arise: What should I do? Why are we here? What is life about? What is the meaning of my life? Is there meaning to life? There have been many answers to these questions, and they vary according to the philosophical, scientific, theological, and metaphysical contemplation of the matter. Many other issues are also involved, such as symbolic meaning, ontology, value, purpose, ethics, good and evil, free will, the existence of one or multiple gods, conceptions of God, the soul, and the afterlife. In religion, life has a deeper meaning. In philosophy it is debated whether life has a deeper meaning. However, the scientific contemplation of life is really the one that matters. Science focuses primarily on describing related empirical facts about the universe, exploring the contexts and parameters concerning the how of life. Science can provide recommendations for the pursuit of well-being and the necessity of morality.[112]

The masses do not bother to ask the questions, but every rational being does ask the questions: "What is the meaning of my life?" "Where do we come from?" "What we are and where are we going?" "Has life any meaning or purpose?" What everyone is doing, without distinction between the intelligentsia and the masses, is the pursuit of happiness. Happiness can be defined as the satisfaction of living conditions. This can include several positive emotions such as joy, pleasure, peace, tranquillity, and happiness. The living conditions of much of the world's population are poor. There is, after all, a constant fight against poverty, and so life comes down to a struggle for existence. It is difficult to contemplate that the pursuit of happiness is the conclusive purpose and meaning of life. All life forms, humanity included, are part of the nature of the universe and cannot have a purpose of meaning different from the universe itself. After all, if life is absurd, as considered by atheistic existentialists, then the universe must be labelled as absurd because life makes inseparable a part of the universe that answers to all physical laws and thereby earned the admiration of Einstein.

Since the first civilisations, religions all over the world have held mankind under the yoke. Only in the twentieth century was humankind able to lift the sway, and then only in the Western world. Theists believe God created the universe and that God had a purpose in doing so. Theists also hold the view that humans find their meaning and purpose for life in God's purpose in creating the universe. Theists further hold that if there were no God to give life ultimate meaning, value, and purpose, then life would be absurd. These beliefs are of course mere inventions by humankind itself and bear no truth, seeing that God did not create the universe.

Religion and philosophy have not provided serious contributions to determine whether there is any purpose or meaning to life. However, it is worth the trouble to return briefly to the considerations we find in religion and philosophy in order to grasp how most humans think.

B. Nonsense of Religion

The worthlessness of religions was explained in detail in chapter 20.

Religious perspectives on the meaning of life are those ideologies which explain life in terms of an implicit purpose not defined by man but by a supernatural deity. In the various religions, we distinguish between the period of the material life that takes place from birth to death and the period after the physical death. Eschatology is dominant in all religions to justify life on Earth. Because of the belief in God's existence, a metaphysical meaning to life is provided. Theists believe that God created the universe and had a goal. Atheists, based on scientific evidence, assume that the universe came into being by the Big Bang, caused by low entropy (disorder or randomness of particles) more than 13.8 billion years ago.

The first and oldest religion that moved from the worship of the pagan gods to a monotheistic religion was Zoroastrianism.[1] Zoroastrianism was founded by the Prophet Zoroaster (Zarathustra) in ancient Iran. The exact date of the creation of the religion is uncertain, and historians do not agree. Through archaeological evidence and linguistic comparisons of the texts of the *Gathas* in the old Vesta language text with the Hindu *Rig Veda,* a probable date of 1500–1200 BC is advanced. Zoroaster was born in a culture of the Bronze Age with polytheistic religion, including the animal sacrifice and ritual use of intoxicants. He was a prophet and reformer who introduced the god of wisdom Ahura Mazda as supreme being and creator. Several other gods, such as the god of evil Angra Mainyu, were demoted with disclaimer of certain rituals.

According to Zoroaster, the purpose of life is to support the god Ahura Mazda, who answers for creation, existence, and free will. Active participation in life through virtuous deeds is necessary to ensure happiness and to keep chaos at bay. The roots of Zoroastrianism are likely found in prehistoric Indo-Iranian religious system, of which the Indian Vedic religions are derived. The importance of Zoroastrianism is huge. All beliefs found in the Abrahamic religions were already present in Zoroastrianism and were copied. Zoroastrianism states that the final saviour of the world, Saoshyant, will be born of a virgin, impregnated by divine seed while swimming in a lake. The saviour will let the dead rise for God's judgement, both those targeted in heaven and in hell, and the sinners will be sent back to hell to be purified of all corporeal sin.[143]

History repeats itself constantly.

Nebuchadnezzar II conquered and destroyed Jerusalem in 587 BC. He deported many prominent citizens along with a large part of the Jewish population of Judea. While in Babylon, the Jews were faced with the pagan religion of the region. They were impressed by the worship of a supergod (Marduk) who dominated all other gods. When Cyrus II conquered Babylon, the Jewish exiles returned to their original country. Cyrus the Great had a policy to respect the customs and religions of the conquered peoples. The Jews returned from Babylonian captivity to Jerusalem in 539 BC. During their stay at Babylon, under the rule of Cyrus II, the Jews also had the opportunity to take knowledge of Zoroastrianism, the state religion of the conqueror.

In the Judaic world view, the meaning of life is to elevate the physical world and prepare it for the world to come, the Messianic era. Even in the Judaic world, there is debate concerning the spiritual afterlife and the eschatological order. Judaism's most important feature is the worship of a single, incomprehensible, transcendent one, indivisible, absolute being who created and governed the universe.

Isaiah, the main prophet of Judaism, is documented by a book in the Hebrew Bible. He would have lived around the eighth century BC during the kingdom of Judah, but the exact relationship between the book and such historical Isaiah is not only complicated but also very doubtful. The book recounts after all matters about three centuries and consequently contains gross errors. The book of Isaiah is suffering from pseudepigraphy (written under false name or alias). Isaiah served as seer under different kings, including Josiah, king of Judah. He is referred to by the Abrahamic religions as the prophet regarding the monotheistic god, although not the least evidence exists. According to Judaism, the meaning of life is the uplift of the physical world (Olam HaZeh) and preparing the world to come (Olam HaBa), the Messianic era, which also includes the spiritual afterlife. Judaism is not focused on personal redemption as in Christianity, but as common (between man and man) and individually (between god and man) spiritualised actions in this world. Many prominent Jewish scientists and scholars such as Albert Einstein, Edward Teller, Richard Feynman, and Lawrence Strauss have abandoned Judaism and have become atheists.

In Christianity, the sacrifice of Christ's passion, death, and resurrection provides the means for transcending the impure state (Romans 6:23). The means for doing so varies between diverse groups of Christians, but all rely on belief in Jesus, his work on the cross, and his resurrection as the fundamental starting point for a relationship with God. Faith in God is found in Ephesians 2:8–9. "For by grace you have been saved through faith; and that not of yourselves, it is the gift of God; not because of works, that no one should boast" (New American Standard Bible). A recent alternative Christian theological discourse interprets Jesus as revealing that the purpose of life is to elevate our compassionate response to human suffering. How can any rational being accept such crap? It is beyond the comprehension of common man and is a mitigation of misery.

Nonetheless, the conventional Christian position is that people are justified by belief in the propitiatory sacrifice of Jesus's death on the cross. The Gospel maintains that through this belief, the barrier that sin has created between man and God is destroyed, and that allows God to change people and instil in them a new heart after his own will, as well as the ability to do it. This is what the terms *reborn* or *saved* almost always refer to. In the Westminster Shorter Catechism, the first question is, "What is the chief end of man?" That is, "What is man's main purpose?" The answer is, "Man's chief end is to glorify God and enjoy him forever." God requires one to obey the revealed moral law, saying, "Love the Lord your God with all your heart, with all your soul, with all your strength, and with all your mind; and your neighbour as yourself." The Baltimore Catechism answers the question "Why did God make you?" by saying, "God made me know him, to love him, and to serve Him in this world, and to be happy with him forever in heaven."[149] The Apostle Paul also answers this question in his mystic speech on the Areopagus in Athens: "And He has made from one blood every nation of men to dwell on all the face of the earth, and has determined their pre-appointed times and the boundaries of their dwellings, so that they should seek the Lord, in the hope that they might grope for Him and find Him, though He is not far from each one of us" (Acts 17:26–27). Catholicism's way of thinking is better expressed through the principle and foundation of St Ignatius of Loyola:

> The human person is created to praise, reverence, and serve God Our Lord, and by doing so, to save his or her soul. All other things on the face of the earth are created for human beings to help them pursue the end for which they are created. It follows from this that one must use other created things, in so far as they help towards one's end, and free oneself from them, in so far as they are obstacles to one's end. To do this, we need to make ourselves indifferent to all created things, provided the matter is subject to our free choice and there is no other prohibition. Thus, as far as we are concerned, we should not want health more than illness, wealth more than poverty, fame more than disgrace, a long life more than

> a short one, and similarly for all the rest, but we should desire and choose only what helps us more towards the end for which we are created.[153]

To believe all this, one must have an enormous imagination. The main purpose of life being to glorify a deity is absurd and reduces humankind to mental slavery during his short existence on earth. A human does not have to live as a martyr! The sacrifice of Jesus Christ holds the message that his death occurred to mitigate the life of mankind, but unfortunately that has not been realised! Therefore, deists believe that since his creation of the universe, God has no longer intervened in his creation. Jesus cannot be considered the son of God. How can God then be the symbol of virtue? Morality cannot be associated with him, and religions are human inventions.

In Islam, man's ultimate life objective is likewise to worship the creator Allah by abiding by the divine guidelines revealed in the Koran and the tradition of the Prophet. Earthly life is merely a test, determining one's afterlife either in Jannah (paradise) or in Jahannam (hell). Beliefs differ about the Kalam. The Sunni and the Ahmadiyya concept of predestination is divine decree; likewise, the Shi'a concept of predestination is divine justice. In the esoteric view of the Sufis, the universe exists only for God's pleasure; creation is a grand game wherein Allah is the greatest prize. Islam is merely a copy of Judaism adapted to the way of living of the original heathen tribes of Arabia. It is preposterous to imagine that the purpose and meaning of life could be to spend your life in worship and prayer to obtain a life hereafter. Islam is a worthless religion and is even dangerous to mankind. Since Averroes, Islam has not had a thinker worth mentioning who has contributed to the elevation of humankind.

Long before the way of life was stressed in religion, Hindu philosophy figured out the meaning of life. The aim is to realise the fundamental truth about oneself.

In all schools of Hinduism, the meaning of life is tied up in the concepts of karma (causal action), Ansara (the cycle of birth and rebirth), and moksha (liberation).[139] Existence is conceived as the progression of the atman (similar to the Western concept of a soul) across numerous lifetimes, as well as its ultimate progression towards liberation from karma. Particular goals for life are generally subsumed under broader yogas (practises) or Dharma (correct living), which are intended to create more favourable reincarnations, though they are generally positive acts in this life as well.[140] Traditional schools of Hinduism often worship Devas, which are manifestations of Ishvara (a personal or chosen God). These Devas are taken as ideal forms to be identified with, as a form of spiritual improvement. Hindi philosophy is dominated by the divine.

Buddhists practise to embrace with mindfulness the ill-being (suffering) and well-being that is present in life. Buddhists practise seeing the causes of ill-being and well-being in life. For example, one of the causes of suffering is an unhealthy attachment to material or non-material objects. The Buddhist sūtras and tantras do not speak about the meaning of life or the purpose of life, but about the potential of human life to end suffering—for example, through embracing (not suppressing or denying) cravings and conceptual attachments. Attaining and perfecting dispassion is a process of many levels that ultimately results in the state of Nirvana. Nirvana means freedom from both suffering and rebirth.

The Mohist philosophers (cf. chapter 20, supra) believed that the purpose of life was universal, impartial love. Mohism promoted a philosophy of impartial caring: a person should care equally for all other individuals, regardless of their actual relationship to the person. The expression of this indiscriminate caring is what makes man a righteous being in Mohist thought. This advocacy of impartiality was a target of attack by the other Chinese philosophical schools, most notably by the Confucians who believed that though love should be unconditional, it should not be indiscriminate. For example, children should hold a greater love for their parents than for random strangers.

Confucianism recognises human nature in accordance with the need for discipline and education. Because mankind is driven by both positive and negative influences, Confucians see a goal in achieving virtue through strong relationships and reasoning as well as minimising the negative. This emphasis on normal living is seen in the Confucianism scholar Tu Wei-Ming's quote: "We can realise the ultimate meaning of life in ordinary human existence."

Taoist cosmogony emphasises the need for all sentient beings and all men to return to the primordial or to rejoin with the oneness of the universe by way of self-cultivation and self-realisation. All adherents should understand and be in tune with the ultimate truth. Taoists believe all things were originally from Taiji and Tao, and the meaning of life for the adherents is to realise the temporal nature of the existence. "Only introspection can then help us to find our innermost reasons for living ... the simple answer is here within ourselves." This is all genuinely nice, but it's very theoretical and contributes little to real life.

Shinto is the native religion of Japan. Shinto means "the path of the kami" (the spirits or the phenomena that are worshipped), but more specifically it can be taken to mean "the divine crossroad where the kami chooses his way". The "divine" crossroad signifies that all the universe is a divine spirit. This foundation of free will, choosing one's way, means that life is a creative process. Shinto wants life to live, not to die. Shinto sees death as pollution and regards life as the realm where the divine spirit seeks to purify itself by rightful self-development. Shinto wants individual human life to be prolonged forever on earth as a victory of the divine spirit in preserving its objective personality in its highest forms. The presence of evil in the world, as conceived by Shinto, does not stultify the divine nature by imposing on divinity responsibility for being able to relieve human suffering while refusing to do so. The sufferings of life are the sufferings of the divine spirit in search of progress in the objective world. From the divinity of the world is sought purpose and meaning from which at the same time is derived a philosophy of goodness, admirable but little believable.

In the Bhà'i religion, they believe the purpose of life is focused on spiritual growth and service to humanity. It's a much more noble purpose in life than those stressed in Islam.

There are many other old and new religions, each with their own specific, often unique, meanings of life in East Asia. However, in modern times it is often difficult to distinguish new religions from cults.

In the new Tenrikyo religion, life has a joyous meaning by participating in acts that provide happiness not only for themselves but also for others.

The most recent religions form a paradigm par excellence of the worthlessness of religions. They even border on the ridiculous.

The last established religion of any significance (currently around 15,000,000 believers) is the Mormon Church, or the Church of Jesus Christ of Latter-day Saints. Its founder was Joseph Smith, who claimed to have had a vision at fourteen years old in response to his search for truth. In the following years, he got more heavenly messages, including those from Jesus, that he should not join in any Christian denomination because they were all wrong and all their creeds were an abomination. In 1830, he wrote the Book of Mormon. In it are the instructions contained, which Smith obtained from the Angel Moroni to translate an ancient chronicle. The chronicle would be written on golden plates by the historian Mormon, who lived around four hundred years after Christ on the American continent. Before Smith rendered the plates to the Angel Moroni, he could show the plates to eleven witnesses, whose statements are recorded in the Book of Mormon. Although some of these witnesses have left the church, they never returned on their testimony. On 6 April 1830, the church was officially founded under the name Church of Christ, and later the Church of Jesus Christ of Latter-day Saints. After a life of constant persecution due to scams, bank fraud, betrayal, and multiple marriages (at least twenty-seven women), Smith was lynched on 27 June 1844 when he was in prison in Carthage, Illinois, and was attacked by a mob. After the assassination of Smith by an anti-Mormon crowd, Brigham Young held the Mormon community together. He organised an exodus to the west, to Utah, which then belonged to Mexico. In 1871, Young was tried for polygamy; he had twenty wives and commitments with fifty-five other women

This is sad history of a religion in the nineteenth century. Religion still plays a key role in the United States, and their political supporters even compete to become president of the United States. It is no different from what occurred in the past. It would be exaggerated to call all prophets of ancient times quacks. However, it cannot be denied that prophets act as fortune tellers and take their imagination, dreams, and alleged revelations as reality and poison their gullible fellow men with their dragons.

The scenario of the nineteenth century was repeated in the twentieth century when L. R. Hubbard, a prolific science fiction writer, founded the religion Scientology in 1952 on the basis of his book *Dianetics: The Modern Science of Mental Health*. The concept of the book mentions Hubbard auditing, a process he described during a TV interview as dehypnotising, based on the neutralisation of the destructive power of stored registration of traumatic events. Each scientific journal refused to take the script as serious. Nevertheless, his movement was a success in the United States, where it was as a faith exempt from tax. The church claims 10,000,000 followers, though 500,000 seems more realistic. Hubbard was a poor student in high school, was unsuccessful at university, and was a navy officer who was found unfit to act as a commanding officer. All his life, he had to contend with persecutions because of corruption, scams, and bank fraud. His followers wrote praising hagiographical manuscripts which are full of lies. In many countries of Europe, the Church of Scientology is classified as a cult and is prosecuted. The oldest son of Hubbard left Scientology in 1959, called his father a charlatan, and changed his name to Ronald Dewolf.

It is remarkable to what extent the human spirit has a potential for her affection and bears witness to far-reaching credulity that makes him completely irrational. One might ask whether man is not actually a silly mammal.

A curious story in the religion and the philosophy is one regarding Antony Flew, author of a famous article in philosophy, "*Theology and Falsification*".[166] In this paper, Flew demonstrates, in the view of a parable, how assertions (a state of belief) end by dissipation of its qualifications. In the same paper, he states that religious intellectuals are driven to double think (power of holding two contradictory beliefs simultaneously). During his life, in all his books and papers, he was a strong advocate of atheism, arguing that one should presuppose atheism until empirical evidence of a god surfaces. He was against religion and criticised the idea of life after death. He died in dementia. A few years before his death at the age of eighty-one, he suddenly admitted doubts about atheism and started leaning towards pantheism. His lifelong Plato's Socrates commitment to go where the evidence leads, he suddenly now believed in an inoffensive inactive god, because he had been misled on abiogenesis and that the recent philosophical and scientific findings (complexities of a living cell) make it impossible to provide a naturalistic theory of the origin of DNA of the first reproducing species from inanimate matter.

In 2007, Flew published the book *There Is a God: How the World's Most Notorious Atheist Changed His Mind* with Roy Abraham Varghese, his friend and philosophical adversary, as co-author. The book was heavily criticised for having been solely written by Varghese because Flew's serious mental state did not allow him to write any more, which was confirmed in several interviews. He died on 8 April 2010 in an extended care facility in Reading, England, suffering from severe dementia. Varghese bears the heavy burden of using the dementia of his friend to push his own convictions. At the death of the deist Voltaire, the Catholic Church pretended that he'd repented and called upon God in his pangs of death. Believers are always ready to distort the truth to justify their convictions.

The controversial book of Flew gives a philosophical interpretation based on alleged recent scientific achievements. The world view of the Big Bang ousted the idea of an endless and static universe. If the universe has a discernible beginning, the demand for an explanation of that beginning can no longer be dodged. But there is more, they claim. There exist in our universe constant and precise laws of nature, such as gravity and electromagnetism. Those natural laws provide the development of the universe. The values of the physical constants of those laws of nature seem so precisely tuned that their combination is seemingly inconceivable and unlikely. The anthropic principle makes the origin of human life possible and feels called upon the idea of creation by an infinitely intelligent designer. In chapter 4, the folly of the anthropic principle was already exposed. These so-called recent scientific achievements are not new at all and are always invoked by intellectual believers. What is new is the invoked theory of the orthodox Jewish nuclear physicist Gerald Schroeder, who is trying to reconcile religion and science, and which is based on the theory of time dilation. It advances the divine creation of six days recounted in Genesis as one billion years per day. Of course, Schroeder's theory has hardly any hearing by his peers. Experiments with muons have indeed shown that the effect really exists but in a very minute measure (the difference between the space station and Earth is 0.005 seconds, but on larger space distances, the difference can be significant) without approaching the assumption of Schroeder.

Religions have no foundation if you eliminate the miracles and the supernatural. Thus, when one believes in religion, he must be classified as a believer in superstition.

Believers make up the majority in the world. Most have no need to judge whether or not God exists. They are lazy-minded and simply believing is sufficient. Those who think have trepidation about the problem, perhaps out of fear of hallucinating. Others think about it but are unable to provide a satisfactory answer. After all, who or what is God? Who designed the designer, as Richard Dawkins put it? Is the designer physical or incorporeal?

What supports the Abrahamitic religions to explain that God is male or that man was created in his image? To create, one must itself exist (dasein).

If a supernatural entity caused the spark that induced the Big Bang, a lot of questions arise that highlight the nonsense of a religious principle, which has no place in the rational world of mankind. Where was God before the Big Bang? Where is he now? Does he still exist, or is he dead as Nietzsche puts it? If God created the universe and fathered man, why did he breed dinosaurs that have nothing to do with the evolution of man? Or does it form a striking confirmation of the theory of abiogenesis? God is considered perfect, but his creation is a catastrophe where the happiness of man is concerned. Religions claim that he is everywhere, an observer *par excellence* to behold the suffering of his people, and yet he does not act. Thus, he is a ruthless figure. The only scientific theory for the origin of life is abiogenesis, which is seriously questioned by the faithful.

Still, there is no reason to cling to the fairy tale of a supernatural entity. What supports the churches to declare that it is man's destiny to overcome the harshness of life as a martyr in order to acquire the happiness of the hereafter? All these pertinent questions point out the nonsense of religion!

Religions have little integrity. In the past, they gave rise to a very dark history with inhuman persecution and execution of dissidents. In addition, the world is constantly plagued by wars of religion. In the twentieth century, there were the scandals of the nunneries, where the single mothers, after they were deprived of their new- born, were obliged to work as slaves. The widespread paedophilia of priests is also a stain on the Catholic Church. Today, we have the atrocities of the Islamic State and the continued hatred between Sunni and Shia.[1]

There are many pseudoscientific theories (time dilation, anthropism, genesis interpretation based on creationism, intelligent design, irreducible complexity, etc.) proclaimed that use only teleological argument from pure religious considerations.[1, 161] Man has not only invented the supernatural god as a placebo against the frustration of life, but he has also found it necessary to hold out a prospect of eternal life to counter the fear of death—but only for those who live in accordance with the standards of that particular religion.

The question arises as to why Catholic intellectuals, all of whom assume that the Big Bang took a divine intervention, never stand still at the refusal of Georges Lemaître, the founder of the Big Bang theory, to the request of Pope Pius XII, to put forward his finding as proof of God. Lemaître diplomatically replied that science has nothing to do with religion. Lemaître was undoubtedly confronted with the same ordeal that Charles Darwin underwent when he, to the consternation of his religious wife, was obliged to forsake his faith while positing his evolution theory. In the past, Catholic scientists often have been the victims of persecution when they released opinions which were contradictory with the doctrines of the Church (e.g., Copernicus, Galileo Galilei, and Giordiano Bruno).

C. Senselessness of Philosophy

Philosophy is the study of general and fundamental problems, such as those related to reality, existence, knowledge, values, reason, mind, and language. In religion, feeling and faith play a role. Philosophy is a science. It is a theoretical discipline that expresses the desire and striving for knowledge and wisdom.[162] The term was originally used for general knowledge.

The philosophical perspectives on the meaning of life are those ideologies which explain life in terms of ideals or abstractions, as defined by man.

All over the world, East and West (India, Iran and China included), people have asked the same questions and built philosophical traditions.

The traditional fields of philosophy can be divided in three directions.

- Those focused on the human being, such as philosophical anthropology, ethics, aesthetics, social philosophy, and theology
- Those focused on nature, such as metaphysics (existence or being) and natural philosophy
- Those focused on human knowledge, such as logic, epistemology (theory of knowledge), rhetoric, and philosophy of science

Western philosophy has its origin in ancient Greece, which was transmitted to Europe via Arab-Islamic philosophy (Abulcasis, Al-Farabi, Al-Kindi, Averroes, and Avicenna) by translations from Greek into Arabic and which was present in Spain during the Moorish reign, where it was further developed. During the golden age of Islam, many medieval Islamic thinkers wrote humanistic, rational, and scientific discourses in their search for knowledge, meaning, and value. The reason why those in Islam of the Middle Ages flourished was that then an emphasis on freedom of speech prevailed, which unfortunately has now completely disappeared in the Arabic world.

The sixth century BCE pre-Socratic Greek philosophers Thales of Miletus and Xenophanes of Colophon were the first in ancient Greece to attempt to explain the world in terms of human reason rather than myth and tradition. Thales questioned the notion of anthropomorphic gods, and Xenophanes refused to recognise the gods of his time.

The philosophers disagree as to the meaning of life.

For Plato, the meaning of life is achieving the highest form of knowledge, which forms the idea of good and from which all good and righteous things, utility, and value are derived. Aristotle, the pupil of Plato, added, "To be good is to be virtuous." Everything happens for a purpose and that purpose is well-being. According to Aristotle, every skill, question, action, and choice of action shall be deemed to relate to any property as an object. This is the reason why good is rightly defined as the object of any effort. Everything happens for a purpose, and that purpose is the virtue (Ethics 1.1). But what is the greatest good in all matters of action? This is what applies to both the educated as the low-skilled—namely, the happiness which corresponds to the virtuous life and successful life. But they do not agree as what happiness is and means (Nicomacheaan Ethics 1.4). It is a way of life and no more, as evidenced by the following philosophy of ancient Greeks.

Antisthenes a pupil of Socrates, first outlined the themes of cynicism, stating that the purpose of life is living a life of virtue which agrees with nature. Happiness depends on being self-sufficient and master of one's mental attitude; suffering is the consequence of false judgments of value, which cause negative emotions and a concomitant vicious character.

Aristippus of Cyrene, also a pupil of Socrates, founded an early Socratic school that emphasised only one side of Socrates's teachings—namely, that happiness is one of the ends of moral action and that pleasure is the supreme good. It is a hedonistic world view wherein bodily gratification is more intense than mental pleasure. Cyrenaics prefer immediate gratification to the long-term gain of delayed gratification; denial is unpleasant unhappiness.

Epicurus (cf. Chapter 20, “Religion”, A. generalities, supra), supporter of atomism and pupil of the Platonist Pamphilus of Samos, is wrongly considered by the believers as a hedonist. In fact, he was a very sober man and was in favour of modest pleasures, almost ascetic abstinence of sex and appetite, with a view to achieving peace and lack of fear (ataraxia) via knowledge, friendship, virtue, and a moderate life. Bodily pain (aponia) is missing through a knowledge of the working of the world and the limits of one’s desires. Combined, lack of pain and fear means happiness in its highest form. To live well means fear of death and fear of the gods is unnecessary.

Zeno of Citium, a pupil of Crates of Thebes, established the stoic school. According to stoicism (but also according to Epictetus, Seneca, and Marcus Aurelius), God is the universe or nature. With that reason as the basis of humanity and the universe, it follows that the purpose of life is to live according to reason (logos)—that is, to live a life in accordance with nature. The meaning of life is “freedom from suffering” through apatheia—that is, being objective and having clear judgement, not indifference. The stoic philosophy presents itself as the preferred way to make man happy. Christianity has drawn much from stoicism, but the inherent pantheism was deemed by Emperor Justinian in 529 to be inconsistent with the Christian faith, and its distribution was prohibited.

In his didactic poem “The Rerum Natura”, the Roman Lucretius teaches about the manifestations of nature and their genesis. He preaches the philosophy of Epicurus and assigns the people that they must get rid of the fear of death and should not cherish superstitions or fear the power of the gods.

The greatest philosopher of the twentieth century, Ludwig Wittgenstein, defined philosophy as the discipline of nonsense, whereas the ingenious physicist and Nobel Prize laureate Richard Feynman ruled that philosophy meant to humans what ornithology meant to the birds.

In philosophy, there are many schools of thought, each of which has a separate life. But there is no decisive scope to really serve humanity. Therefore, there is actually very little interest in philosophy. The philosophical reflection is the result of a reasoning that bears no evidence, notwithstanding it is an excellent discipline for the development of reasoning. In the face of the overwhelming predominance of science, less and less attention to philosophy is paid in universities. The University of Rotterdam (Netherlands) is even considering cancelling the faculty of philosophy.

The different tendencies are distinguished from one another to the extent that they go out of theists, agnostics, deists, pantheists, and atheists. The philosophy of a believer is different from that of the unbeliever, though they both belong to the same flow, such as the existentialism of Heidegger and Sartre.

From the beginning, a major theme of philosophy was being (dassein), while the meaning of life and the purpose of life got less bidding. Existence means the being of a particular entity. Within the ontology, the most important branch of metaphysics, there are different views on the concept of existence. According to some philosophies containing transcendentalism, such as Platonism, a distinction should be made between the physical, material existence and the disembodied, the thought. According to other philosophies, such as materialism, in immanence, there are no objects that have no material existence. According to the materialists, all exists there is. In theology, there are a lot of questions. The existence of God should be awarded, or should he be regarded as transcendent, elevated beyond any human ontological understanding? What is the relationship between God and reality? Finally, theology preaches that God is proof of existence and the basis of absolute reality.

The existence of God remains an important debate. Epistemology examines criteria of truth, which define "primary truths", inherently accepted in research and knowledge. Consequently, nature cannot be doubted. Materialism holds that the only thing that exists is matter and that all phenomena, including consciousness, are the result of material interactions. Life is a characteristic that distinguishes objects that entertain biological processes from inanimate objects.

The concept of essence in philosophy is rather vague and highly contested. Essence (being) is derived from the Latin *esse* and is used to indicate the nature of something, what is characteristic and essential for something. In metaphysics and religion, essence is a synonym for soul, which is rejected by the existentialists.

The religious philosopher Soren Kierkegaard, a fierce opponent of the church, stressed essence on nature while human nature according to him does not exist because it does not determine human behaviour or direct it. Essence is only an attribute preceded by existence. This existentialist tenet was further elaborated on by Jean-Paul Sartre and the like of the Parisian intellectualised movement around 1950, with the understanding that all related to metaphysical essence and the soul was completely rejected. The teachings of Sartre that "existence precedes essence" is a rejection of the idealist philosophy of Georg Hegel and of the phenomenological philosophy (pure nature of perceiving) of the Catholic thinkers Husserl (originally a Jew) and Heidegger. What distinguishes the modern existentialists from their predecessors is that each person is responsible for his own actions and destiny. The challenge of man consists, in the absence of a transcendent God, to use within his absurd and meaningless existence his freedom to build his ethos and so give meaning to his existence.

The concept of reality, related to the notion of existence, is an interpretation of the world. It is controversial because it is too dependent on the sensory perceptions. Kant emphasised that one cannot prove that the knowledge we possess about the world causal relates to the world. In the academic discipline, the concept of reality pertains to clarity or evidence. According to Einstein, the belief in an external world, independent of the observer, is the basis of all science. However, because the sensory perception allows only indirect information from the external world, we can only think with speculative meanings so that the understanding of the physical reality is never final.[62]

Classical liberalism is a set of ideas that arose in the seventeenth and eighteenth centuries out of conflicts between a growing, wealthy, propertied class and the established aristocratic and religious orders that dominated Europe. Liberalism cast humans as beings with inalienable natural rights (including the right to retain the wealth generated by one's own work, which is opposed to socialism), and it sought out means to balance rights across society. Broadly speaking, it considers individual liberty to be the most important goal because only through ensured liberty are the other inherent rights protected. There are many forms and derivations of liberalism, but their central conceptions of the meaning of life trace back to three main ideas. Early thinkers such as John Locke, Jean-Jacques Rousseau, and Adam Smith saw humankind beginning in the state of nature and then finding meaning for existence through labour and property, as well as using social contracts to create an environment that supports those efforts.

Notwithstanding the admiration that one cherishes for the declaration of human rights resulting from the French Revolution of 1789 and the writings of Thomas Paine, man has no natural rights or duties. What he has are rules that he himself draws up for a harmonious society and its well-being.

Trade unions and syndicates who call for strikes in season or out of season when they feel that their members are wronged have no right to call "right upon work". Neither are they entitled to call for "inequality of tax assessments".

The highest good of man is his freedom.

When there is disparity in the treatment of the people, there is violation of the principle of equality. Slogans like "right upon work" is based on nothing. Another slogan, "the toughest shoulders must bear the heaviest burden is political nonsense and populism", is a transgression of the equality of people. The curtail of the freedom of man is a serious threat for the stimulus of life. It means entering mediocrity, the end of civilisation, and the hopes of Homo *sapiens.*

Utilitarianism is an ethical movement that measures the moral value of an act by the contribution that this act brings to the common good, whereby the well-being and happiness of all people is meant. The origins of utilitarianism can be traced back as far as Epicurus, but as a school of thought, it is credited to Jeremy Bentham, who found that "nature has placed mankind under the governance of two sovereign masters, pain and pleasure". From that moral insight one derives the rule of utility: "that the good is whatever brings the greatest happiness to the greatest number of people". He defined the meaning of life as the "greatest happiness principle". However, it is considered that this is probably impossible to achieve in practise. Utilitarianism was started by David Hume, who was inspired by the hedonism of Epicurus. It was further developed by Jeremy Bentham and by John Stuart Mill.

Arthur Schopenhauer has a special place in philosophy. He was a bon vivant who preached asceticism. Therefore, he was violently criticised by later philosophers, including Bertrand Russell. Nevertheless, his influence was great on important artists as Richard Wagner, Leo Tolstoy, Marcel Proust, Thomas Mann, and Gerard Reve, as well as on philosophers like Friedrich Nietzsche and Henri Bergson.

According to Schopenhauer (cf. chapter 14, supra), the human will be guided by motives, but the man himself is blind and stupid. It is the urge to exist that is working in everything and in the infinite life of the world. In the living nature, no desire is finally fulfilled, and all that without any reason and without any purpose. His way of life holds that one must make the best of life in a difficult existence.

For Schopenhauer, human desire was futile, illogical, and directionless—and by extension, so was all human action in the world. He wrote, "Man can indeed desire what he wants, but he cannot what he wants." He is credited with one of the most famous opening lines of philosophy, "The world is my representation", whereby he answers all discussions about the reality of things.

Nietzsche is the philosopher who proclaimed the death of god and thus the end of the classic, sacred umbrella Christian story. He characterised nihilism as emptying the world (an especially human existence) of meaning, purpose, comprehensible truth, and essential value. Nihilism is the process of "the devaluing of the highest values". He saw the nihilist as a natural result of the idea that God is dead, insisting it was something to overcome but questioning whether the nihilist's life-negating values meant a return to the meaning of earth. He considered that life is only worth living if there are goals inspiring one to live, and so all ideations take place from a particular perspective.

Nihilism suggests that life is without objective meaning.[63]

The philosophy of life (lebensphilosophie) is a philosophical school of taught which emphasises the meaning, value, and purpose of life as the foremost focus of philosophy. It was inspired by the critique of rationalism in the works of Schopenhauer, Kierkegaard, and Nietzsche. It emerged in nineteenth-century Germany as a reaction to the rise of positivism and the theoretical focus prominent in much of post-Kantian philosophy. The philosophy bears relation to the subjectivist philosophy of Vitalism (élan vital), developed by Henri Bergson (a Jew converted to Catholicism), who convinced many thinkers that the processes of immediate experience and intuition are more significant than abstract rationalism and science for understanding reality.

Philosophy of life pays special attention to life as a whole, which can only be understood from within. It rejects Kantian abstract philosophy or scientific reductionism of positivism.

The human situation is considered a struggle between what is (existence) and what ought to be (essence). Normative situations are alternatives, choice, freedom, values, standards, ideals, obligations, and responsibility, whereas the existential predicament bears on finitude, alienation, anxiety, guilt, ambivalence, and thrownness. Denial of essence refers to regression and pre-human existence. Nihilism is a denial of meaning. Denial of existence is found in Eastern mysticism and essentialism. Humanism, religion, and Zen hold affirmation of essence and existence. Religion is an attempt to overcome the existentialism predicament. Existentialism has two basic forms of existentialism, a religious one and an atheistic one. Religious existentialism is best exemplified by St Augustine and Blaise Pascal, who hold that there are two levels of reality: essence (which is the ground of being) and existence. Atheistic existentialism is best exemplified by Nietzsche and Sartre, who hold that there is one level of reality, existence. In this view, each person constructs his own unique and temporary essence. However, to the theist Martin Heidegger, nihilism is the movement whereby being is forgotten and is transformed into value—in other words, the reduction of being to exchange value. Heidegger, in accordance with Nietzsche, saw in the so-called death of God a potential source for nihilism: "If God, as the supra-sensory ground and goal of all reality, is dead; if the supra-sensory world of the ideas has suffered the loss of its obligatory, and above it, its vitalizing and up-building power, then nothing more remains to which man can cling, and by which he can orient himself."

The French philosopher Albert Camus (cf. chapter 14, supra) asserts that the absurdity of the human condition is that people search for external values and meaning in a world which has none and is indifferent to them. Camus writes of value nihilists such as his absurd hero Meursault in his book *The Stranger*, but also of values in a nihilistic world, where people can instead strive to be "heroic nihilists", living with dignity in the face of absurdity, living with "secular saintliness", having fraternal solidarity, and rebelling against and transcending the world's indifference. The outlook of Camus is indeed beautiful in the face of a cruel world. We shall further see that his philosophy is the only one that somewhat corresponds to a purely scientific view.

According to existentialism (cf., chapter 14, supra), people create the essence (meaning) of their lives. Life is not determined by a supernatural God or an earthly authority—one is free. As such, one's ethical prime directives are action, freedom, and decision, and thus existentialism opposes rationalism and positivism. In seeking meaning to life, the existentialist looks to where people find meaning in life, in the course of which using only reason as a source of meaning is insufficient. This gives rise to the emotions of anxiety and dread felt in considering one's free will and the concomitant awareness of death. According to Jean-Paul Sartre, existence precedes essence. The essence of one's life arises only after one comes to existence.

Søren Kierkegaard spoke about a leap, arguing that life is full of absurdity, and one must make one's own values in an indifferent world. One can live meaningfully (free of despair and anxiety) in an unconditional commitment to something finite, devoting that meaningful life to the commitment, despite the vulnerability inherent to doing so. He argued that the absurdity of certain religions prevents humans from reaching God rationally.

In absurdist philosophy, the absurd arises out of the fundamental disharmony between the individual's search for meaning and the apparent meaninglessness of the universe. As beings looking for meaning in a meaningless world, humans have three ways of resolving the dilemma. Kierkegaard and Camus describe the solutions in their works *The Sickness Unto Death* and *The Myth of Sisyphus*, respectively.

- Suicide (or "escaping existence"): a solution in which a person simply ends one's own life. Both Kierkegaard and Camus dismiss the viability of this option.
- Religious belief in a transcendent realm or being: a solution in which one believes in the existence of a reality that is beyond the absurd and as such has meaning. Kierkegaard stated that a belief in anything beyond the absurd requires a non-rational but perhaps necessary religious acceptance in such an intangible and empirically unprovable thing (now commonly referred to as a leap of faith). Camus, however, regarded this solution as "philosophical suicide".
- Acceptance of the absurd: a solution in which one accepts and even embraces the absurd and continues to live despite of it. Camus endorsed this solution (notably in his 1947 allegorical novel *The Plague*), whereas Kierkegaard regarded this solution as "demoniac madness". "He rages most of all at the thought that eternity might get it into its head to take his misery from him" (*The Sickness unto Death*).

Humanism is the philosophical and ethical stance that emphasises the value and agency of human beings individually and collectively, and it generally prefers critical thinking and evidence (rationalism, empiricism) over established doctrine and faith (fideism). In modern times, humanist movements are typically aligned with secularism. Today, humanism refers to a non-theistic life stance centred on human agency, looking to science instead of religious dogma in order to understand the world.

From the fourteenth to the sixteenth century, humanism was the name given to the intellectual, literary, and scientific movement that the form of knowledge based on the culture, literature, and sciences of classical antiquity and the Renaissance of Western culture.

Per secular humanism, the human species came to be by reproducing successive generations in a progress of unguided evolution, free of supernatural sources, as an integral expression of nature, which is self-existing.[63] People determine human purpose without supernatural influence; it is the human personality that is the purpose of human's life. It is an ethical life of personal fulfilment that aspires to the greater good of all humanity.[63] Humanism posits that every living creature has the right to determine its personal and social "meaning of life", in so far as it has no negative effects on humanity as a whole.

During the French revolution, and soon after in Germany under the influence of the Left Hegelians (David Friedrich Strauss and Ludwig Feuerbach), humanism began to refer to an ethical philosophy centred on humankind, without any bearings to the transcendent or supernatural.

From a humanistic-psychotherapeutic point of view, the question of the meaning of life is reinterpreted as, "What is the meaning of my life?" This approach emphasises the fact that the question is personal and avoids focusing on the cosmic or religious questions about the overarching purpose. There are many therapeutic responses to this question. For example, the neurologist Viktor Frankl advocates dereflection, which can be translated as "no longer endlessly reflect on oneself but instead participate in life". Overall, the therapeutic response is the question itself ("What is the meaning of life?") evaporated at a full involvement in life. (The question then results morphologically in a more specific concern such as, "Which delusion do I undergo? What is blocking my ability to enjoy things? Why do I neglect my loved ones?")

Humanism has a long history that's more closely tied to the modern concept and different from what it meant in the Renaissance. In Asia, human-centred philosophy, which rejects the supernatural, is found around 1500 BC in the Lokayata system of Indian philosophy. "Nasadya Sukta" (hymn of creation of the universe), a passage in the Rig Veda, contains one of the first recorded statements of agnosticism. In the sixth century BC, Gautama Buddha posited in the Pali literature a sceptical attitude towards the supernatural. Old humanism, as an organised system of thinking, can also be found in the Gathas (Sanskrit for song or verse) of Zarathustra (Zoroaster), written between 1500–600 BC in ancient Iran. In the sixth century BC, the Taoist teacher Lao Tzu created a series of naturalistic concepts with some elements of the humanist philosophy, which can be found in the teachings of Confucius.

Thomas Paine was a most remarkable humanist. He was an English American political activist, philosopher, political theorist, revolutionary, and founding father of the United States. His ideas reflected Enlightenment-era rhetoric of transnational human rights. He arrived in the American colonies in 1774 with the help of Benjamin Franklin, just in time for the American Revolution, for which he wrote in 1776 the all-famous pamphlet "Common Sense". John Adams stated, "Without the pen of the author of 'Common Sense', the sword of Washington would have been raised in vain." Paine became notorious because of his pamphlet "The Age of Reason", in which he advocated deism, promoted reason and free thought, and argued against institutionalised religion in general and Christian doctrine. When he died in 1809, only six people attended his funeral because he had been ostracised for his ridicule of Christianity. The conservative author and politician Edmond Burke was an opponent of Paine's philosophy. The erudite, author, and journalist Christopher Hitchens was an ardent admirer of Paine.

The philosophical subgenres of humanism and transhumanism, sometimes used synonymously, are extensions of humanistic values.[137] One should seek the advancement of humanity and of all life to the greatest degree feasible and seek to reconcile Renaissance humanism with twenty-first-century culture.[138] In this light, every living creature has the right to determine its personal and social "meaning of life".

Logical positivists ask, "What is the meaning of life? What is the meaning in asking? And If there are no objective values, then is life meaningless?" Ludwig Wittgenstein, the greatest philosopher of the twentieth century, and the logical positivists said that "Expressed in language, the question is meaningless" because *in* life the statement the "meaning of x", usually denotes the *consequences* of x, or the *significance* of x, or *what is notable* about x. Thus when the meaning of life concept equals x in the statement the "meaning of x", the statement becomes recursive and therefore nonsensical. Or it might refer to the fact that biological life is essential to having a meaning in life. Biological life is part of the nature of the universe.

Pragmatism, which originated in the late nineteenth century in the United States, concerned itself mostly with truth, positing that "only in struggling with the environment" do data and derived theories have meaning, and that consequences, like utility and practicality, are also components of truth. Moreover, pragmatism posits that anything useful and practical is not always true, arguing that what most contributes to the most human good in the long course is true. In practise, theoretical claims must be practically verifiable—that is, one should be able to predict and test claims—and that ultimately the needs of humankind should guide human intellectual inquiry. Pragmatic philosophers suggest that the practical, useful understanding of life is more important than searching for an impractical, abstract truth about life. William James argued that truth could be made but not sought. To a pragmatist, the meaning of life is discoverable only via experience. Indeed, experience forms humans and contributes to its evolution.

The current era has seen radical changes in both formal and popular conceptions of human nature. The knowledge disclosed by modern science has effectively rewritten the relationship of humankind to the natural world. Advances in medicine and technology have freed humans from significant limitations and ailments of previous eras, and philosophy—particularly following the linguistic turn—has altered how the relationships people have with themselves and each other are conceived. Questions about the meaning of life have also seen radical changes, from attempts to re-evaluate human existence in biological and scientific terms (as in pragmatism and logical positivism) to efforts to meta-theorise about meaning-making as a personal, individual-driven activity (existentialism, secular humanism). Serious doubt should be expressed whenever metaphysics conflicts with science.

The things (people, events) in the life of a person can have meaning (importance) as parts of a whole, but a discrete meaning of life, itself, aside from those things, cannot be discerned. A person's life has meaning (for himself and others) as the life events resulting from his achievements, legacy, family, et cetera, but to say that life itself has meaning is a misuse of language because any note of significance or of consequence is relevant only *in* life (to the living), rendering the statement erroneous. Bertrand Russell wrote that although he found that his distaste for torture was not like his distaste for broccoli, he found no satisfactory, empirical method of proving this.

> When we try to be definite, as to what we mean when we say that this or that is "Good", we find ourselves involved in very great difficulties. Bentham's creed, that pleasure is the Good, roused furious opposition, and was said to be a pig's philosophy. Neither he nor his opponents could advance any argument. In a scientific question, evidence can be adduced on both sides, and, in the end, one side is seen to have the better case—or, if this does not happen, the question is left undecided. But in a question, as to whether this, or that, is the ultimate Good, there is no evidence, either way; each disputant can only appeal to his own emotions, and employ such rhetorical devices as shall rouse similar emotions in others. Questions as to "values"—that is to say, as to what is good or bad on its own account, independently of its effects—lie outside the domain of science, as the defenders of religion emphatically assert. I think that, in this, they are right, but I draw the further conclusion, which they do not draw, that questions as to "values" lie wholly outside the domain of knowledge. When we assert that this, or that, has "value", we are giving expression to our own emotions, not to a fact, which would still be true if our personal feelings were different.

Broadly speaking, postmodernist thought sees human nature as constructed by language, or by structures and institutions of human society. Unlike other forms of philosophy, postmodernism rarely seeks out a priori or innate meanings in human existence, but instead focuses on analysing or critiquing *given* meanings to rationalise or reconstruct them. Anything resembling a "meaning of life" in postmodernist terms can only be understood within a social and linguistic framework and must be pursued as an escape from the power structures that are already embedded in all forms of speech and interaction. As a rule, postmodernists see awareness of the constraints of language as necessary to escaping those constraints, but different theorists take different views on the nature of this process: from radical reconstruction of meaning by individuals (as in deconstructionism) to theories in which individuals are primarily extensions of language and society, without real autonomy (as in post-structuralism). In general, postmodernism seeks meaning by looking at the underlying structures that create or impose meaning, rather than the epiphenomenal appearances of the world.

According to Steven Pinker,[163] in the mid-twentieth century, psychology was no longer "the science of mental life" (as William James had defined it) but "the science of behaviour". Mentalistic concepts—thoughts, memories, goals, and emotions—had been banned as unscientific, replaced by associations between stimuli and responses.

But new ideas about computation, feedback, information, and communication were in the air, and psychologists realised they had enormous potential for a science of mind. Four Harvard scholars used them to launch the "cognitive revolution".

George Miller noted that people could label, quantify, or remember about seven items at a time, whether they were tones, digits, words, or phrases. That meant the human brain must be constricted by a bottleneck of seven (plus or minus two) units, which Miller called chunks.

Linguist Noam Chomsky, while at the Harvard Society of Fellows, noted that people can produce and understand an infinite number of novel sentences. They must have internalised a grammar, or set of rules, rather than having memorised a list of responses. Children are not taught this grammar and so are equipped with a "language acquisition device" that instantiates a "universal grammar".

Jerome Bruner co-authored *A Study of Thinking*, which analysed people as constructive problem-solvers rather than passive media as they mastered new concepts. His colleague Roger Brown analysed the relationship of concepts to language and initiated a new science of language development in children.

In 1960, Bruner and Miller founded the Harvard Centre for Cognitive Studies, which institutionalised the revolution and launched the field of cognitive science. Today, the study of the human mind is amongst the most exciting frontiers of science. Its practical applications include the design of software, the diagnosis of neurological disease, and the formation of public policy. Its theories have revolutionised our understanding of ancient problems such as consciousness, free will, and human nature.

On the other hand, Yuval Noah Harari, a secular Jew, a homosexual in a same-sex marriage, a professor of history at the university of Jerusalem, considers in his bestseller *Sapiens: A Brief History of Humankind*[164] that cognitive revolution is the evolution of mankind which endowed Homo *sapiens* with rationality and language fifty thousand years ago. This revolution is only a stride in evolution, which has no end.

A particular aspect in Harari's book is his argument about the agricultural revolution that asks a lot of thought. He is of the opinion that the evolution of man from hunter-gatherer to farmer, though yielding more safety, meant loss of freedom and at the same time a decrease in happiness. He agrees with the view of Jean-Jacques Rousseau that man in his state of "noble savage" was happiest (cf. chapter 7, supra). This would mean that the evolution of man brings about less happiness and that the simplest way of life is the happiest—in other words, the dumber, the happier! What a blow to intellectualism.

Man considers himself a superior being and gives himself the title of Homo *sapiens*. Man is indeed the most developed being on earth but is far from being a wise being. The man is at the most an *animal rationale*, with all its faults. In a world of more than seven billion people, perhaps 10 per cent of the population can be considered significantly developed. The term *rational animal* refers to a classical definition of humanity or human nature, associated with Aristotelianism.[152]

In the *Nicomachean Ethics*, I.13, Aristotle states that the human being has a rational principle (Greek: λόγον ἔχον) on top of the nutritive life shared with plants and the instinctual life shared with other animals (i.e., the ability to carry out rationally formulated projects). That capacity for deliberative imagination was equally singled out as man's defining feature in *De Anima* III.11. While seen by Aristotle as a universal human feature, the definition applied to wise and foolish alike, and it did not in any way imply the *making* of rational choices as opposed to the *ability* to make them.

Neoplatonic philosopher Porphyry defined man as a "mortal rational animal", and he also considered animals to have a (lesser) rationality of their own.[5]

The definition of man as a rational animal was common in scholastic philosophy. *Catholic Encyclopaedia* states that this definition means that "in the system of classification and definition shown in the Arbor Porphyria, man is a substance, corporeal, living, sentient, and rational".

In "Meditation II" of *Meditations on First Philosophy*, Descartes arrives at his famous "I think; therefore I am" claim. He then goes on to wonder, "What am I?" He considers and rejects the scholastic concept of the rational animal: "Shall I say 'a rational animal'? No; for then I should have to inquire what an animal is, what rationality is, and this one question would lead me down the slope to other harder ones."[7]

Freud was as aware as any of the irrational forces at work in humankind, but he nevertheless resisted what he called too much "stress on the weakness of the ego in relation to the id and of our rational elements in the face of the daemonic forces within us".

Neo-Kantian philosopher Ernst Cassirer, in his work *An Essay on Man*, altered Aristotle's definition to label man as a symbolic animal. This definition has been influential in the field of philosophical anthropology, where it has been reprised by Gilbert Durand, and it has been echoed in the naturalist description of man as the compulsive communicator.

Sociologists in the tradition of Max Weber distinguish rational behaviour (means-end oriented) from irrational, emotional, or confused behaviour, as well as from traditional-oriented behaviour, but they recognise the wide role of all the latter types in human life.

Ethnomethodology sees rational human behaviour as representing perhaps one-tenth of the human condition, dependent on the nine-tenths of background assumptions which provide the frame for means-end decision-making.

Bertrand Russell satirised the concept that man is rational, saying, "Man is a rational animal—so at least I have been told. Throughout a long life I have been looked diligently for evidence in favour of this statement, but so far I have not had the good fortune to come across it." The humour of his observation derives from an equivocation between describing mankind as rational (i.e., that all members of the species has the potential to think, whether that potential is realised or not) and describing an individual person as rational (i.e., the person can think well, avoid biases, and make valid inferences).

What's important is that man has the ability to think, but the question is whether the ability to think is realised. Superficial thinking is present daily, but thinking in depth is hardly realised by the human beings.

God is a supernatural entity, invented by humans in order to be able to understand the universe. Religions are false institutions to honour and serve a fictitious deity. They have manipulated humankind and forced upon it a way of living which was far from beneficial and certainly not benevolent. In its historicity, the rule of the Church has been a disaster, and in the case of Islam it continues to be so. Religions seduce their followers with the ludicrous prospect of a fictitious afterlife to compensate for a hard existence on Earth. The tenets of religion, bearing no truth, do not allow a judicious approach to the matter of purpose and meaning of life. Neither does metaphysics.

Metaphysics is the oldest branch of philosophy and perhaps the least important because it completely takes the line of abstract thinking. It tries to explain the fundamental nature of being and the world that encompasses it.

- Ultimately, what is there?
- What is it like?

Metaphysics deals with the first principles of things, including such concepts as being, knowing, substance, essence, cause, identity, time, and space. Originally called natural science, it was demoted by the scientific method to philosophical enquiry of a non-empirical nature. Some philosophers of science, such as the neo-positivists, say that natural science rejects the study of metaphysics, but other philosophers of science disagree. Some philosophers advance the anthropic principle to adjudge a meaning to life.

The anthropic principle is the philosophical consideration that observations of the universe must be compatible with the conscious and sapient life that observes it. It lacks the deeper physical understanding of the universe and seems a resignation. The anthropic principle is in contradiction with the modern, evolved Copernican principle. As metaphysics embraces no hard facts and examines what lies beyond existence, it cannot be considered to examine purpose and meaning of life.

In his book *Known and Unknown: Memoir*, prominent ex-politician and businessman Donald Rumsfeld wrote, "There are known knows. There are things we know that we know. There are known unknowns. That is to say, there are things that we know we don't know. But there are also unknown unknowns. There are things we don't know we don't know."

D. Scientific Approach to the Meaning of Life

After having exhausted every aspect of the universe regarding life and humans, an approach can be made regarding the mystery of life in scientific terms of purpose and meaning.

The universe is the way it is, whether we like it or not. We are as we are and live as we do on Earth because of the interplay of our inherent natures and the environment of the universe. This much is uncontroversial, nevertheless the quest of humankind has always been which and for which do we exist. All cultures have wondered about their origins and the paradox of how something came from seemingly nothing.

The current era has seen radical changes in both formal and popular conceptions of human nature. The knowledge disclosed by modern science has effectively rewritten the relationship of humankind to the natural world. Advances in medicine and technology have freed humans from significant limitations and ailments of previous eras, and philosophy (particularly following the linguistic turn) has altered how the relationships of people with themselves and each other are conceived. Questions about the meaning of life have also seen radical changes, from attempts to re-evaluate human existence in biological and scientific terms (as in pragmatism and logical positivism) to efforts to meta-theorise about meaning-making as a personal, individual-driven activity (existentialism, secular humanism). Serious doubt should be expressed whenever metaphysics conflicts with science.

The scientific method[165] is a body of techniques for investigating phenomena, acquiring new knowledge, or correcting and integrating previous knowledge. To be termed scientific, a method of inquiry is commonly based on empirical or measurable evidence subject to specific principles of reasoning. Oxford Dictionaries Online defines the scientific method as "a method or procedure that has characterised natural science since the 17th century, consisting in systematic observation, measurement, and experiment, and the formulation, testing, and modification of hypotheses". Experiments need to be designed to test hypotheses. Experiments are a valuable tool of the scientific method.

The method is a continuous process that begins with observations about the natural world. People are naturally inquisitive, and so they often come up with questions about things they see or hear. They often develop ideas or hypotheses about why things are the way they are. The best hypotheses lead to predictions that can be tested in many ways. The strongest tests of hypotheses come from carefully controlled experiments that gather empirical data. Depending on how well additional tests match the predictions, the original hypothesis may require refinement, alteration, expansion, or even rejection. If a particular hypothesis becomes well supported, a general theory may be developed.

Although procedures vary from one field of inquiry to another, they are frequently the same from one to another. The process of the scientific method involves making conjectures (hypotheses), deriving predictions from them as logical consequences, and then carrying out experiments based on those predictions. A hypothesis is a conjecture, based on knowledge obtained while seeking answers to the question. The hypothesis might be very specific, or it might be broad. Scientists then test hypotheses by conducting experiments. A scientific hypothesis must be falsifiable, implying that it is possible to identify a possible outcome of an experiment that conflicts with predictions deduced from the hypothesis; otherwise, the hypothesis cannot be meaningfully tested.

The purpose of an experiment is to determine whether observations agree with or conflict with the predictions derived from a hypothesis. Experiments can take place anywhere from a college lab to CERN's Large Hadron Collider. There are difficulties in a formulaic statement of method. However, though the scientific method is often presented as a fixed sequence of steps, it represents a set of general principles. Not all steps take place in every scientific inquiry (nor to the same degree), and they are not always in the same order. Some philosophers and scientists have argued that there is no scientific method; they include physicist Lee Smolin and philosopher Paul Feyerabend (in his *Against Method*). Others consider that the whole idea of a theory of scientific method is yesteryear's debate.

The beginning and the end of life requires an answer to the question of the meaning of life. Apart from religion (where it is an important part), the meaning of life is a topic in philosophy that's often raised, but it's never explored in depth because it is the whole concept of existence, consciousness, and happiness as well as the symbolic mind with respect to ontology, value, purpose, ethics, good and evil, monotheistic god or multiple gods, soul, the afterlife, and many other issues, which are dealt with separately but never as a whole. The demand for the nature, purpose, and meaning of life also has meaning outside philosophy and religion. There are two mutually exclusive objectives.

* life has a deeper meaning
* life has no deeper meaning

Each rational being asks, "What is the meaning of my life? Where do we come from? What are we, and where are we going?" What everyone is seeking, without distinction between the intelligentsia and the large mass of the world's population, is the pursuit of happiness. Happiness can be defined as the satisfaction with its living conditions. This can include several positive emotions such as joy, pleasure, peace, tranquillity, and happiness. The living conditions of most of the world's population is far from ideal. There is, after all, a constant fight against poverty, and so life comes down to a struggle for existence; the necessary positive emotions are missing. This is exploited in religion by presenting to the stumper a paradise in the hereafter.

Has life any purpose or meaning? To be able to answer this question, one must go back to the roots of life.

The singularity of the Big Bang caused the beginning of the universe. It was first seriously envisaged by Belgian mathematician and physicist Monsignor Georges Lemaître in 1927, as an implication of his work on Einstein's 1915 equations of general relativity and early observational indications of an expansion of the universe. The theory was initially repudiated and denounced by the astronomer Fred Hoyle as the Big Bang theory, and the label stuck. However, the theory became firmly established by the later scientific observations of expansion and radiation and the analysis of data concerning very distant supernova explosions.

The Big Bang started the whole universe with an utterly stupendous explosion. The Big Bang was not localised at some particular region of space. In accordance with Einstein's perspective of general relativity, at the time of the Big Bang, the Big Bang encompassed the entire spread of the universe and included all physical space, not merely the material contents of the universe. Accordingly, space is taken to have been, in an appropriate sense, infinitely small (zero size) and infinitely dense and hot. The established wisdom is that the energetic fireball of the Big Bang nearly fourteen billion years ago spawned matter and antimatter in perfect balance. Intense heat and light, with huge energy, emerged from the Big Bang and congealed into counterbalance pieces of matter and antimatter. This transubstantiation of radiant energy into particles and antiparticles is not a one-way voyage; if these opposites subsequently come into contact, they annihilate one another, with the energy that was previously entrapped within them being liberated as gamma rays. In the dense cauldron of the infant universe, such collisions would have been very common, and the new-born material would not have lasted very long. If in the first moment matter and antimatter emerged equally from the Big Bang, an instant later they should have annihilated one another. The Big Bang is the creation of all energy, all matter, and all the known universe, together with space and time. This is profound and seemingly beyond common comprehension. Here arises a problem concerning *memorabilia* and *imponderabilia*. According to Stephen Hawking,[4] time started with the Big Bang because the universe did not exist before the Big Bang. This is not an absolute truth because there must have been a period before the singularity. If time started with the Big Bang and advanced with time plus (T+), then there was time minus (T-) when there was dense, hot matter or energy. Science remains discrete on the pre–Big Bang, which is quite normal considering that, contrary to the proven singularity due to the known facts and measuring the consequences, the period of hot density is without absolute facts and measurement because observations of consequences of facts are excluded. Hawking considers speculations on this period useless. However, one must accept a pre–Big Bang period about which our knowledge is minimal. At the same time, this should not result in a fairy story of a supernatural entity having created the universe. What we do know is that an explosion took place. Energy or matter (M= (EC^2), thus there was something before the Big Bang, matter or energy. What existed we ignore because there is no possibility of discovering it. So, there was time before the Big bang? Another query is whether there was space in which the explosion took place. All scientists agree that space started with the big bang and did not exist before. What existed before the big bang will always remain a mystery. There are no remains of light because existence of light only started by the big bang. For an ignoramus as myself it rests an enigma (cf. Kraus, 53).

No intelligence intervened in the Big Bang. The happening of the Big Bang was autochthonous, arising without apparent cause. The universe was created in terms of physical forces acting under impersonal laws. The spontaneous generator of something out of seemingly nothing is the singularity of the Big Bang. If the Big Bang is spontaneous and accidental, then it is not autotelic, and it is not possible to attach any cause or meaning to this genesis. Pope John Paul II realised the danger of cosmology for religion. In 1981, he let the Jesuits organise a conference on cosmology. At the end of the conference, the participants were invited to an audience. He told the participants that it was all right to study the evolution of the universe after the Big Bang but that the scientists should not inquire into the Big Bang itself because that was the moment of creation and therefore the work of God (who was responsible for the spark that set off the explosion). John Paul II was a fundamentalist and was not a very intelligent man. At that moment, he was ignorant that Stephen Hawking had told the conference that there was the possibility that space-time was finite but had no boundary, in which case it had no beginning and thus no moment of creation.

Out the chaos of the Big Bang came order from disorder. This order pervades the universe and establishes physical laws.

The first-generation stars converted some of the original hydrogen and helium into elements like carbon and oxygen The solar system is about five billion years old. The first one or two thousand million years of Earth's existence were too hot for the development of anything complicated. The following three billion years have been taken up by the slow process of biological evolution, which have led from the simplest organisms to the beings of humankind.

Although the weak anthropic principle seems obvious, without any utility, it is highly contested in the scientific world as being metaphysical and contrary to the evolved Copernican principle. Some go much further and propose a strong verse of the anthropic principle. According to this theory, there are either many different universes or many different regions of a single universe, each with its own initial configuration and, perhaps, with its own set of scientific laws. In most of these universes, the conditions would not be right for the development of complicated organisms; only in the few universes that are like ours would intelligent beings develop and ask, "Why is the universe the way we see it." The answer is that if it had been different, we would not be there! This reasoning relies on a hypothetic multiverse proposed in quantum mechanics. The reasoning is abstract, belongs to the sphere of metaphysics, and is foreign to science.

The weak anthropic principle also restricts the principle to carbon-based life, rather than being based on the presence of observers. It proposes that the purpose of the universe is to give rise to intelligent life within the laws of nature and their fundamental constants set to ensure that life as we know it will emerge and evolve, based on quantum physics. It is beautifully put but is pseudoscience. Moreover, it is in violence of the Copernican principle that states that humans do not occupy a privileged position in the universe. It is not because humans are able to observe that they are the dominant species in the universe, and neither is it their ability to observe a reason of purpose, a universe designed with the goal of generating observers.

Though scientists have intensively studied life on Earth, defining life in unequivocal terms is still a challenge. Physically, one may say that life feeds on negative entropy, which refers to the process by which living entities decrease their internal entropy at the expense of some form of energy taken in from the environment. Biologists generally agree that life forms are self-organising systems which regulate their internal environments as to maintain this organised state. Metabolism serves to provide energy, and reproduction causes life to continue over a span of multiple generations. Typically, organisms are responsive to stimuli and genetic information changes from generation to generation, resulting in adaptation through evolution; this optimises the chances of survival for the individual organism and its descendants. Non-cellular replicating agents, notably viruses, are generally not considered to be organisms because they are incapable of independent reproduction or metabolism. This classification is problematic, though, because some parasites and endosymbionts are also incapable of independent life. Astrobiology studies the possibility of different forms of life on other worlds, including replicating structures made from materials other than DNA.

- We do not know how life started on Earth. The exact mechanisms of abiogenesis are unknown; notable theories include the RNA world hypothesis (RNA-based replicators) and the iron-sulphur world theory (metabolism without genetics). The process by which different life forms have developed throughout history via genetic mutation and natural selection is explained by evolution. At the end of the twentieth century, based on insight gleaned from the gene-centred view of evolution, evolutionary biologists George C. Williams, Richard Dawkins, and David Haig, amongst others, concluded that if there is a primary function to life, it is the replication of DNA and the survival of one's genes. Some people, such as the heavily contested biologist Jeremy Griffith, maintain that the meaning of life is to be integrative. Dawkins asked James Watson, "What it is all for?" James Watson stated, "I don't think *we're for anything*. We're just the products of evolution."

There are good reasons to think that all life is carbon-based, as it is on earth. Carbon is much more versatile as a building block for complex molecules than other elements for speculation about alternative alien biochemistries. Making the building blocks of life, like sugars and amino acids, is the easy part. There are lots of chemically plausible ways to do that, starting with the simple molecules found in young solar systems. The hard bit is persuading these complicated molecules to assemble into something capable of life-sustaining processes like replication and metabolism. Up till now, it was possible to create a bacterium in a laboratory, which is a crucial step in creating life, but no further. We know that other building blocks of life can be formed from different chemical reactions. Some of the key building blocks can be produced under harsh conditions mimicking those of interstellar space. The molecular chemist Cornelia Meinert headed a team of scientists at the university of Nice, and they recently showed that a mixture of frozen water, methanol, and ammonia (all compounds known to exist in the vast molecular clouds from which stars form) can be transformed into a wide range of sugar molecules when exposed to ultraviolet rays, which pervade space. The sugars included ribose, which is a part of the DNA-like molecule RNA. This suggests that the fundamental molecules of life might be formed in outer space and delivered to planets like earth by icy comets and meteorites. Other life in the universe must not necessary be similar to that on earth. Life in the universe could be ubiquitous, not necessarily carbon-based and requiring water.

Why is the urge to reproduce so dominant in living beings? Why, if the only intention is to survive, have the living organisms not learned to be immortal? Organisms have not evolved for any purpose, but those organisms who do not feel compelled to reproduce are swiftly crowded out by those that do so. On the other hand, there are a lot of single-celled organisms which are nearly immortal unless they meet with an accident. Senescence is a feature of the complex organisms such as humans; it is in the interest of the genes that death occurs. The evolution of humans brings longevity. Primitive man lived only thirty years, but today humans nearly attain one hundred years.

It is difficult to disagree with the French biologist and Noble Prize laureate Jacques Monod, who is a proponent of the view that life on earth arose by freak chemical accident even in the vast universe. Monod became famous for his work on the *E. coli lac* operon, which encodes proteins necessary for the transport and breakdown of the sugar lactose (lac). In his book *Chance and Necessity*, he wrote that the freak chemical accident of life may not have been simply of low probability but of identically *zero* probability, a unique event that never will be repeated.

At last knows he is alone in the unfeeling immensity of the universe, out of which he has emerged only by chance. His destiny is nowhere spelled out, and neither is his duty. The kingdom above or the darkness below—it is for him to choose. His bleakness of life pushed him to atheism and the absurdity and pointlessness of existence. He stated that first scientific postulate is the objectivity of nature. Nature does not have any intention or goal. Neither is the universe pregnant with life or the biosphere. We are merely chemical extras in a majestic but impersonal cosmic drama. We find this bleak assessment of life in the nihilism of Friedrich Nietzsche. Humanity has no goal, according to the modern existentialists of Jean Paul Sartre and colleagues. These existentialists, however, do affirm that one must make the best of an absurd life.

The biophysical chemist and Noble Prize laureate Manfred Eigen wrote a preface to Jacques Monod's book *Chance and Necessity*. In 1975, he wrote a book on the same theme with his assistant Ruthild Winkler, *The Laws of the Game: How the Principle of Nature Govern Chance*. In their book, Eigen and Winkler show that all that in the world happens is a great game in which only the rules from the start are established. They try to both understand the factor chance and tame it. They point to the overestimation of the coincidence by Monod. They argue that what affects everyone, everyone must solve. What affects everyone are the insights that allow freeing atomic powers, and that are also the possibilities of the biologists and pharmacologists to influence genes and behaviour. We all must learn together to create the conditions for a liveable life, retain it, and secure it. In fact, what Eigen and Winkler propagate is repeating the ancient Greek philosophers' "live according to nature and as happy as possible".

The famous psychiatrist Carl Jung introduced the concept synchronicity, which holds that events are "meaningful coincidences" if they occur with no causal relationship yet seem to be meaningfully related. He used the concept to justify the paranormal. Jung was a pantheist who believed that spiritual experience was essential to our well-being. His ideas on religion gave a counterbalance to the Freudian scepticism of religion. Synchronicity influenced the scientist Wolfgang Pauli in his quantum mechanics because he likewise believed in metaphysical spirituality. Jung was convinced that life has a spiritual purpose beyond material goals, based on the belief that human must discover and fulfil a deep innate potential. The writings of Jung are today considered by many scientists to be mumbo jumbo.

The universe has physical and chemical aspects. Are there biological aspects to the universe? If life is derived from chemical reactions, then the answer is affirmative. The inorganic universe generated organic life. The universe was created by chance, and so was life. Once created, the universe had its own impersonal laws to which life forms on earth, as part of the universe, had to adapt. The universe is the progenitor of life. The universe is severe. Life is not a game. Life forms must struggle to survive and are cruel to each other. The human is the product of evolution and has found that in order to survive, civilisation was necessary. Not every human is ready to accept civilisation, and that is why there is unrest in the world.

Some have difficulty accepting reality, the fact that life has no goal, and that the meaning of life only resides in survival (and then only in the easiest way). When someone as the prominent scientist Roger Penrose can't get around the difficulty of lack of purpose of the universe and considers that in the shelter of the universe, there must be something deeper than a mere existence, then he is governed by metaphysical reasoning. A rather strange view for a scientist and atheist, which must be classified as wishful thinking, being an occult cause for purpose and meaning.

Quality of life is an end in itself and is dependent on the purpose of improving life and achieving it. The meaning of life is so strict personal. It is man himself who provides sense to his life, but that means nothing in terms of content. The fate of man, as part of nature (which constitutes the universe), is inseparably linked with the fate of the universe. A stone on earth is merely a part of the universe with no purpose or meaning. This subscription may seem materialistic, but it is simply the naked truth that must be accepted by humans.

Since the human civilisation of Mesopotamia ten thousand years ago, there have been many successive civilisations of various kinds that have had their place in history by their conquests, bequeathed buildings, art treasures, and mainly their writings. In the past, religion has always played a key role and affected the quality of life. History shows barbaric treatment of fellow men by people who kept slaves for their own quality of life. History reveals a steady growth of knowledge, especially the last hundred years, in which the high flight of science and the resultant technology has drastically improved the quality of life. Some consider that the evolution of human is the goal and meaning of life, because if there is no purpose or meaning of life, humankind is confronted by a doomsday syndrome that leads to the destruction of life. People with unhappy lives will be ready to take farewell of an aimless and meaningless existence; only the fear of death may impede suicide. However, the false promises of paradise afterlife induce Islam fanatics to become self-destructing terrorists.

The nature and origin of consciousness and the mind itself are also widely debated in science. The explanatory gap is generally equated with the hard problem of consciousness, and the question of free will is also considered to be of fundamental importance. These subjects are mostly addressed in the fields of cognitive science, neuroscience (e.g., the neuroscience of free will), and philosophy of mind, though some evolutionary biologists and theoretical physicists have also made several allusions to the subject.[86]

When one considers purpose and meaning of life, it is not possible to neglect the ultimate fate of the universe, implicitly humanity as all biological life, when a Big Freeze, a Big Rip, or a Big Crunch causes the end of the universe. Life on Earth is extremely short, and the existence of the universe is extremely long but not timeless. However, both remain temporal and thus affect purpose and meaning. The destruction of galaxies also causes renaissance of new galaxies and so postpones the destruction of the universe indefinitely. We should be conscious of these facts before clinging to considerations or explanations without any truth. Only the pursuit of the truth can be the object of the human will he survive?

Has life purpose or meaning? But what is the meaning of the struggle for survival? Is it instinct, nature, nurture, or innatism? In any case, survival is the aspiration and drive of all life forms, humans included. Evolution is not the optimising for the survival of organisms, but according to Charles Darwin, evolution is the survival of the fittest. The evolution of man has led to civilisation, where man has found safety and life less hard.

Primitive man (50,000–40,000 years ago) was a hunter while his spouse supplemented the meat or fish with gathering roots and fruits. Life was hard, and the man had to constantly defend himself and his issues against wild animals and fellow human beings, who were always ready to steal his meagre possessions or hijack his spouse. The people were nomads, always looking for better places where it was easier to find food or where more security was offered. When it was possible to grow crops, settlements came into being where the collective was safer to live for the individual. Gods were invented to explain the imponderable of existence. From the settlements grew cities and later empires, which formed the first civilisations. Civilisation brought culture.

Civilisation is any complex society characterised by urban development, social stratification, symbolic communication forms (typically, writing systems), and a perceived separation from and domination over the natural environment by a cultural elite. Civilisations are intimately associated with and often further defined by other socio-politic and economic characteristics, including centralisation, the domestication of both humans and other organisms, specialisation of labour, culturally ingrained ideologies of progress and supremacism, monumental architecture, taxation, societal dependence upon farming as an agricultural practise, and expansionism. Historically, civilisation was a so-called advanced culture in contrast to more supposedly primitive cultures. In this broad sense, a civilisation contrasts with non-centralised tribal societies, including the cultures of nomadic pastoralists, egalitarian horticultural subsistence, Neolithic societies, or hunter-gatherers. The earliest emergence of civilisations is generally associated with the final stages of the Neolithic Revolution, culminating in the relatively rapid process of Urban Revolution and state formation, a political development associated with the appearance of a governing elite. The earlier Neolithic technology and lifestyle was established first in the Middle East (for example, at Göbekli Tepe from about 9130 BCE), and later in the Yangtze and Yellow river basins in China (for example, the Pengtoushan culture from 7500 BCE). Similar pre-civilised Neolithic revolutions also began independently from 7000 BC in such places as the Norte Chico civilisation in Peru and Mesoamerica at the Balsas River. These were amongst the six civilisations worldwide that arose independently. Mesopotamia is the site of the earliest developments of the Neolithic Revolution from around 10,000 BC, with civilisations developing from 6,500 years ago. This area has been identified as having "inspired some of the most important developments in human history including the invention of the wheel, the development of cursive script and mathematics".[136] The civilised Urban Revolution in turn was dependent upon the development of sedentarism, the domestication of grains and animals, and the development of lifestyles which allowed economies of scale and the accumulation of surplus production by certain social sectors. The transition from complex cultures to civilisations, while still disputed, seems to be associated with the development of state structures in which power was further monopolised by an elite ruling class who practised human sacrifice. The process of sedentarisation is first thought to have occurred around 12,000 BCE in the Levant region of southwest Asia, though other regions around the world soon followed. The emergence of civilisation is generally associated with the Neolithic, or Agricultural Revolution, which occurred in various locations between 8,000 and 5,000 BCE, specifically in south-western/southern Asia, northern/central Africa, and Central America. At first the Neolithic was associated with shifting subsistence cultivation, where continuous farming led to the depletion of soil fertility resulting in the requirement to cultivate fields further removed from the settlement, eventually compelling the settlement itself to move. In major semi-arid river valleys, annual flooding renewed soil fertility every year, with the result that population densities could significantly rise. It was associated with the state monopoly of violence, the appearance of a soldier class and endemic warfare, rapid development of hierarchies, the appearance of human sacrifice, and a fall in the status of women. Towards the end of the Neolithic period, various elitist Chalcolithic civilisations began to rise in various "cradles" from around 3300 BCE. Chalcolithic civilisations, as defined above, also developed in Pre-Columbian Americas and (despite an early start in Egypt, Axum, and Kush) much later in Iron Age sub-Saharan Africa. The Bronze Age collapse was followed by the Iron Age around 1200 BC, during which a number of new civilisations emerged, culminating in the Axial Age transition to Classical civilisation. A major technological and cultural transition to modernity began at approximately 1500 CE in Western Europe, and from this beginning new approaches to scicncc and law sprcad rapidly around thc world, incorporating earlier cultures into the industrial and technological civilisation of the present.[81]

Civilisations have generally ended in one of two ways: through being incorporated into another expanding civilisation (e.g., as Ancient Egypt was incorporated into Hellenistic Greek, and subsequently Roman civilisations), or by collapse and reversion to a simpler form (as happened in what are called Dark Ages).

There have been many explanations put forward for the collapse of civilisation. Some focus on historical examples and others on general theory.

> The decline of Rome was the natural and inevitable effect of immoderate greatness. Prosperity ripened the principle of decay; the cause of the destruction multiplied with the extent of conquest; and, as soon as time or accident had removed the artificial supports, the stupendous

> fabric yielded to the pressure of its own weight. The story of the ruin is simple and obvious; and instead of inquiring why the Roman Empire was destroyed, we should rather be surprised that it has subsisted for so long (Gibbon, Decline and Fall of the Roman Empire, 2nd ed., vol. 4, edited by J. B. Bury, London, 1909, pp. 173–174).

It is argued that the defining characteristic of the twenty-first century will be a clash of civilisations. Conflicts between civilisations will supplant the conflicts between nation-states and ideologies that characterised the nineteenth and twentieth centuries. These views have been strongly challenged by others who argue that the "true clash of civilisations" between the Muslim world and the West is caused by the Muslim rejection of the West's democratic values, equality of women, freedom of expression, and choice of religion.

There was always a desire for better living conditions—not an end in itself but a necessity to survive. All life forms have the urge to survive. Overpopulation can suffocate the world. Overcrowding is worse in less developed regions. Sexual satisfaction brings children in the world who are doomed to die early or undergo an existence of misery. In addition, in many parts of Asia (e.g., India and China), children are conceived to be part of the economic cycle and even as an investment to the maintenance of the aging parents. In the hinterland of Asia, the elder of the villages still exert the power upon patriarchal lines, which are outright barbaric.

Overpopulation and warfare lead to migration. There are two types of immigration. In numerous war zones, there are refugees who try to reach a safer area to continue living and prefer an area where the economic living conditions are a lot more favourable. These war refugees must be helped, of course, but after the war, they should be returned. The second kind of migrants is economic refugees looking for a higher standard of living. There is no civilisation able to accommodate massive economic migrants without bringing itself difficulties. This seems hard, but it is the naked truth. Besides, such migrants also have a duty to help their fellow countrymen to improve the living conditions in their country of origin rather than flee. Pity is out of place and should concede to realty. Exception should be made for reasons of persecution.

Europe is undergoing the phenomenon of mass migration of people who not only cause overpopulation but are also unwilling to integrate into the laws of democracy of the country of refuge. They remain obstinately practising the manners and customs of their homeland, and in doing so, they inevitably collide with the autotochtons. Employers were at first excited with the phenomenon of migrants, acquiring cheap labour, but they were quickly disappointed to find that the immigrants were averse to learning skills required to work and consequently remained for the most part unemployed, becoming susceptible to deteriorating into a mass of troublemakers. In the countries where mass migration occurs, extremist groups arise to combat the immigrants, which in turn ensures turmoil reminiscent of the days of Fascism and Nazism. In North America, there is also a problem of migration, but it's less acute. Mexicans and other Latinos of the South American continent try to enter the United States, and to a lesser extent Canada, to the great annoyance of the members of the Republican party, who consider them a danger to the labour market. These immigrants are generally Christians whose life stand does not pose the same spiritual differences as in Europe. Populists such as Boris Johnson, the ex-mayor of London, and Donald Trump, the Republican president of the United States, are smart but are not intelligent drivers of humanity; they provoke and cause turmoil. What is alarming is that these individuals can depend on such a large following.

To those who consider that the above argumentation is incompatible with humanism, it is recommended to subject their own reasoning to a dialectical analysis in order to determine what good is for mankind. Migration has nothing to do with purpose and meaning of life. It is a by-product of the incongruities on earth caused by overpopulation, warring factions, poverty, and ignorance.

The scientific community and philosophy of science communities believe that science can provide a relevant context and set parameters necessary for dealing with topics related to the meaning of life. In this vision, science can offer a wide range of insights on to topics of achieving happiness and avoiding death anxiety. The parameters which they expose are the realities of life, such as the Big Bang, the origin of life, and the evolution of life. The difficulty of course is the assimilation by the people of the scientific facts to achieve a life stand by which one can live happily. First, people must be able to assimilate knowledge, which demands a certain education, and which is not present in most of the people. Scientific research makes it possible to reveal what aspects of life are of fundamental value and, if realised, grant peace of mind and satisfaction. A full deployment of activities in a career (work, sports, charity) will surely enhance happiness. Materialistic philosophies such as dialectical materialism challenge the idea of an absolute value of the meaning of life. As said before, neuroscience describes pleasure and motivation in terms of neurotransmitter activity, particularly in the limbic system of the ventral tegmental area of the brain. The parameters that science makes available to people to approach the concept of meaning of life are undoubtedly concrete. However, the information of that nature barely reaches the world's population. Scientific information requires not only skill but also willingness to assimilate knowledge. Someone who believes in God finds no need to take note of scientific knowledge about the origin of the universe, but whether he is happy with his life is another question.

Humanity must face the fact that the universe is not autotelic (having within itself the purpose of its existence and happening) and acquiesce to it. Life, being part of nature without goal and meaning, does not hold that humans, during their exceedingly short existence on Earth and in the presence of a quasi-eternal universe, should not strive for an agreeable existence. The struggle for survival is real. The essence of evolution is survival of the fittest—not the strongest but the most apt and most intelligent. Today, the evolution of humans has not reached a standard beyond a creature of being too much animal and too little rational. Many will prance at this statement. The naked truth is often offensive. Most humans are shallow; though equipped with thought and reasoning, they barely use these faculties. But time gnaws at the ignorance of man, and the ratio gradually takes the upper hand. Nevertheless, there waits for man a long journey into the future. Humans are the only beings that can do something that natural selection does not achieve, just because of natural selection. Humans must be conscious of the fact that if they do not have a reason to exist, they cannot survive. This seems contradictory to the lack of purpose and meaning of life. However, humans, as part of the nature of the universe, have their roles to play. Biologists are convinced that living organisms can act only according to their nature.

The philosophical perspectives on the meaning of life are those ideologies which explain life in terms of ideals or abstractions defined by humans.

Science has unravelled the secrets of the universe and freed Homo *sapiens* from the supernatural faith. Unfortunately, the most people do not have the mental potential to follow science. This applies not only to the underdeveloped man but also for the establishment, even though the latter often abuses the naivety of the people. In addition, science is the foundation of all technological inventions that has contributed to human welfare.

Science has made God redundant. It is a very disturbing fact for the theists. The non-existence of God deprives theists of their life stand and their reason for living. Do they have the mental strength to overcome this? Of course, they can continue the lie of their belief and continue to live as sheep.

The universe, including humans, has no purpose or meaning. There are many hypotheses (most science fiction) of how humans will further evolve. We only use 20 per cent of our brainpower. In what state will we be when we access full brainpower? The universe gave birth to humans, perhaps by chance. It remains possible but improbable that humans, descendants of the universe, dominate their progenitor and redirect its course, in which case humans do have a goal to fulfil. The fully developed human would be a godlike creature, in the sense of a being with the potential accorded to the human-invented God, in full command of the universe (compare to Yuval Noah Harari)[164]. The monotheistic God is making a place for pantheism.

Today, life itself remains a conundrum. The memorabilia do not assess the imponderable.

The [53]conclusion is that the universe, which has not been created by a supernatural entity, has no real purpose or meaning. To survive, humans need to adapt to conditions on Earth. The universe itself is the progenitor of life. Humans form an integral part of the universe and no more than the universe have humans any purpose or meaning. The fact that life started so late on earth is quite natural. The solar system was only formed five billion years ago, 8.5 billion years later than the Big Bang. It took many billion years to stabilise Earth and create an environment susceptible to start life.

In so far as we know, humankind is the only intelligent species in the universe. The inorganic universe is the progenitor of all organic life and includes the evolved *Homo sapiens.* Living organisms form the animate part of the universe. Before the universe, humankind is minute and short-lived, however the potential of reproduction assures a quasi-eternal existence. Humans are essential in the universe because we are the consciousness of the universe. Thus, we are the universe in the full flow of evolution. However, we must not forget that the stupidity of many factions of the world's population hampers our evolution.

Religions with their tales of a god-being and a life hereafter, provide the poor unstable human a soporific which grants that life has a meaning and a purpose.

Philosophical thought has no value, unless the reasoning is based on scientific facts.

The universe is inorganic and responds solely to physical laws, but the inorganic universe generated organic life, fauna, and flora. Humankind belongs to the fauna on Earth and constitutes an exceedingly small part of the universe. Inorganic matter such as a stone on Earth, which is part of the universe, has no cognition.

Space is not empty[53]. If there is nothing then there is no substance. However, energy has substance and can be transformed into matter ($E=MC^{2)}$.

Purpose or meaning are nothing of the sort, but human has an important choice. He can choose for a harmonious life with his fellowmen or he can choose a life of dissent. A harmonious life with the fellowmen ensures an existence of peace, prosperity, and happiness. Dissent in the world opens the possibility for a labile leader to press the button to start a nuclear war, thereby returning Earth to the time the dinosaurs disappeared from our globe.

It is evident that present-day human in many places of Earth does not meet the qualifications necessary for a harmonious living. The intellectual faculties must increase not only in the third world but also in the western world where still most do not have an open mind. In the modern world the march of technology brought about by science has been remarkable; but the social aspect of life regretfully did not follow and fell behind.

Homo sapiens to deserve his denomination has a long way to go; evolution takes time.

The next big question for humankind is whether it is going to remain prisoner of its solar system or whether it will be able in the future to explore outer space, in which case the role of human in the universe may be susceptible to a far more understandable.

LITERATURE

1. Luke VandenBerghe, *God, Fact or Fiction* (AuthorHouse, 2014).
2. Carroll Sean, *Dark Matter, Dark Energy, The Dark Side of the Universe* (Cal Tech, 2007), 59.
3. Edward Witten, "String Theory Dynamics in Various Dimensions", *Nuclear Physics*, B, 443 (1995).
4. Stephen Hawking, *A Briefer History of Time* (Bantam Books, 2005). Stephen Hawking, *The Universe in a Nutshell* (University of Cambridge, 2002).
5. Kitty Ferguson, *Stephen Hawking: His Life and Work* (Bantam Books, 2012). Jane Wilde, *Travelling to Infinity: My Life with Stephen Hawking* (Alma, 2007).
6. Stephen Hawking, *The Grand Design* (Bantam Books, 2010).
7. Richard Dawkins, "Another Ungodly Squabble", *The Economist* (9 May 2010).
8. Nature (October 2013).
9. Taxonomy: The Science of Classification of Species.
10. Oparin Alexander, The Origin of Life (New York, 1952). Bryson Bill, A Short History of Nearly Everything. Miller Stanly, "A Production of Amino Acids under Possible Primitive Earth Conditions", Science, 117, 903–915.
11. *Science* (20 May 2010).
12. B. F. Skinner, *About Behaviourism* (New York, 1974).
13. J. B. Watson, *Behaviourism* (revised edition, Chicago, 1930).
14. Sir Francis Galton, *English Men of Science: Their Nature and Nurture* (Google Books).

15. Jesse Bering, *The Godinstinct. The Psychology of Souls, Destiny, and the Meaning of Life* (London, 2010).
16. Richard Dawkins, *God Is a Delusion*,Bantam Press, 2006.
17. Thomas of Aquino, Sent IV, 26, Summa Theologica, Sacrament of Matrimony, http://www.newadvent.org/summa/5041.htm.
18. Internet Encyclopedia of Philosophy, "Sigmund Freud", http://iep.utm.edu/freud.
19. Homework Help, "What Is Human Sexuality?", http://www.notes.com/psychoanalysis- encyclopedia/three essays-theory
20. Gary B. Ferngren, *Science and Religion: A Historical Introduction*, (JHU Press, 2002), http://books.google.com/books.
21. Anselm of Canterbury, *Proslogion*, 1078.
22. Thomas van Aquino, *Summa Theologica* (1274), http://www.newadvent.org/summary.
23. Richard Dawkins, "Why There Is Almost Certain No God", The Huffington Post (23 October 2006), http://www.huffingtonpost.com/Richard-dawkins/why-there-almost-certainl. b32164.html.
24. Stephen Hawking and Leonard Mlodinow, *The Grand Design* Bantam Books, 2010.
25. Thomas Piketty, *Le Capital au XXI e Siècle*, (Editions du Seuil, 2013).
26. Paul S. Mueller, David J. Plevak, and Teresa A. Rummans (http://download.journals.elsevierhealth.com/pdfs/journals/00256196/PIIS002561961116279 97.pdf).
27. *USA Today*, "Spaghetti Monster Is Noodling around with Faith" (http://usatoday.com/life/books/2006-03-26-spaghetti-monster.htm).
28. "Giordano Bruno: His Life and Thought, (1548–1600)", http://www.positiveatheism.org/hist/brunoOO.htm.
29. George A. Lindbeck, *Nature of Doctrine,* (Louisville,1984).
30. R. G. Swinburne, "*God*", in *The Oxford Companion to Philosophy*, Ted Honderich, ed. (Oxford University Press, 1995).
31. *City of God,* Book VIII, I, http://logicmuseum.googlepages.com/civitate-8.htm.
32. Aristoteles, *Metaphysics,* Book Epsilon, http://etext.library.adelaide.edu.au/mirror/classics/mit/edu/Aristotle/metaphy.

33. Protagoras, *On the Gods,* Internet Encyclopaedia of Philosophy, http.www.iep.utm.edu/Protagoras.
34. Thomas Paine, *The Age of Reason* (New York, 1945), 601.
35. Ludwig Feuerbach, *Principles of the Philosophy of the Future,* translation by Manfred H. Vogel (Indianapolis, 1986), 5.
36. Ludwig Feuerbach, *The Essence of Christianity,* translation by George Eliot (New York, 1989).
37. James Joyce, *Ulysses* (Random House, 1986), 414.
38. Robert Green Ingersoll, Positive Atheism (11 August 1954), http://www.positiveatheism,org.hist/quotes/Ingersoll.htm.
39. Charles Bradlaugh, Positive Atheism, (11 November 2012), http://positiveatheism.org/hist/quotes/bradlaugh.htm.
40. Charles Bradlaugh, "Humanity's Gain from Unbelief", Positive Atheism (11 November 2012), http://positiveatheism.org/hist/bradloOO1. htm.
41. Richard Dawkins, *The Emptiness of Theology,* 10 May 2006, http://richarddawkins.net/aricles/88-the emptiness-of-theology.
42. Jerry Coyne, *Why Evolution Is True,* (25 January 2009), http://www.forbes.com/2009/02/12:evolution-creation-proof-opinions-darwin/02-12-2009/jerrycoyne.html. "Does the Empirical Nature of Science Contradict the Revelatory Nature of Faith", Edge.org (21 January 2009), http://edge.org./conversation/does-the-empirical-nature-of-science-contradict-the-revelatory-nature-of-faith. "The Case Against Intelligent Design", Point of Inquiry (16 June 2006), http://pointofinquiry.org/jerrycoyne-the-case-against-intell. "The Faith That Dare Not Speak Its Name", New Republic, http://pondsde.uchicago.eduee/faculty/coyne/pdf/newrepublic.
43. Jerry Coyne, "*Why Am I Reading Theology*", The Richard Dawkins Foundation, http://richarddawkins.net/articles/642023-why-am-i-reading-theology. "The Case against Intelligent Design", Point of Inquiry, http://pointofinquiry.org/jerrycoyne-the-case-against-intell. "The Faith That Dare Not Speak Its Name", New Republic, http://pondsde.uchicago.edu.ee/faculty/Coyne/pdf/NewRepublicII.

44. "Directory of Mark Twain's Maxims, Quotations, and Various Opinions". Twainquotes.com, http://twainquotes.com/Religion.htm.
45. Karen Armstrong, *Fields of Blood: Religion and the History of Violence* (Canada, 2014).
46. Philip Birnbaum, *Encyclopaedia of Jewish Concepts* (Wadsworth, 1979).
47. John Riches, *The Bible: A Very Short Introduction* (Oxford, 2000).
48. Weekly Haaretz, *Deconstructing the Walls of Jericho* (1999).
49. I. Finkelstein and N. A. Silberman, *The Bible Unearthed: Archeology's New Vision of Ancient Israel and the Origin of its Sacred Texts* (New York, 2001).
50. Puin Gerd, *The Koran* as Text, ed. Stefan Wild, E. J. Brill, 1996, reprinted as *What the Koran Really Says,* ed. Ibn Warraq (Prometheus Books, 2002).
51. "*What Is the Koran", The Atlantic* (January 1999), http://www.theatlantic.com/magazune/archive/1999/01/what-is-the-koran/304024.
52. Elisabeth Puin, *Ein fruher Koranpalimpsest aus San'a* (Berlin,2008), http://books.google.de/?id=wOMO2s7RRsY&pg=PA461"pg=PA461. Verlag Hans Schiller, https://www.worldcat.org/oclc/496960079.
53. Lawrence Krauss, *A Universe from Nothing: Why There Is Something Rather Than Nothing* (Atria Books, 2012).
54. Tahafut Al-Falasifah and Al-Ghazali, *The Incoherence of the Philosophers,* translation in English by Sabih Ahmad Kamali (Lahore, 1963).
55. Tahafut al-tahafut and Ibd Rushd, *The Incoherence of the Incoherence,* (London, 1954). Seyyed Hossein Nasr, *An Introduction to Islamic Cosmological Doctrines* (Albany, 1993).
56. Matthew 22:23–33, http://www.biblegateway.com/passage/?search=matthew%2022:22-33; &version=47.
57. Jacques Derrida, *The Acts of Religion,* https://books.google.no/books?id=5n-kpSC8m2YCH.
58. Blaise Pascal, *Pensées*, volume II (1670).
59. *Identity and Death Anxiety* (Central Michigan University, 1985).

60. William, Lane, Craig, *Philosophy Now Magazine* (December 2013).
61. Maimonides, World Digital Library (22 January 2013).
62. Albert Einstein, "Maxwell's Influence on the Evolution of the Idea of Physical Reality", in J. C. Maxwell, *A Commemoration Volume* (Cambridge, 1931).
63. American Humanist Association, "Human Manifesto" (1933), http://www.americanhumamanist.org/about/manifesto1.html.
64. Wei-Ming Tu, *Confucian Thought: Selfhood as Creative Transformation* (Albany: 1985).
65. Cavendish, Richard; Ling, Trevor Oswald 1980), Mythology: An Illustrated Encyclopedia, http://books.google.com/books?id=GdENAAAAYAAJ, Rizzoli, 40–45.
66. Richard Lynn, John Harvey, and Helmuth Nyborg, "Average Intelligence Predicts Atheism Rates across 137 Nations" (2009), http://www.sciencedirect.com/science/aIntelligence37:11-15.
67. Ian King, *How to Make Good Decisions and Be Right All the Time: Solving the Riddle of Right and Wrong* (Continuum, 2008), 74.
68. Immanuel Kant, *Critique of Pure Reason.*
69. Burton L. White, *Raising a Happy, Unspoiled Child* (rev. ed., Touchstone, 1995).
70. Phil Zuckerman, *Society without God: What the Least Religious Nations Can Tell Us about Contentment* (New York University Press, 2008).
71. Gregory Paul, "Cross-National Correlations of Quantifiable Societal Health with Popular Religiosity and Secularism in the Prosperous Democracies", *Journal of Religion and Society* (Baltimore, 2005).
72. James D. Watson, *The Double Helix: A Personal Account of the Discovery of the Structure of DNA* (New York, 1968).
73. Evan Goodmalen, *Islamic Humanism* (Oxford University Press, 2003).
74. Thomas Bergin and Jennifer Speake, *The Encyclopedia of the Renaissance* (Oxford), 216–217.
75. C. B. Collins and S. W. Hawking, *The Astrophysical Journal* (1973), 317–334.

76. Don Page, "Inflation Does Not Explain Time Asymmetry", *Nature* (1983), 304.
78. https://en.wikipedia.org/wiki/cognition.
79. D. J. Grothe, "Podcast: Steven Pinker—Evolutionary Psychology and Human Nature", *Point of Inquiry with D.J. Grothe* (23 February 2007).
80. https://en.wikipedia.org/wiki/Big_Bang.
81. https://en.wikipedia.org/wiki/Civilisation.
82. https://en.wikipedia.org/wiki/Sun.
83. https://en.wikipedia.org/wiki.Chronology_of_the_universe
84. https://en.wikipedia.org/wiki/Life.
85. https://en.wikipedia.org/wiki/Martin-Bojowald.
86. https://en.wikipedia.org/wiki/Meaning-of-life.
87. https://en.wikipedia.org/wiki/Origin-of-life.
88. https://en.wikipedia.org/wiki/What-Is-Life%3F.
89. https://en.wikipedia.org/wiki/Schr%C3%B6inger%27s_cat.
90. https://en.wikipedia.org/wiki/Anthropic_principle.
91. https://en.wikipedia.org/wiki/Lee_Smolin.
92. https://en.wikipedia.org/wiki/Andrei_Linde.
93. https://en.wikipedia.org/wiki/Human_evolution.
94. https://en.Wikipedia.org/wiki/Leonard_Susskind.
95. https://en.wikipedia.org/wiki/Human_nature.
96. https://en.wikipedia.org/wiki/Instinct.
97. https://en.wikipedia.org/wiki.Existence.
98. https://en.wikipedia.org/wiki.Existentialism.
99. https://en.wikipedia.org/wiki/Mythology.
100. https://en.wikipedia.org/wiki.Deity.
101. https://en.wikipedia.org/wiki.Theodicy.
102. https://en.wikipedia.org/wiki/.religion.
103. https://en.wikipedia.org/wiki/Judaism.
104. https://en.wikipedia.org/wiki/ Tzipi_Hotovely.
105. https://en.wikipedia.org/wiki/Christianity.
106. https://en.wikipedia.org/wiki/Islam.
107. https://en.wikipedia;org/wiki/Muhammad.
108. gttps://en.wikipedia.org/wiki/Koran.
109. https://en.wikipedia.org/wiki/Truth.

110. https://en.wikipedia.org/wiki/Belief.
111. https://en.wikipedia.org/wiki/Happiness.
112. https://en.wikipedia.org/wiki/Meaning-of-life.
113. Bertrand Russell, *History of Western Philosophy* (Routledge, 1995).
114. William James, *Pragmatism* (1907), 91. William James, *Pragmatism: A New Name for Some Old Ways of Thinking?* (Hackett Publishing, 1981).
115. http://www.budsas.org/ebud/ebdha019.htm.
116. https://www.en.wikipedia.org/wiki/Epigenetics.
117. https://www.en.wikipedia.org/wiki/Innatism.
118. https://www.en.wikipedia.org/wiki/Morality.
119. https://en.wikipedia.org/wiki/G.E.M.Anscombe.
120. https://en.wikipedia.org/wiki/The_Most_Good_You_Can_Do You Can Do.
121. https://en.wikipedia.org/wiki/GiveWell.
122. https://en.wikipedia.org/wiki/Subjectivity.
123. https://en.wikipedia.org/wiki/Empathy.
124. https://en.wikipedia.org/wiki/Mind.
125. https://en.wikipedia.org/wiki/Human-Sexuality.
126. https://en.wikipedia.org/wiki/Death.
127. https://en.wikipedia.org/wiki/Theology.
128. http://www.physlink.com/Education/essay-Weinberg.cfm.
129. https://en.wikipedia.org/wiki/Nature.
130. https:/en.wikipedia.org/wiki/Big Bang.
131. https://en.wikipedia.org/wiki/James_Watson.
132. https://en.wikipedia.org/wiki/Spacetime. https://en.wikipedia.org/wiki/Spacetime"time.
133. https://en.wikipedia.org/wiki/Instinct.
134. Francis Crick, *What Mad Pursuit: A Personal View of Scientific Discovery* (Basic Books, 1990).
135. http://www.budsas.org/ebud/ebdha019.htm.
136. https://en.wikipedia.org/wiki/Mathematics"athematics. https://en.wikipedia.org/wiki/Agriculture"griculture.
137. https://en.wikipedia.org/wiki/Posthumanism. https://en.wikipedia.org/wiki/Posthumanism"humanism.

138. "Techno Scientific Culture", https://en.wikipedia.org/wiki/Techno scientific.
139. https://en.wikipedia.org/wiki/Sansara.
140. https://en.wikipedia.org/wiki/Dharma.
141. http://www.gotquestions.org/Sanctity-of-life.html.
142. Catholic Encyclopedia, *Nature and Attributes of God,* Newadvent.org (9 January 1909). *Particular Judgement,* Newadvent.org (10 January 1910).
143. http://www.gotquestions.org/Sanctity-of-life.html.
144. http://plato.stanford.edu/entries/belief.
145. Cavendish, Richard; Ling, Richard; Mythology: an Illustrated Encyclopedia, 1980, Rizzoli, 40–45.
https://themuslimissue.wordpress.com/2013/02/03,when-iman khomeini-ayatollah-raped-a-4-year-old-girl.
147. https://en.wikipedia.org/wiki/Tannaim"annaim.
148. https://en.wikipedia.org/wiki.Koran.
149. https://en.wikipedia.org/wiki/Cathechism.
150. https://books.google.come/books?.151.
151. https://en.wikipedia.org/wiki/Homo_Sapiens.
152. https://en.wikipedia.org/wiki/Rational_Animal.
153. gaillardi@bc.edu
154. Edward Hong and Edna Hong, *The Essential Kierkegaard* (Princeton University Press, 2000).
155. *Theories of Truth: A Critical Introduction* (Cambridge, 1992).
156. https://nl.wikipedia.org/wiki/Waarheid. https://en.wikppedia.org/wiki/Truth.
157. https://en.wikipedia.org/wiki/Civilisation. https://nl.wikipedia.org/wiki.Beschaving.
158. https://en.wikipedia.org/wiki/Culture. https://nl.wikipedia.org/wiki/Cultuur.
159. https://en.wikipedia.org/wiki/Intelligence. https://nl.wikipedia.org/wiki/Intelligentie.
160. Catholic Encyclopedia, *Nature and Attributes of God,* NewAdvent.org (9 January 1909). *Particulat Judgement,* NewAdvent.org (10 January 1910).
161. https://en.wikipedia.org/wiki/Intelligent_Design.

162. https://en.wikipedia.org/wiki/Philosophy.
163. *Harvard Gazette* (October 12, 2011), https://news.harvard.edu/gazette/story/2011/10/the-cognitive-revolution.
164. Kizur Toldot Ha-Enos, Kinneret Zmora-Bitan Dvir, and Or Yehuda, *A Brief History of Mankind*, (Israel). https://en.wikipedia.org/wiki/Yuval_Noah_Harari.
165. https://en.wikipedia.org/wiki/Sientific_method.
166. http://www.ratbags.com/rsoles/comment/flew.htm.
167. https://en.wikipedia.org.wiki/Intelligent_design.

REGISTER

T

U

V

W

Z

ABOUT THE AUTHOR

After being expelled from the university in 1947, because his studies at an English grammar school during the war were not homologated (later well), the author started work at the Belgian Treasury Department at the lowest rank. He became a tax law expert and published many articles on the subject. His main work was a ten-volume commentary on value-added tax (VAT). He ended his career as director of VAT of the province of West-Flanders and as a commander of the realm. When he retired in 1993 at the age of sixty-five, he started studying religion, philosophy, and cosmology. A convinced atheist, in 2014 he published his essay "God, Fact or Fiction". Immediately afterward, he started his research for this book.

www.ingramcontent.com/pod-product-compliance
Ingram Content Group UK Ltd.
Pitfield, Milton Keynes, MK11 3LW, UK
UKHW041633190726
13854UKWH00006B/2481